THE

Holistic Dog

BOOK

THE
Holistic Dog
BOOK

Canine Care for the 21st Century

DENISE FLAIM

HOWELL
BOOK
HOUSE

For general information on our other products and services or to obtain technical sup-port please contact our Customer Care Department within the U.S. at 800-762-2974, outside the U.S. at 317-572-3993 or fax 317-572-4002.

Wiley also publishes its books in a variety of electronic formats. Some content that appears in print may not be available in electronic books.

Library of Congress Cataloging-in-Publication Data:

Flaim, Denise.
  The holistic dog book : canine care for the 21st century / Denise Flaim.
       p. cm.
  ISBN 978-0-7645-1763-1
  1. Dogs. 2. Dogs—Health. 3. Dogs—Diseases—Alternative treatment.
4. Holistic veterinary medicine. I. Title.
  SF427 .F56 2003
  636.7'08955—dc21

                                    2002152376

Book design by Marie Kristine Parial-Leonardo
Cover design by José Almaguer
Photographs by Theresa Lyons/LyonsDen Inc.

For Fred, my husband and friend

Contents

Foreword

This book is an important contribution to improving the health, well-being and care of our closest animal companion, the dog. It does, as the subtitle states, take us into the 21st century of canine care, and the author, Denise Flaim, has provided an outstanding review of a diversity of subjects—some relatively new, such as veterinary acupuncture and chiropractic, others more controversial, such as the pros and cons of commercial pet foods and vaccination protocols.

Ms. Flaim has thoroughly covered the relevant literature and coupled this research with personal interviews with leading veterinarians and other experts in the various related fields of holistic canine care and understanding. The beauty of this book is that it effectively integrates these many fields and therapies to provide a truly holistic approach to canine care, disease prevention and treatments for different ailments. By so doing, the reader is informed and empowered to assume a more active role in providing optimal care for his or her canine companion.

The book includes a useful directory and resource guide of holistic and alternative veterinary therapies and practitioners, and each chapter includes key reference materials for further reading. Such information will greatly enhance the competence and confidence of those who want the best for their dogs, and will provide a more informed basis for their discussions with the attending veterinarian, other health care providers and dog trainers, as the occasion may demand.

Prevention is the best medicine, and the core of this book provides the cardinal components: sound nutrition, emotional security through proper understanding and communication and appropriate use of vaccines and dietary supplements. As this book shows, the cost savings in thus helping either prevent or more quickly recognize various health problems and nip them in the bud are significant. However, this does not mean trying out various home remedies when a dog is ill; I do not advocate home-doctoring in the absence of initial veterinary diagnosis and oversight. What is particularly impressive about this book is that the author provides a balanced view of selected topics and does not go overboard advocating one alternative therapy or diet or training method over another.

No one with a dog should be without this book, which should be mandatory reading for first-year veterinary students, veterinary nurses and animal health technicians. While some of the therapies may not yet be "scientifically proven" (aspirin was used for decades as an analgesic long before there was a scientific basis for its effectiveness), positive clinical benefits—such as improved rate of healing, general comfort and remission of symptoms—are proof enough. Furthermore, many alternative and supportive therapies do not have the same, if any, harmful side effects that many of the costly conventional drugs have.

After thousands of years as our dedicated companions and guardians, and with a long history of serving humanity in countless ways (often without reciprocal respect and loving kindness), we are eternally indebted to the dog. Dogs deserve the best that we can provide for their physical and psychological well-being, and this will foster a deeper and more fulfilling relationship—a mutually enhancing bond that this book most certainly advocates and so clearly helps establish.

Michael W. Fox, D.Sc., Ph.D., B.Vet.Med., M.R.C.V.S.
Veterinarian, bioethicist, author
Washington, D.C.

Acknowledgments

Nobody does it alone, and this book is no exception.

My deepest thanks go to the many veterinarians whose expertise and experience illuminate all the chapters of this book: Ian Billinghurst, Nancy Brandt, Eric Clough, Jean Dodds, Marcie Fallek, Roger De Haan, Terry Durkes, Bruce Ferguson, Martin Goldstein, Donna Kelleher, Jody Kincaid, Barbara E. Kitchell, Shawn Messonnier, Antony Moore, Richard Pitcairn, Nancy Scanlan, Allen Schoen, Anna Maria Scholey, Cheryl Schwartz, Robert Silver, Sharon Willoughby and Susan Wynn. Your help was priceless.

I also want to thank all the holistic practitioners and experts who shared their time and knowledge just as generously, including herbalist Gregory Tilford, aromatherapists Kristen Leigh Bell and Jeanne Rose, accupressurists Amy Snow and Nancy Zidonis, massage therapist Jean-Pierre Hourdebaigt, clicker guru Karen Pryor, positive trainer Jean Donaldson, behavioral specialist Larry Lachman, and animal communicators Penelope Smith and Gretchen Kunz.

Thanks especially to Michael Fox for reviewing the manuscript and writing the Foreword. His 1981 book *The Healing Touch* was the first in its genre and is still going strong.

I'm grateful to my friends Theresa Lyons, whose photographs in this book speak more eloquently than words of her eye for dogs; and Maryanne Russell, for her nuanced portrait photography. More thanks go to Howell editors Beth Adelman and Dale Cunningham for believing in this book, and to my agent David Hendin for making it all happen.

I'm grateful to Howard Schneider, Phyllis Singer and Barbara Schuler, my editors at *Newsday*, the Long Island newspaper where I write a weekly column on companion animals, for recognizing the importance of our creatures in our everyday lives and for encouraging me to write about them. I'm also indebted to the many *Newsday* readers whose daily letters, e-mails and phone calls are a constant reminder of the unbreakable bond we have with the animals we love.

This book wouldn't have been possible without the support and suggestions of Susan Marino, founder of Angel's Gate, a residential hospice for animals in Fort Salonga, New York. Susan came into my life as the subject of what I thought would be just another story, and she has stayed on to become a dear friend. Her insights on this manuscript were invaluable, and she more than anyone has taught me the importance of a healer's intention.

My love to my parents for a lifetime of encouragement. And last but never least, thanks to my husband Fred Eder for his endless patience and support, as well as to Blitz and Diva, the two Ridgebacks who share our life, not to mention our queen-size bed. They have been my greatest teachers.

Introduction:
The Holistic Balance

Holistic. It's the latest, greatest buzzword these days, for our animal companions as much as for ourselves. Marketers have latched onto it big time, from the dog food company that sells a line of "holistic" kibble to neighborhood veterinarians who now offer "alternative" services such as chiropractic and acupuncture.

But what exactly does it mean?

A true holistic approach is all about balance—emotional and spiritual as well as physical. It means taking into consideration the entire dog, factoring her individual circumstances and her unique qualities into an approach that will best support her overall well-being. In the holistic model, disease isn't simply the result of some opportunistic microbe that comes lurking in the night; it's more global than that. Instead of being an isolated instance, disease is a symptom of a larger problem—a lack of integration of the physical, mental and spiritual. It's the body's way of manifesting an imbalance, a disconnect or blockage, of the central life force that animates us all. And the only way to regain that balance—and the well-being that comes with it—is to consider the whole picture of who your dog is.

Holistic veterinarian Susan Wynn of Marietta, Georgia, who is the coeditor (with fellow holistic vet Allen M. Schoen) of *Complementary and Alternative Veterinary Medicine: Principles and Practice*, uses this definition: "Holistic is what's best for the animal, taking into account the animal's environment, including what the owner can do and the animal's total health."

Most conventional—sometimes called "allopathic"—vets would argue that this is precisely what they do. But one difference, say holistic vets, is that the tools their more conventional colleagues use—drugs and surgery among them—are designed to treat the symptoms of disease, not the imbalances that created it to begin with. In that respect, conventional treatments often address parts of the individual, not the whole. As an example, consider cancer. The non-holistic approach would be to cut out the tumor or kill the cancer cell. The holistic route, by contrast, goes deeper, seeking to find and correct the imbalances that enabled the cancer to grow in the first place.

Despite the growing popularity of holistic medicine, training is not routinely offered to veterinary students, and the curious must go afield to find it. Most modalities, with the growing exception of chiropractic and acupuncture, are not taught in veterinary school. They are simply not part of that culture. "One problem is you're limited by your training and own prejudices," says Roger De Haan, a holistic vet from Kings Mountain, North Carolina, who started exploring holistic medicine in 1983 when his wife became ill and did not respond well to conventional drugs and medicine. "You're down on what you're not up on."

Perhaps prompted by the interest of their clients—according to a 1997 study, 4 in 10 Americans say they have sought out alternative medical therapies—more and more vets are turning to holistic approaches, from herbs to homeopathy. "Things are opening up more and more—it's actually very heartwarming," says De Haan. "For instance, acupuncture is now accepted as a mainline modality in veterinary medicine. That's a dramatic change."

Despite its current "new age" label, holistic medicine is hardly new. Based on traditions that are hundreds, sometimes thousands of years old, these ideas have been there all along: They've just been overlooked—or dismissed or demonized by a medical profession that often refuses to acknowledge any discipline that falls outside of what is traditionally taught in veterinary school.

ALLO-WHAT?

A holistic approach is often contrasted to an allopathic one. What is the difference? Allopathic medicine is a fancy phrase used to identify the current system used by conventional doctors. The word comes from the Greek *allos*, meaning "other," and *pathos*, meaning "suffering" or "disease," and this definition explains the intent of conventional Western medicine: to define the disease, which is "other than" the body, and then use methods opposed to the disease to eliminate it.

Allopathic medicine assumes that disease is caused by a foreign "renegade" in the body itself, and the course of treatment is often drugs or surgery to drive out the invader. In contrast, a holistic approach doesn't seek to kill what is causing disease, but rather to support and bolster the body so it can correct itself and become balanced and healthy again. It's for this reason that holistic writers often hyphenate the word dis-ease— disease is simply a lack of ease within the body itself.

Some words migrate from their linguistic roots over time, and allopathic is no different. Although today it is most commonly used as a catch phrase to capture all that holistic therapies are not, its original meaning was not anywhere near as encompassing. "Allopathic medicine was a term coined by homeopaths, and using their context, many, many medicines are actually allopathic," says holistic veterinarian Susan Wynn. "Herbal medicine may contain a drug that suppresses an inflammatory reaction by balancing cell membrane mediators, but it also contains nutrients that support healing. Acupuncture is potentially allopathic, since we don't know how it works. I think the phrase 'allopathic medicine' is misunderstood and overused."

As holistic modalities become more popular, a whole host of adjectives have sprung up to describe them. Some are more appropriate than others. I don't use the word "alternative" to describe holistic modalities because it implies that they are apart from the mainstream, that you must choose them and reject all else. Since the goal is for holistic medicine to join the mainstream, not be marginalized from it, I find "complementary" medicine to be much more accurate.

This book is an introduction to holistic ideas and natural modalities for your dog, exploring everything from raw-meat

THE NAME GAME

Throughout this book, you may notice that I don't use the word "pet." It's a conscious choice. That three-letter word implies a certain degree of domination and condescension. Although I know I am a bigger-brained mammal who also has the advantage of opposable thumbs, when I interact with my dogs, I am really trying to work *with* them, more as part of a partnership than a hierarchy. While I'm not violently opposed to the word "pet," I just think "companion" has a gentler ring to it, and better describes the relationship we have. When most people say "pet," they really do in their deepest understanding of the word mean "companion." So why not just say what you mean?

As for another area of politically correct canine terminology, I don't use "guardian" instead of "owner." Guardian implies that my dogs have a larger degree of self-determination in our society than they really do; legally speaking, dogs are considered property, and I do *technically* own my dogs. Though I know I don't own their spirits or their selves, and I'm not entirely thrilled with "owner," it's what I'm using for now, until I find a truer description. (I keep trying: Every once in awhile I trot out "caretaker," but it feels too forced.) Might I feel differently about the "owner" versus "guardian" debate in the future? Undoubtedly, since I was blithely using the word "pet" in my animal-related writing up until recently. That's the beauty—and spirit—of the holistic approaches outlined in this book: We are not static creatures. We can and do and should adapt. And any approach that seeks to nurture and heal us should be expected to do the same.

diets to chiropractic to flower essences. You or your vet may have never heard of some of these modalities. Some may seem unorthodox, or just plain silly, which is fine: We're not living in a one-size-fits-all society, and what works for one person—or dog—may not work for another. Here you'll find the basic information you need to sort out what will—and won't—suit you and your dog. And that epitomizes the true spirit of holistic care—taking into account your individuality, and your dog's.

Consider this book a starting point for your exploration of holistic practices. It's a diving board into the ocean of information available out there. If one approach or modality appeals to you, use the basic information provided to learn more about it—which should propel your interest even further. From there, you can find holistic-minded vets who accept and use that practice, and get a more in-depth understanding by reading more and finding others with the same interest and who have experience and knowledge to share with you.

GETTING STARTED

Before you continue, here are some important concepts to consider. They have little to do with your dog, but everything to do with you. In our society, where providing food and toys and supplies and medical care for your dog is a multi-billion-dollar business, you've been "trained" to react a certain way to alternative ideas, thanks to sophisticated marketing and, often, fear tactics. This book doesn't ask you to reject the advice of conventional medicine; it just asks you to consider that there may be other modalities you can explore and possibly use to augment or complement what the mainstream approach is.

Forget "Either/Or"

Just because you want to consider holistic care for your dog doesn't mean you must abandon conventional veterinary care or disregard sound medical advice. You don't have to trade in your common sense for a tambourine. A holistic approach is all about individuals, and one size doesn't fit all. Your dog can have both a veterinarian and an acupuncturist—often they are the same person. You're not trying to find the singularly "right" way to raise your dog; you're trying to find out what works for you. Sometimes those philosophies will seem diametrically opposed, and that's perfectly fine. "Do I contradict myself? Very well then, I contradict myself," the great poet Walt Whitman wrote. "I am large. I contain multitudes."

Needless to say, it will help if your vet isn't intimidated by or dismissive of holistic medicine. One of the greatest deficits among medical practitioners—veterinary and otherwise—is the ability to listen. Find a vet who has an open mind and is not afraid of new things.

That said, *this book is in no way a substitute for professional veterinary care.* Always consult your vet first when there is a medical problem or before you try any holistic modality on your dog.

Be Active, Not Reactive

A lot of people become interested in holistic concepts in the face of a crisis. When a dog becomes very ill, and conventional medicine is unable to provide a tidy solution, desperation prompts people on to open-mindedness.

This is typically how most people discover raw food diets. Your dog has allergies, which don't go away or get even worse. Allergy testing is inconclusive. After trying antihistamines and fatty-acid supplements, the only remaining course of treatment your vet offers is cortisone shots. You start surfing the Internet and asking around for a solution, and you keep hitting on this raw food diet, which you'd never even considered before. But suddenly, the idea of feeding your dog a raw chicken wing isn't so scary, considering the alternative: watching him scratch himself so violently his skin turns bloody. Desperation makes you more willing to take the plunge.

Despite that very human instinct to react in a crisis and enjoy oblivion during the good times, the best time to explore something new is when you are not under pressure to make a decision. Dabble a little here and there—consider it an adventure. If you discover, then, that your dog loves massage, or that after a chiropractic session he doesn't hop on his rear leg as much, you may have played a large part in averting a crisis.

At the same time, just because something is holistic does not mean it is safe. Some herbs, for example, can be toxic and even deadly if used in inappropriate doses or in conjunction with incompatible herbs. Deciding to be more active about your dog's care means you have the greater burden of doing more research to make sure you understand the risks posed by the course you are taking.

Think for Yourself

Conventional medicine—whether human or animal—has conditioned us to see doctors and veterinarians as omniscient. Intellectually, of course, we know this isn't true. Medical professionals make mistakes, just as we all do. But when we are in a position of needing help, we want to have an authority figure to turn to and tell us what to do. It not only makes us feel comforted to have someone powerful and all-knowing in charge, but, frankly, on a psychological level it absolves us of culpability. If something goes wrong, we are not to blame because we were not part of making that decision.

But by taking yourself out of the equation, you are depriving your dog of an important advocate. Yes, the vet has years of academic and practical experience, and she knows all sorts of technical terms that have so many syllables that they seem downright intimidating. But *you* are the expert on *your dog*, his daily routine, habits and quirks. You know what is normal and abnormal for him. You know when he is feeling well and when he is not. You know whether a treatment is working or not. Your input and observations are crucial, and will help the vet determine the best course of treatment for your dog.

Learn When *Not* to Think

As important as it is to think for yourself, it's just as important to know when not to think at all. Conventional medicine loves facts and data—anything that can be explained by a chart or a controlled study. But some things in life are intuitive, not logical. Some things can be known but not proven. And some of those things are no less valuable or effective simply because they currently cannot be explained.

Consider flower essences, for example. If one of your prerequisites before you try them is to have empirical evidence that these distillations of buds and blooms can affect an animal's emotional state, then you're not going to make much progress. The same goes for vibrational therapies, such as reiki, or animal communication, which many medical experts would dismiss as not harmful but certainly kooky.

But if you set aside those criteria and choose to act on the intuitive, and not the intellectual, side of yourself, the worst thing that can happen is that nothing will happen at all. Thinking at the wrong time—demanding explanations and proof of something that cannot be measured in scientific terms (at least not yet, anyway)—means you will close yourself off to a lot of possibilities.

This happens in conventional medicine, as well. Some drugs and therapies work, but scientists don't know precisely *why* they work. That doesn't necessarily mean doctors don't use them. When penicillin was discovered, it was enough to know that it fought infections; no one refused to administer it to wounded World War I soldiers because they didn't understand how a moldy piece of bread could accomplish such miracles. And it could be that some day, many of the modalities outlined in this book will be better explained and their methods of action teased out and enumerated.

Be Aware of Hidden Motives

Holistic care is not about conspiracy theories. But it is important to recognize that many segments of the animal-care industry are not solely motivated by the well-being of our animals. Financial and corporate considerations loom large.

Consider, for example, the dog food industry. The great majority of dog food companies are subsidiaries of megacorporations dedicated to producing human food. Making breakfast cereal and other processed foods creates many byproducts that are not fit for human consumption. The dog food industry exists in large part to make use of these byproducts and turn a profit on them.

Another prime example is annual vaccines. Vaccinations are big business for veterinarians, and fear of not adequately protecting our dogs from dangerous diseases such as distemper and parvovirus propels many owners into the vet's office every year. Whether or not your dog actually *needs* a particular vaccine sometimes never gets discussed.

All this is not to say that you should avoid Milkbones like the plague or never vaccinate your dog. But you should understand that it is one reason why holistic approaches—say, a raw diet or titering to determine immunity—are not automatically offered to you. As a consumer, you need to do your research and present it to your vet to start a meaningful dialogue.

Don't Be Overwhelmed

Easier said than done. Our culture has an expectation of take-out-window quickness. But a complex meal requires time, care and thought to prepare, and should be consumed that way, as well. Learning requires an investment—of time and energy. You may find it difficult to absorb the facts and theories of some of the modalities outlined in this book. You'll likely expend a lot of effort seeking out herbs and homeopathic remedies and other things that don't pop up in the supermarket aisle—at least not frequently. You may have to spend lots of time addressing your own fears about going out into uncharted territory, not to mention the fears of others who then project them on to you—"You're feeding *what*? I've never heard of *that*."

Don't Give In to Fear

Some people avoid complementary medicine or a holistic lifestyle for their dog because they are afraid of it. Partly, this fear comes from not understanding the theories behind a particular modality or treatment approach. It can also come from uneasiness in departing from what everyone else is doing. It's natural to feel trepidation about changing the way you do things.

However, sticking with an allopathic approach that feels uncomfortable or invasive simply because you are afraid is usually not a good idea. The best decisions are never made out of fear.

The biggest antidote to fear is the experience you gain after you set aside your first qualms and venture forward. The good news is that the more you learn and the more you explore, the easier the whole process will be. After all, the best decisions are the ones we make based on experience and faith in our own judgment. The more knowledge you gain, the more successes you'll have. That approach feeds on itself, building confidence and curiosity—two things you must have if you're going to integrate a holistic approach into your dog's care and lifestyle.

Once you see success, it will be easier for you to try more new things, to take bigger risks, and then to see, in retrospect, that they were not very risky after all. Follow your common sense, and your heart, and chances are the two won't lead you astray.

A CANINE CHRONOLOGY

For almost as long as humans have existed, there have been dogs by our side. Through our intertwined history, people's attitudes about our canine companions have changed as capriciously as the flip of a coin. During the Middle Ages, most dogs were reviled as pestilence-carrying scourges; during the 19th century, new breeds were created with almost alarming alacrity to satisfy the Victorian demand for diminutive toys to pamper. History has given us all those extremes, and almost everything in between.

Although our attitudes about dogs and the status they hold in our society have changed dramatically with the ages, one thing remains constant: The thread of relationship between our two species, though at times frayed, has never been broken. We've come a long way from the cave, baby.

6 million years ago: *Eucyon*, an early fox-size canid, migrates from North America's Great Plains to the attached continental mass of Asia and Europe. There, this adaptable, omnivorous predator eventually evolves into the modern wolf, coyote and jackal.

800,000 years ago: The gray wolf trots back across the land bridge to Arctic North America.

100,000 years ago: The dog is domesticated. Although earlier theories held that the dog was welcomed to the hearth around 14,000 years ago—when the first fossil evidence of dogs at human encampments was found—current DNA research shows that canines' relationship with humankind actually began much earlier.

12,000 years ago: In Ein Mallaha in northern Israel, archaeologists have found the burial remains of an older woman dating from this period. Her hand, frozen in time, is cupped gently over the skeleton of a puppy.

3000 B.C.E.: Recognizable breeds of dogs begin to appear.

1300 B.C.E.: Anubis, the dog-headed deity, is worshiped in ancient Egypt. As the god of embalming, he guided and protected the souls of the dead. Egyptologists still argue over what species Anubis actually was—a jackal, a dog or a cross between the two.

79 C.E.: Pompeii is engulfed in hot ash from the eruption of nearby Mount Vesuvius. Millennia later, archaeologists uncover the Roman city, where dogs were depicted in household mosaics and homes sported signs with the Latin warning "*Cave Canem*"

(Beware of Dog). Among the remains: a dog stretched protectively across the body of a child.

1014: England's King Canute enacts the Forest Laws, reserving huge swaths of land for the nobility to hunt with their Greyhounds, which could only be owned by aristocracy. "Meane persons," or commoners, found with the prized hounds risked being fined and having their dogs "lawed," or made lame through mutilating the toes.

1876: The Westminster Kennel Club holds its first dog show—considered today to be the second-oldest continuous sporting event in America. (Only the Kentucky Derby predates it.) The popularity of purebred dogs is sealed.

1923: Rin Tin Tin is put under contract with Warner Brothers, making him one of the world's first canine movie stars. Among the perks: a $1,000-a-week salary, a personal chef and limo, and a diamond-studded collar. A rags-to-riches story, this German Shepherd was found in the breed's native land by a U.S. serviceman after World War I, and brought back to the United States as a puppy.

1934: Patsy Ann, a deaf Bull Terrier, is proclaimed the Official Greeter of Juneau, Alaska, for her ability to "hear" the whistles of approaching ships and be the first to greet them at the wharf. Patsy died in 1942, and her bronze likeness still greets the tourists who now disembark from cruise ships onto her beloved docks.

1957: The Soviets send a dog named Laika (meaning "barker" in Russian) up in the Sputnik 2 satellite, making her the first living passenger to orbit the earth. Because safe reentry was not possible, the "space dog" dies during her mission.

2001: The world watches in horror as downtown Manhattan's World Trade Center collapses on a balmy September morning. In the ensuing days and weeks, grief is intermingled with pride and admiration as an army of search-and-rescue and cadaver dogs converges on the city to help find the lost amid the rubble. Working as tireless teams with their human handlers, they demonstrate for the world the unique relationship between our two species.

Don't Stop Here

No one book can tell you everything there is to know, especially on the subject of holistic care. Knowledge is fluid and ever-expanding; you acquire it through reading, through life experience, through talking with others who are willing to share their own knowledge. It's a journey, and this book is just one step.

The information is out there for you. The Web has exploded with hundreds of sites devoted to all sorts of holistic approaches to animal care. (Just keep in mind that anyone with an Internet provider and a keyboard can set up a website; make sure you check credentials and motivations before even considering someone else's advice.) There are also plenty of books (both mainstream and independently published), workshops and seminars that can provide you with more information than you can possibly process in one sitting.

And that's OK; you can't know everything all at once. It's enough to learn a little something at every stop along the way.

Chapter 1

Nutrition: Is Your Dog Eating McFood?

The canine corollary to talking about religion and politics is discussing dog food. At first glance, it might seem silly to get emotional about what you feed your dog. You feed kibble, I feed canned, the guy down the street gives his dog leftovers—what's the big deal?

But on a deeper level, food is about love and nurturing. For someone to suggest that we are not giving our dog the best possible nutrition is to suggest that we are not the best possible dog owner. And as the options for feeding our dogs increase, so does the defensiveness of many people about the decisions they ultimately make.

So before you go any further in this chapter, it's important to know that there is no universally "best" way to feed a dog. There is only the best way to feed *your* dog. The decision you ultimately make about what and how you feed depends not only on the food itself, but other factors, including your own resources. You may not have enough time to commit to home cooking for your dog, or may not have the budget to afford free-range chicken for yourself, let alone your dog. If you have small children, you may not feel comfortable feeding raw meat (one of the options discussed here) because of concerns about salmonella. (Concerns for your children, that is, not your dog. Canine digestive tracts are well-equipped to handle most microbes that would level us bipeds.)

These are valid points, and you should not feel bad about yourself because they factor into your decision-making. Remember: A holistic approach is all about evaluating the entire situation, not getting fixated or stuck on one area. And life is a fluid, changing process. A year from now, your circumstances may change, and you may be ready to try a new approach.

Do your best to do what's best.

A RAW DIET

Raw food diets for dogs have become trendy these days. There are books, e-mail discussion groups, even bumper stickers devoted to what has come to be affectionately referred to as BARF—short for "bones and raw food." While veterinarian Ian Billinghurst of Bathurst, Australia, ignited the most recent interest in raw feeding, other advocates include Richard Pitcairn, Wendy Volhard and Kymythy Schultze.

Each offers slightly different methodologies. Some advocate including cooked grains, others recommend different supplements. But the basic theory behind all their diets is this: Domesticated dogs are not markedly different from their progenitor, the gray wolf. Indeed,

WHY DO THEY CALL IT BARF?

As acronyms go, BARF isn't the most elegant, but that hasn't mitigated its popularity. According to veterinarian Ian Billinghurst, the BARF nickname was coined by someone who disagreed with the diet and referred to those who fed it as Born Again Raw Feeders. "She then tried it herself, became convinced and changed it to mean Bones and Raw Food," says Billinghurst, who also interprets the acronyms to mean Biologically Appropriate Raw Food.

up until less than a century ago, before the advent of commercial dog foods, most dogs ate as wolves did—fresh, oftentimes raw meat, usually scavenged or tossed to them as a leftover. What raw feeders advocate is not a radical departure from the norm, but a return to how dogs were meant to eat in the first place.

Science bears out the dog's close relationship to the wolf. Studies of mitochondrial DNA—the DNA passed down directly from mother to offspring that changes only in the relatively rare occasion of a genetic mutation—show that the genetic difference between domesticated dogs and gray wolves is about 1 percent. (By comparison, the difference between wolves and their wild cousins, coyotes, is a whopping 7.5 percent.) This minute degree of separation from the wild is the cornerstone of the nutritional theory behind raw food: Dogs, like wolves, need raw meat to derive crucial enzymes and nutrients, which are destroyed during the cooking process.

Take a look inside a dog's mouth. Those big teeth are not there for show. They are there to rip and tear and crunch flesh and bones. And dogs have short digestive tracts with powerful enzymes for dealing with harmful bacteria, such as salmonella.

Billinghurst's book *Give Your Dog a Bone* helped drive the current renaissance of raw meat diets. In that raw food guide, he explains that dogs don't just need to eat *what* wolves eat, but *how* they eat as well. Consider Mr. Wolf on a given Monday. He and his pack have managed to bring down a deer, and he greedily eats the innards, including the stomach, which contains half-digested plant material. He returns on Tuesday to eat some choice muscle meat, then chomps on the remaining bones on Wednesday and Thursday. On Friday, he may come across a nest of quail eggs and have a raw omelet. On Saturday, dumpster-diving is on the menu, and he snarfs a half-eaten Big Mac. Sunday might bring slim pickings around town, so (appropriately, perhaps), he fasts.

Billinghurst points out that this dramatic variation in a wolf's diet—from day to day, week to week, month to month—is entirely natural, and depends upon what he calls "balance over time." This is antithetical to the way commercial dog food delivers its nutrition, which is basically the same percentage of nutrients, in the same form and of the same quantity, day in and day out. This is also the reason, Billinghurst suggests, behind the dramatic improvement many dogs show when their owners switch brands of dog food. It's not that the second brand is necessarily any better; it's just that the dog's system is responding to the change in ingredients and sudden variety of nutrition. But once the dog has been eating the second brand for a period of time, that effect will wear off and the dog will begin to show the same problems again.

The staple of the BARF diet is the raw meaty bone—ideally, one that has a 50-50 ratio of bone to meat. Chicken wings and backs fulfill this equation handily, as do turkey necks. These poultry bones are non-load bearing, meaning they do not carry the weight of the animal's body, and therefore are soft and can be easily chewed and swallowed raw. In addition to raw meaty bones, raw feeders give their dogs pulped vegetables, raw muscle meat, offal such as liver and gizzards, nutritional supplements, and other goodies such as raw eggs, yogurt and the occasional leftover lasagna.

The key is to make the raw meaty bones the majority of the diet so that the dog derives benefit from their enzyme and calcium content.

The Benefits of Feeding Raw

Feeling nervous yet? That's normal. Most people have such reflexive reactions to changing or rethinking their dog food—"He'll get sick if I switch." "How will I know if I'm feeding him correctly?"—that the dog food companies are to be commended for all but signing us up as customers for life.

Most everyone who has switched a dog from a commercial dog food to a raw food diet has had twinges of panic. It's understandable, and it's transitory. Once you actually see your dog eating and thriving on a raw diet, once weeks and months go by and nothing horrible happens, you will begin to relax. And soon, feeding this way will feel natural—which is exactly what it is, on a bunch of different levels.

Although it sounds far afield, there is a parallel between the pressure some vets put on dog owners to feed kibble instead of home-prepared meals and the insistence of obstetricians in the 1950s and '60s that women give their newborns formula instead of breast milk. This idea that somehow we are incapable of

providing appropriate sustenance without corporate intervention—
that something artificial is better than something natural—should
seem counterintuitive. Think about it: Are you so incapable of putting together a balanced diet for your dog that you need to feed
him out of a bag every day? You don't feed your human children
that way. And surely their nutritional needs are no less complicated,
or important, than your dog's.

Raw feeding "has all the appearances of becoming mainstream within the next five to ten years," says Billinghurst, adding
that the most common reason people switch is "the need to solve
a health issue for their pet. However, large numbers of people
who have taken an interest in their own health and have
embraced natural therapies for themselves research and adopt the
evolutionary diet for their pet as a logical extension of that way
of thinking."

Here are some of the changes you can generally expect after
switching your dog to a raw diet.

**Enhanced immune system and reduced allergic reac-
tions.** Commercial dog food is taxing on your dog's system, for
a number of reasons. To keep kibble fresher longer, dog food
companies must remove as much moisture as possible, baking it
under extremely high temperatures. Not only is the food overprocessed, with lots of additives to preserve shelf life and provide
nutrients lost during the cooking process, but the quality of the
ingredients varies widely.

In contrast, raw food is much more bioavailable—your dog's
body doesn't have to work as hard to extract the much-needed
nutrients. And since all the ingredients are controlled by *you*, you
can eliminate the cheap grains, low-quality meats and chemical
preservatives that may account for some of the food sensitivities
you see.

Increased hydration. Raw meat contains plenty of water.
Kibble, because of the manufacturing process, does not. People
who switch their dogs to raw food will often notice a decrease in
their dog's water intake. This isn't a cause for alarm; in fact, just
the opposite. It's a sign that the dog is getting the moisture and
hydration she needs from her food, and no longer needs to supplement it.

Smaller volume of stool. Kibble contains fillers, which help bulk up the food—and contribute to the formation of copious amounts of stool. In contrast, the ingredients in a raw diet are fresh, more easily digested and more completely absorbed. Most of what goes in gets used.

As a result, dogs fed raw diets produce a smaller amount of stool—in many cases, about a third less than kibble-fed dogs. And their stools are often hard and round like marbles, turning white in a couple of days and disintegrating into a powder if you get lax with your poop-scooping. Contrast this to the potty products of kibble-fed dogs, which can endure for weeks and months.

Fewer anal-gland problems. The stools of raw-fed dogs aren't made soft and mushy by the preservatives and fillers in kibble. Instead, their bone content gives them a harder consistency. As a result, when stools are passed, they tend to stimulate and empty a dog's anal glands naturally.

Less of a doggy smell. Raw feeders swear that their dogs have less of an objectionable overall odor than kibble-fed dogs.

Cleaner teeth. If you choose to feed your dog whole raw bones, as some raw feeders advocate, you can expect a mouth full of shiny, tartar-free teeth. The reason should be obvious: All that bone crunching and gnawing is better than any brushing or flossing you could ever do. A side benefit—reduced doggy breath.

Fewer ear infections. The yeast and grain content of commercial dog foods can contribute to chronic ear problems in many breeds, especially those with pendulous or drop ears. Raw diets—especially those with no- or low-grain content—can clear up those frustrating infections for good.

Bloat management. Some owners and breeders of large dogs who are prone to bloat, or gastric torsion, believe a grain-free raw diet reduces the risk of a bloating episode. The theory is that a raw diet does not contain fillers that can expand in the stomach, thereby increasing the possibility of bloat.

The Risks of Feeding Raw

Most conventional vets are adamantly opposed to a raw food diet, and will be very persistent in trying to dissuade you from feeding one to your dog. Billinghurst sees this animosity as rooted in a lack of knowledge, and the myth that canine nutrition is somehow more complex than human nutrition.

"Vets have no training in this area," he says. "In fact, they have very little training in nutrition outside the admonition to feed a complete and balanced scientifically produced grain-based processed pet food. They are very much afraid that raw food will pass on deadly bacteria to their patients. They assume—on the basis of nothing more than their own prejudicial belief—that raw foods will cause animals to be overwhelmed with E. coli, campylobacter and salmonella. They also think that such bacteria will be readily passed from the dog to its human companions.

"In practice, none of this has been known to happen. Dogs and cats have, until very recently, been eating this way and doing brilliantly for millions of years—certainly not requiring the army of vets they apparently need today to keep them healthy!" In addition, Billinghurst says, vets often have a vested financial interest in promoting the kibble that is displayed in their waiting room.

Are there risks to feeding a raw diet? Of course, just as there are to feeding a steady diet of kibble. Nothing in life is risk-free. But if you take the proper precautions and educate yourself about this way of feeding, you can mitigate many of the following concerns.

Parasites and Bacteria

Raw meat contains salmonella and other nasty bacteria—that is just a fact of life. You can cook the meat, but, raw food advocates point out, along with those nasty microbes you're also destroying important enzymes and nutrients.

Much of the current concern with bacteria, especially salmonella, in raw diets for dogs results from anthropomorphism. We worry (and rightly so) about ingesting salmonella, and so think we need to have the same concerns for our dogs. But canids do not have the same digestive system as humans. They can handle bacteria that would severely incapacitate, or even kill, a human. Even the United States Department of Agriculture has stated that salmonella is not a health risk for dogs. Instead, it's we humans who should be worried about it. Indeed, if your household includes young infants, the elderly or anyone who is immunologically compromised, you must take precautions to keep your dog's feeding area scrupulously clean. (Also, always wash your hands after handling such popular doggy treats as pigs' ears, as they can and do carry salmonella.)

There is a wide spectrum of opinion among holistic vets about whether most dogs can handle a raw food diet. While Billinghurst says that in his experience, "only the most severely immune-compromised animal genuinely requires a cooked diet," some vets are reluctant to switch all but the youngest and healthiest dogs to raw. Still others advocate a long transition period, especially for elderly or ill animals, moving from kibble to home-cooked to, eventually, raw, if a dog's system can handle it.

And some vets, including Michael Fox, one of the first veterinarians to introduce American dog owners to holistic concepts, feel the widespread contamination of raw meat and unsanitary slaughtering practices are simply too risky. Fox also worries that raw-fed dogs may pass on intestinal food-borne diseases to human members of the family. *He recommends that raw feeders lightly sear all meat before serving.*

There are ways to minimize the amount of harmful bacteria in your dog's raw meat. One way is to soak the meat in grapefruit seed extract, which has antibacterial qualities. You can also use food-grade hydrogen peroxide. Another precaution is to store raw meat for at least a month in your freezer. Recent studies by British researchers found that freezing kills 20 to 25 percent of all micro-organisms.

Best of all, feed naturally raised raw meat. It may be more expensive, but it's likely to be less contaminated and safer than meat that, when it was alive, was injected with hormones, pumped with antibiotics and fed pesticide-sprayed grains.

Impaction and Perforation

The old injunction about not feeding chicken bones to dogs pertains to *cooked* bones, and its wisdom is unassailable. Cooked bones are brittle and prone to splintering, and they should never be fed to dogs. Raw bones, however, are are soft, supple and easily dispatched with a rapid crunch-crunch-crunch-gulp.

Still, some people worry about their dog's ability to properly chew and swallow a whole bone. The overenthusiastic can also

THE MIDDLE GROUND

Increasingly, those who do not feed their dogs kibble diets find themselves confronted by food wars, in which evangelical-sounding proponents of one diet or another insist that it's their way or the highway.

That's precisely what Monica Segal of Toronto discovered while researching a diet for her Zoey, a Cavalier King Charles Spaniel puppy with digestive problems so dire she was literally wasting away. Segal, who is certified in animal care, decided she would look beyond the posturing and the diet gurus, and see where the facts took her.

In the end, Segal wound up with a healthy dog and a firm conviction: Dogs are highly individualistic, and their diets should be, too. One dog may thrive on raw food; another may need cooked. While one dog may not tolerate beef, his housemate may do exceedingly well on it.

Segal organized all her information into a self-published book, *K9 Kitchen, Your Dogs' Diet: The Truth Behind the Hype* (Doggie Diner, $21.99, available from www.doggiedietician. com). In it, she explores the minutiae not just of which nutrients dogs need, but also how those components interact and the factors that affect their absorption. Also invaluable is her nutritional analysis of commonly fed raw meaty bones, the staple of the BARF diet. No matter what guru you follow, Segal's book is an important addition to your bookshelf.

swallow a poultry neck or wing whole, possibly leading to asphyxiation. An alternative is to grind the bones up. Tabletop sausage grinders such as the Maverick (sold, among other places, at www.pierceequipment.com) can process chicken necks and wings into a hamburger-like consistency. The bone content is still there—and so is your peace of mind.

If you want to feed whole bones, stay with bones that are non-load-bearing, such as turkey and chicken necks, and chicken wings and backs. Some people feed bigger bones—such as chicken thighs and lamb necks—without concern. But since there is always a risk of impaction and choking, it is best to supervise your dog while she is eating. And if your dog is a gobbler, you may have to teach her to eat slowly and safely by holding the bone and forcing her to take her time while chewing it.

Nutritional Imbalances

Buying a bag of kibble is a pretty commitment-free act. The label on the side of the package tells you that the company that manufactured it has made sure the contents are nutritionally balanced. But when you are feeding a home-made diet, whether raw or cooked, the burden is on you to make sure your dog is getting a complete and balanced diet.

If you want to start feeding a raw diet, you need to educate yourself. Entire books have been written on the subject, and at the very least, you should read one straight through, following the nutritional requirements it outlines. Most of the diets advocate feeding 60 to 75 percent raw meaty bones and the remainder muscle and organ meat, such as ground beef and gizzards. Feeding a raw diet that includes only meat and no bone (or no bone substitute) can lead to dangerous imbalances, because phosphorus levels will be too high and calcium levels too low.

Most raw diets also require pulverized vegetables (dogs cannot digest whole vegetables because they lack the enzyme to break down cellulose), especially green leafy veggies such as dandelion greens and collard greens. Then, to be sure you have all the essential vitamins and minerals covered, you need to add a good multivitamin, olive oil or vegetable oil for omega-6 fatty acids and fish body oil or flax seed oil for omega-3 fatty acids. (Some dogs show a sensitivity to flax seed oil, so watch for itching or other signs of sensitivity.) Some raw food authorities advocate adding cooked grains such as millet or bulgur. Still others encourage you to add trace minerals in the form of kelp and alfalfa, and supplemental antioxidants such as vitamins C and E. Then there are the yummy extras that dogs love, and that are good for them too, such as raw egg yolks and plain yogurt.

Sound complicated? Not really, once you understand the theory behind it and have established a routine to feeding. But you should not embark on a raw diet until you have done your homework and have found a detailed diet to follow. "Many people hear about feeding raw and start doing so before reading this book and others like it," says Billinghurst. "As a result, they don't

Reading Up on Raw

Here are some of the more popular raw diet books. Most are available from www.amazon.com, as well as www.dogwise.com.

The BARF Diet: Raw Feeding Using Evolutionary Principles is an updated book by raw-feeding guru Ian Billinghurst (Barfworld, $17.95). His earlier books, which are equally as commonsense and reassuring, are the self-published *Give Your Dog a Bone* ($27.95) and *Grow Your Pups With Bones* ($34.95).

Natural Nutrition for Dogs and Cats: The Ultimate Diet by Kymythy R. Schultze (Hay House, $8.95). A little pithier than Billinghurst, this is a good choice for those who find "Dog" in the details, as Schultze provides approximate amounts and sample monthly menus.

Dr. Pitcairn's Complete Guide to Natural Health for Dogs and Cats by Richard H. Pitcairn and Susan Hubble Pitcairn (Rodale Press, $17.95). A discussion of raw feeding (supplemented with grains) kicks off this popular book, which also includes an in-depth look at homeopathy.

Holistic Guide for a Healthy Dog by Wendy Volhard and Kerry Brown (Howell, $16.95). Volhard developed her Natural Diet two decades ago, and she describes it in this classic bestseller, along with complementary therapies and vaccine concerns.

Raw Meaty Bones: Promote Health by Tom Lonsdale (Rivetco, $29.95). Written by an Australian veterinarian, this is the latest addition to the raw feeding *oeuvre*.

Also worth a cyber-visit are the many websites of dog owners and breeders who have had practical experience feeding a raw diet for years, even generations. While visiting someone's site is not a substitute for buying one of the raw diet books and doing in-depth research, those personal Web pages will show you how people are integrating this natural feeding regimen into their lives.

supplement properly or give the correct ratio of raw meaty bones to muscle meat."

The most common mistake, says Billinghurst, is feeding an all or mostly meat diet, with no bone content. "This mistake is particularly critical in the case of young animals," he says, leading to severe calcium deficiencies and, in turn, weak and easily broken bones. Holistic veterinarian Susan Wynn says this is precisely why she is reluctant to encourage the wholesale adoption of raw food

SWITCHING GEARS

Gung-ho about going raw? While that's understandable and commendable, be sure to give your dog time to make the switch, especially if you are going from a poor-quality kibble to a raw diet.

While some raw feeders advocate going cold turkey—switching from kibble to raw in one meal and never looking back—many animals, no matter how young or healthy, can be overwhelmed by the sudden influx of healthy and healthful ingredients. A sudden change could trigger a "healing crisis"—basically, a full-blown detoxification. While the end result may be good—the dog eliminates all the toxins in his body—the process itself can be unpleasant and messy for both you and your dog, including bouts of diarrhea, vomiting, mucous discharge and skin eruptions.

Instead, make the change slowly, feeding small amounts of raw food and gradually decreasing the amount of kibble. Because feeding raw meat and kibble simultaneously can cause diarrhea, consider breaking up meals into several feedings over the course of the day.

In the case of elderly or ill animals, proceed very carefully—and maybe not at all. Some animals may simply not have the constitution to handle a raw-food diet.

diets. "I personally have seen smart people who read the books and who drifted to feeding pure meat"—a disaster waiting to happen.

Bottom line: If you are going to start your dog on any non-commercial diet, you must be able to do it correctly, or not at all.

Minimizing the Hassle

One of the biggest drawbacks to a raw diet is that it can be time-consuming to prepare. Pulping vegetables, grinding bones (if you choose to take that added precaution) and ferreting out sales in the meat department can take as much time as cooking for your own family. Here are some shortcuts.

Get chummy with your local health-food store. Most of these establishments have a juice bar where they use organically grown fruits and vegetables. Juicing produces lots of wonderful pulp that is perfect for raw-fed dogs (or any dog—even if you feed kibble or cook for your dog at home, you can supplement with freshly pulped veggies). Most health-food stores would be happy to give you their excess pulp.

Find bargains in numbers. Chances are there are many folks in your area who are feeding raw—you just don't know about them. Search for e-mail groups of BARF feeders in certain geographic areas on websites such as www.yahoogroups.com. If enough of you band together and approach your butcher, you might be able to persuade him to start buying preservative- and pesticide-free meat for you in bulk. My local butcher found that the demand among raw feeders was so high that he invested in a grinder, and now prepackages ground meat and vegetables in two-pound sleeves. They fit easily in the freezer, and can be defrosted and served in a snap. His business has skyrocketed, and his customers have a convenient, healthy and cost-effective way to feed their dogs. Remember, if there is an economic advantage to supplying raw feeders, a smart butcher (like mine) will try to accommodate you.

A HOME-COOKED DIET

Let's say for whatever reason, you can't or won't feed your dog a raw diet. Home cooking is another option. The downside, raw food advocates say, is that you are destroying beneficial enzymes and nutrients in the food during the cooking process. But even if it is cooked, the food will still be far more healthy and bioavailable than commercially prepared dog foods. Because you are not feeding bones, you will have to supplement with a calcium source such as calcium carbonate or bone meal. As with a raw diet, be sure to pulp the vegetables, since dogs cannot digest them whole and they would then pass through the digestive system unused.

And, of course, be sure to feed a veterinarian-approved multivitamin daily.

Most traditional vets are supportive of home-cooked diets, and often will provide you with recipes and instructions. There are also plenty of suggested menus and recipes on the Internet; plug the words "home-cooked dog food" into any search engine to find them. As with a raw diet, if at any time you are worried

Recipes for Home Cooking

There are some wonderful books available that outline easy home-cooked recipes for dogs.

Barker's Grub by Ruth Edalati (Three River Press, $12)

Home-Prepared Dog & Cat Diets: The Healthful Alternative by Donald R. Strombeck (Iowa State University Press, $37.99)

Natural Food Recipes for Healthy Dogs by Carol Boyle (Howell Book House, $14.95)

that your dog is not getting proper nutrition, you can always ask your vet to run a blood chemistry panel to check your dog's overall health.

KIBBLE

For the vast majority of consumers, dry commercial dog food, or kibble, is the dog food option of choice. But from a holistic point of view, kibble is probably the least appropriate option for feeding your dog. In order to be converted into dry form for a long shelf life, kibble goes through a process called extrusion, in which it is dried at high temperatures so that much of the moisture is removed. This also removes many naturally occurring enzymes, nutrients and antioxidants that are vital for your dog's health. The dog food companies then add back additives to compensate for the lost nutrients, and spray the desiccated food with flavor enhancers to make it palatable.

It hardly sounds natural, and it isn't.

Another thing to consider is the source of the ingredients that go into dog food. Many dog food companies—especially the mass market name brands in your supermarket aisle—are not in business solely to make dog food. In fact, most of the major dog food companies are subsidiaries of larger companies that make the food we eat. Nestle, for example, owns Ralston Purina, Colgate-Palmolive is the parent company of Science Diet,

Procter & Gamble has Eukanuba and Iams under its corporate umbrella, and the list goes on and on. This isn't coincidence. It's good business: When a company makes, say, cereal or granola bars, there are a lot of byproducts from the process that are not fit for human consumption. They are, however, fodder for dog food.

The meat used in dog food is almost always the leftovers from slaughterhouses after the human-grade meat is removed. Some animals may have died from disease, others may have been road kill or euthanized. Although dog food companies say they do not use the carcasses of euthanized companion animals—including cats and dogs—in their foods, it is perfectly legal for them to do so. Rendering companies can and do use carcasses picked up from shelters in the rendered—basically, melted down—meat they sell to dog food companies. Since the sodium pentobarbital often used in euthanization does not degrade during the rendering process, residue can find its way into dog food that uses rendered meat meal. And the nutritional label on that bag of dog food is no help whatsoever in determining the source or quality of its ingredients.

All that said, if you do decide to feed a commercial dry dog food, be aware that not all kibbles are created equal. Some have better quality ingredients and less fillers than others. A look at the ingredients label can be a real eye-opener if you know what you're looking at. And don't stop at the so-called "premium" foods sold in pet supply stores, or even the waiting rooms of vet offices, because there are lots of private-label kibbles that are much healthier. It may take a while to find them, but searching the Internet and talking to fellow dog owners can get you started.

Despite all the quality control associated with the commercial manufacture of dog food, kibble does have risks of its own—just as every feeding method does. One concern is mycotoxins, which are toxins produced by mold or fungus from contaminated grains. Responsible for several kibble recalls in the 1990s, mycotoxins can cause vomiting, appetite loss, liver damage and in some cases even death. Be sure to check the expiration date on your bag of kibble.

Reading the Label

If you need any special skill in selecting a kibble for your dog, it's mastering the art of label reading. Here are just some of the ingredients you might find in that tiny box on the back of your bag of kibble. (Ingredients are listed on the label in descending order of weight, so that theoretically the first ingredient listed makes up the most content of the food. However, some manufacturers will split up a poor quality ingredient into several different entries, so they appear lower on the list. See "Corn," below, for more on how this can happen.)

Animal fat. A blended, rendered product that includes, among other things, restaurant grease. It is sprayed onto kibble to make the little food pieces more palatable.

Beet pulp. The dried residue from the processing of sugar beets, this ingredient is used to add dietary fiber. There is debate over whether this is desirable or not. But having beet pulp high up in the first several ingredients is probably not a good thing.

BHA (butylated hydroxyanisole), BHT (butylated hydroxytoluene) and **ethoxyquin.** These preservatives were once widely used to increase the shelf life of kibble. Concerns over the possibility that all three might be carcinogens prompted dog food companies to start using more "natural" preserving agents such as vitamin C (**ascorbic acid** and/or **sodium ascorbate**) and vitamin E (**alpha tocopherol**).

Byproduct. This is a euphemism you will encounter frequently on dog food labels. Basically, these are proteins that by law cannot be used in food consumed by humans. "Meat byproducts" are the non-rendered parts of slaughtered mammals that do not include meat but can contain lungs, spleens, kidneys, brains and most other organs. Hair, teeth, horns and hoofs are excluded. Generally speaking, it's better to buy a food with a named byproduct (such as "lamb byproduct") rather than the vaguer "meat byproduct."

Byproduct meal. This is a very cheap—and usually not good quality—source of animal protein. Avoid it.

Corn. In and of itself, corn isn't necessarily a bad ingredient. But warning bells should go off if it is listed high up in the ingredient

Resources for Kibble

If you have decided that your lifestyle and budget compel you to continue to feed kibble, your work has just begun. There are many brands of dog food, all claiming to be the best. One cyber-source for label comparisons is the popular and long-lived home.hawaii.rr.com/wolfepack/, which lists the ingredients of many brands.

Another ongoing source of information about canine nutrition is the *Whole Dog Journal*. To subscribe, call (800) 424-7887 or visit their website at www.Whole-Dog-Journal.com. The online address is a good place to research and order back articles, including commercial food reviews and the magazine's recommendations for dry and wet dog foods.

The ominously titled *Food Pets Die For* by Ann N. Martin (NewSage Press, $13.95) is a no-holds-barred look at how commercial food is manufactured. It also offers some recipes for a home-cooked diet for dogs. The author does not support raw feeding.

list under several guises, such as "ground corn" and again as "corn gluten meal." It means that the manufacturer has split up the overall corn content by listing it in several categories, allowing other, more desirable ingredients, such as meat-based ones, to climb up the ingredient list.

Meal. This is the euphemism for animal tissues and bone that have been ground and rendered—basically, heated until they turn to liquid. Excluded are blood, hair, hide trim, manure, hoofs, contents of the intestines or "extraneous materials." Lamb, turkey and chicken meal is self-explanatory. As with byproducts, avoid the generic term "meat meal," and choose brands that use a *named* meal.

Natural. Using this word on a bag of dog food simply means the food does not use synthetic ingredients (except for vitamins or minerals). It does not mean it contains organic or healthy ingredients.

Propylene glycol. A chemical preservative, often added to keep semi-moist dog food chewy.

Sodium nitrite. A color fixative and flavor enhancer, this food additive has been shown to create cancer-causing agents called nitrosamines.

Soy. Soybeans are a major ingredient in some dog foods. Many dogs have difficulty digesting this protein, leading to flatulence.

CANNED FOOD

Perhaps the greatest difference between canned dog food and dry is the moisture content. Canned dog food is mostly water, but check the label to see where the water comes from. Unlike kibble, good-quality canned food often uses whole meats in their natural state, which is where the high moisture content comes from. Yes, the ingredients are still cooked and processed, losing much of their original nutritional value, but they are still more bioavailable than dry kibble.

Canned foods tend to contain better quality ingredients, such as whole meats instead of meat byproducts—again, read the label to be sure. And, by virtue of their packaging, they also usually contain less preservatives. The big drawback is that they are much more expensive than kibble, especially if you opt for a very high-quality brand that uses human-grade meat.

THE MIDDLE GROUND

Because many dog lovers feel very strongly about their feeding methods, this subject can degenerate into judgmental posturing and take-it-or-leave-it standoffs. The implication, sometimes, is that if you don't feed raw or home-cooked, you're a bad person who doesn't care about your dog's well-being.

As I've already said, there may be very legitimate reasons of lifestyle and economics that prevent you from taking a more natural approach to your dog's nutrition right now. Instead of getting caught up in black and white, look for shades of gray. Many dog owners successfully feed a half raw, half kibble diet, giving one in the morning and the other in the evening. Since raw meat and kibble have different rates of digestion, feeding them together in the same sitting may very well cause diarrhea. But many dogs do well on this "split-personality" diet.

WATER WISDOM

Up until a few years ago, I used to think it was the height of indulgence to give dogs bottled water to drink. Here's what happened to change my mind.

We had moved into an old Victorian house in a geographic area known for its high breast-cancer rates. Growing up in nearby New York City, which has a high-quality water supply, we could literally *smell* the difference in the water that came out of our suburban tap. So as a precaution, we decided not to drink it—we used bottled water for making coffee, even for boiling pasta.

Enter Blitz, our Rhodesian Ridgeback puppy. As he grew through puppyhood, his coat was a disappointment—blotchy and tweedy, it always looked like he had just come in out of the rain. We chalked it up to genetics, and thought little more about it until a year later, when we acquired Diva, another Ridgeback from the same breeder. After a month or so at our house, Diva's coat turned the same ugly color as Blitz's. When we went to visit her littermate brother outside of Philadelphia, we were shocked to see the disparity in their coats: His was a gleaming, deep red; hers was a speckled, dull tweed.

We racked our brains for possible environmental causes. Both dogs ate a hormone- and pesticide-free raw meat diet. We don't use chemicals in our yard, and neither do most of our neighbors. The only possible culprit was the water.

So we switched from tap water to bottled spring water, and within weeks, the difference was miraculous. Each dog's coat was transformed into what it should have been all along. Diva's became a rich red to match her brother's; Blitz's was a warm honey-tinged wheaten that we had never seen before.

While I didn't perform a double-blind study to confirm my hunch, my dogs never again drank tap water and their ugly coats never returned. And that experience drove home an important lesson: If something is not good enough for you, it's not good enough for your dog.

Bottled natural spring water is best for your dog. Some holistic practitioners recommend distilled water; others consider it to be "dead," stripped of the energy found in spring water. If your budget or lifestyle preclude giving your dog spring water, filter your tap water to try and screen out as many impurities and contaminants as possible.

Even if you are committed to an all-kibble diet, resist the temptation to believe that everything your dog needs is contained in that brightly colored bag. Here are some things you can do to make commercial food more healthful.

Add Fresh Ingredients

Just because you're feeding kibble doesn't mean you can't supplement with healthy, whole foods. Pulp some veggies in the food processor and pour them over your dog's food. (Anything but raw onions, that is. They are toxic to dogs.) Cook some chicken and brown rice and mix it in. Just be sure to subtract an equivalent amount of kibble if you are adding significantly more calories.

Add Enzymes

One of the biggest drawbacks of overprocessed foods—whether for humans or animals—is that they are stripped of the naturally occurring enzymes that help in the process of digestion and in aiding the body to assimilate nutrients in the food. Adding an enzymatic supplement, such as Prozyme, to your dog's kibble can help increase the absorption of its nutrients.

Switch Brands

Although some dogs have sensitive stomachs and delicate digestive systems, the vast majority of canines can gradually switch from one brand of food to another over several days and be no worse for wear. Switching brands has two advantages: First, it gives your dog that diversity of nutritional intake that is a little closer to the wolf model mentioned earlier in the chapter; second, it ensures that you are not wedded to one company's formula. By varying the brands, you're increasing the chances that your dog is getting as balanced a diet as possible.

How often should you switch? I know one person who changes brands every few days; another who switches foods every three months. The best answer is to use your own judgment, and take into consideration the habits of your own dog when making your decision.

Add Supplements

These can include nutritional "pluses." Some to consider:

Apple cider vinegar. This common pantry item is a health booster for you and your dog alike. It kills germs and bacteria, flushes out toxins, oxygenates the blood and boosts fertility. Apple cider vinegar—*not* white distilled vinegar—can be added to your dog's water bowl daily; just a teaspoon or two will do. (Make sure your dog does not find the taste offensive, and will still drink his water.) Buy an organic brand that contains "the Mother"—a cloudy weblike sediment that indicates the vinegar has not been overprocessed and depleted of vital minerals and enzymes.

Kelp. This food supplement contains important trace minerals and amino acids. It helps clear up dry skin and dull coats, and aids thyroid function, making it a good choice for dogs with hypothyroidism. Make sure the kelp is deep-ocean harvested, so it is as pure as possible. Supplement with kelp about twice a week—don't overdo it.

Vitamin C. Dogs can and do manufacture their own vitamin C, which helps boost the immune system, but their stores of this antioxidant can be depleted rapidly by stress and environmental toxins. Most experts suggest supplementing with doses "to bowel tolerance"—that is, build up slowly and if the dog develops diarrhea, lower the dose you are feeding. Generally, most large dogs can handle a minimum of 500 mg a day.

Vitamin E. Another powerful antioxidant, vitamin E helps deactivate

A PANTRY MUST-HAVE

Pumpkins aren't just for Halloween. In fact, you should keep a supply of canned pumpkin on your kitchen shelf year-round. (Be sure to buy only *plain* pumpkin, *not* pumpkin pie mix, which has added sweeteners and spices.) Pumpkin is a very effective and natural remedy for diarrhea. It is also a very helpful antidote for constipation. Most dogs like the taste, and it can be added to your dog's food or given alone. Because pumpkin contains a lot of fiber, it is very filling and can be given to a dieting dog to create a feeling of fullness.

free radicals that can trigger cell damage that leads to heart disease and cancer. Figure 200 IUs of this fat-soluble vitamin to be an appropriate daily dose for a large dog. More is not better, so do not overdose.

Yogurt. There is some debate about whether it is a good idea to include dairy products in a canine diet, because dogs have difficulty digesting lactose. So while you don't want to overdo it, an occasional dollop of yogurt containing active cultures such as acidophilus will help with intestinal functioning.

Chapter 2

Herbs and Essential Oils: Healing Gifts From the Plant World

Familiarity breeds contempt, the old saying goes. And maybe, to some degree, that characterizes our relationship with the healing plants that surround us. Perhaps because they are everywhere— marigolds enlivening a garden path, mature trees swaying over- head, shrubs bursting into bloom—we tend to vastly underesti- mate plants. We see them as pleasing to the eye, but incapable of making a meaningful contribution beyond their decorative value in the landscape or their culinary impact in the saucepan.

This is a far cry from how plants were regarded in cultures older and wiser than our own. Connecting us to the earth with their cycles of growth, death and renewal, plants were more than just objects for a window box display. They were regarded as sources of powerful medicine, our partners in health and healing.

Animals intuitively recognize the healing power of plants and will seek them out. How many times have you watched a dog "grazing" in her backyard, stopping to nibble on some chickweed here, a blade of grass there? Have you ever admonished her without thinking about it, because if she eats too much grass she'll throw up that slimy yellow bile? But have you stopped to think that this cleansing effect is why she seeks out the grass in the first place?

Zoopharmacognosy—the study of how animals seek out certain plants to treat disease—has provided ample scientific evidence that animals self-medicate. A 1985 study, for example, looked at chimpanzees in an African rain forest who not only sought out young aspilia leaves when they had upset stomachs, but chewed the leaves for long periods before swallowing them with a grimace. Researchers found that the leaves contained thiarubrin, a natural antiobiotic that kills intestinal parasites, fungi and retroviruses.

Often, animal wisdom is more intuitive than our own.

In our modern-day craving for the new, the cutting edge and the high tech, we tend to ignore the fruits of the rich black soil in favor of chemical cocktails produced in a test tube. While drugs are an important tool for any veterinarian, they are not the only one. Plants are gentler, more organic and sometimes more effective in the long run.

Plants are nothing if not incredibly versatile, and this chapter looks at two of the many healing forms they can take. Herbs—whether fresh or dried, crushed into powder, dissolved into tinctures or made into salves—are nature's primordial drugs, and when we turn to them to heal our animals, we return to a wholeness that is connected to the earth, not the laboratory.

Essential oils are the concentrated, aromatic products of distilled plants, and they unlock another level of healing from the flora around us. To the degree that herbs are currently trendy, essential oils are correspondingly unexplored. But as with all things holistic, their time will come.

"Each year I'm seeing an increased acceptance" among more conventional colleagues on the subject of herbalism, says holistic veterinarian Robert Silver of Boulder, Colorado. "At conferences they'll ask, 'Can you tell me about milk thistle?' and 'What's this about ginkgo?' Things are changing as the old guard is retiring and the new guard is coming through the ranks."

And with that change in attitudes and practices, the medical pendulum is slowly swinging back in a direction that it has not seen for quite some time.

HERBS

Herbs are hot these days. Just walk down the vitamin aisle of your local supermarket, and look at all the "natural" supplements on the shelves. Like most holistic remedies, however, herbs are hardly new. They are the original "drugs," used by shamans, medicine men and midwives long before technology enabled us to take them into the laboratory and create synthetic versions. Indeed, almost a quarter of the drugs on the market today were derived from botanical sources.

Although they are the closest thing nature offers to the synthesized compounds of chemicals that we call drugs, herbs aren't exactly drugs. And though they have a culinary element to them and can be vital nutritional supplements, they aren't quite food, either. They occupy a middle ground between the two.

This is why most herbs are theoretically safer to use than drugs. They have active ingredients that can and do make biochemical changes in the body, but those powerful agents exist within the context of the whole plant. A complete herb has an internal synergy that offers checks and balances.

This also explains why it's often unwise, even dangerous, for manufacturers to isolate the active ingredient in an herb. In their effort to scientifically validate the effect herbs have on the body, many studies isolate their individual constituents to find the one "responsible" for biochemical reactions in the body. But that kind of reductionist thinking takes us in the wrong direction, says Gregory Tilford, an herbalist from Hamilton, Montana, who, with his wife, Mary, is the author of *All You Ever Wanted to Know About Herbs for Pets.* "All we're doing is repeating history—picking apart plants to create more drugs."

Instead, we need to accept the fact that herbs work as safely and effectively as they do because the whole plant acts in synergy. "It's about accepting what science can't understand in terms of the synergistic properties of the plants," Tilford says. "It exists—even if we can't see it under a microscope."

When it comes to using herbs with animals, veterinarian Roger De Haan groups herbs into three categories, based on their degree of safety:

- *Nutritional* herbs, such as burdock and alfalfa, are recognized as the safest to use and have an overall tonic effect on the body. "They can be given just about any time and to anybody," De Haan says.
- *Medicinal* herbs, such as hawthorn, are used to treat a specific condition. Although generally recognized as safe to use, as with any herb, care must be taken in terms of dosage.
- *Toxic* herbs are just that. Most, like poinsettia, are poisonous and are not used medicinally. A minority, however, might be used in microdoses under proper medical supervision.

Dosage is a tricky subject. "There are people who think a little is good and more must be better," says De Haan. Conversely, "there are those who are so afraid that they don't give enough to do enough good. It takes a certain amount of an herb for it to be medically or physiologically active, and it does very little good by giving too small an amount." This is particularly true of nutritional herbs, he notes. "It's like drinking a half cup of water a day when you need eight cups a day."

Dosage also depends on the severity of the condition being treated. "I use a lot of hawthorn berry for heart problems," says De Haan. "If a dog has a minor condition, like a mild heart murmur, I might want to add that herb in smaller quantities to try and treat it nutritionally and preventively." But if a dog has congestive heart failure, the dose of hawthorn would be significantly higher.

Tilford encourages would-be herbalists not to get hung up on the idea of a quick fix. "The most important thing to consider when using herbs is to learn how to put them in proper context," he says. "If you want to use them for their best potential, they shouldn't be considered as a replacement for drugs. They shouldn't necessarily intervene with illness or infection, but instead support what the body's designed to do in the first place."

In other words, a truly holistic approach doesn't use herbs to knock out symptoms without seeking to understand the deeper causes that generated the symptoms in the first place. Used in that way, herbs take time to work, and expecting quick results will only lead to disappointment. "The hardest part of using herbs as a holistic modality isn't finding the herb that works," Tilford says, "but getting through that mindset in order to let them work."

While "herbs are relatively benign, even when misused," he continues, "they still require respect and common sense." It's important to properly research an herb to learn about possible side effects and toxicity, and to discover whether it has been used safely in animals. Kava-kava, for example, is becoming popular as people discover its calming qualities. But the herb has never been tested extensively on animals, and it is possible that overuse can cause liver damage. With herbs, as with many other modalities, "natural" is not synonymous with "safe."

"The difference between a medicine and a poison is dosage and application," Silver warns. And some commonly used herbs should be used with great caution: Comfrey has a centuries-long tradition of use for burns, skin irritations, mastitis and respiratory conditions, but there are concerns about its toxicity when taken internally in too great a quantity. Black walnut, touted as a natural wormer, can also be dangerous at high doses.

Quality of ingredients is another significant concern. "The problem out there is what's on the label doesn't always match what's in the product. Make darned sure you are very familiar with the company," stresses holistic veterinarian Shawn Messonnier of Plano, Texas, who is the author of several holistic-care books, including *Natural Health Bible for Dogs & Cats*. "They should use human-grade products and have independent lab testing of their products, which costs more."

Messonnier says he tends to use combination proprietary products instead of individual herbs. This is not only practical—instead of giving a dozen different pills, he chooses a formulation that contains all those herbs—but it takes advantage of synergy. The many herbs work together to support and bolster one another's effects, making the total far greater than the sum of the individual parts.

If all this sounds complicated, that's because it is. Any herb that has the ability to help can also hurt, and this relationship is often proportionate. As veterinarians expand their knowledge to include herbs in their treatment protocols, finding an herb-savvy practitioner is not very difficult. Seek one out for guidance when using herbs. The cost of a consultation pales in comparison to the price you might pay for misusing an herb.

And, of course, make your own education as deep as possible. "The biggest mistake people make when they learn about herbal medicine is they spend a lot of time learning about what the herb does in the body, but they don't get to know the nature of the herb itself," says Tilford. "Learn about the plants first. Learn from the field up—what they look like, what they smell like, what stage they are harvested at. From this you can learn how to recognize a quality product."

An Herbal Sampler

Herbs are very versatile and can be prepared in a number of different ways—in teas or tinctures, ointments or infusions, compresses or poultices, dried or fresh. Each has its advantages and disadvantages, and you'll need to do some research to determine which preparation is the safest and most effective for the use you are considering.

When possible, use products that have been made especially for animals. The Tilfords, for example, sell a whole line of herbal tinctures under the label Animals' Apawthecary. Tinctures are more rapidly absorbed than pills in a dog's short digestive tract, and because most animals dislike the taste of alcohol-based tinctures, theirs use vegetable glycerin, which is sweet like corn syrup.

There are thousands of herbs, used in hundreds of different cultures, and it would be impossible to list them all. Instead, here is a list of some useful "beginner" herbs that are relatively easy to locate and use.

Pay close attention to the source of the herbs you are buying. In addition to making sure they are whole and not chemically synthesized, check to see that they are as pure as possible—that is, organically grown and naturally harvested. Take into account

THE DOPE ON DOSAGE

With herbs, as with most things in life, size does matter. As a general guideline, Roger De Haan suggests using one-tenth to one-quarter of the recommended human dose for a 10-pound dog; half the human dose for a 50-pound dog; and approximately the equivalent of a human dose for a dog who weighs 80 pounds or more.

that dosage recommendations are for an average-sized human adult, and that your dog will likely need less.

Most important, do not use herbs in the place of consulting a veterinarian for a serious or life-threatening condition. Herbs are best used to support and complement traditional medicine, not supplant it. Generally speaking, herbs are not often used in emergency situations, but more for chronic conditions that don't have a pressing time element. In using herbs, the very best ingredient is common sense.

As always, be sure to check with your veterinarian or a holistic practitioner before using any herb, especially one that can have side effects.

Aloe (Aloe vera)

This delicate succulent cannot survive in most non-tropical climates. But many cooks keep a potted aloe on a sunny kitchen counter, at the ready in case they burn themselves. The jelly-like pulp inside the leaves of the aloe vera plant is soothing to skin irritations such as insect bites, minor burns, lick granulomas and hot spots.

Because aloe has antibacterial qualities, it can be used on surgical incisions, where it will stimulate healing. Most animals will avoid licking the area, because of the juice's bitter taste.

To administer the aloe, simply snip off a piece of a leaf, squeeze out the juice, and apply topically.

While aloe can be given internally, primarily as a laxative, it can cause severe digestive upset. It's best to stick to topical applications and consult an herbalist for internal treatment.

Burdock (Arctium lappa)

Burdock is the deep cleaner of the herb world, and when used over time, it can help clear the body of toxic elements—hence its reputation as a "blood cleaner." Its ability to flush out wastes and toxins makes it useful for treating arthritis, and liver and kidney diseases.

If you live in an area where pesticide and chemical use is high, consider adding burdock as a nutritional supplement to your dog's diet, as it can help filter those dangerous environmental toxins from your animal's system. Burdock is also useful in treating chronic skin conditions such as eczema.

Burdock is an extremely safe herb, and can be used without fear of toxicity or side effects. Many dogs also like the taste of it and will eat it readily. You can buy fresh burdock root at health and ethnic food stores and grate it atop your dog's food, or buy the dried root.

Calendula (Calendula officinalis)

The pot marigold is good for skin conditions, healing and reducing inflammation in the area as it inhibits infection. Use it in cream form on irritations such as insect bites, poison ivy, small cuts, lesions and minor burns. Because calendula heals and closes skin rapidly, make sure wounds are clean and free of infection before applying.

Coltsfoot (Tussilago farfara)

This herb's Latin name means "cough dispeller," and it has been used for centuries as an expectorant and antispasmodic. It is useful for respiratory infections and deep coughs, including kennel cough and pneumonia. Coltsfoot does not just suppress cough symptoms, but actually aids the body in flushing out what caused them in the first place.

Because coltsfoot contains potentially dangerous alkaloids, some countries have restricted its use. If you plan to use this herb for any length of time, consult with an herbal practitioner.

Dandelion (Taraxacum officinale)

Another detoxifier, this common lawn weed cleans the blood-stream and liver, and improves the workings of the kidneys and stomach. It helps regulate bowel movements and aids in moving toxins and poisons out of the body. A valuable diuretic, dandelion improves elimination efforts by the kidneys and liver, all the while helping the body maintain its potassium levels.

Provided you do not garden with pesticides or chemicals, the nutrient-rich leaves can be plucked right from your lawn, pulped and added to your dog's food bowl.

Garlic (Allium sativum)

This is the too-good-to-be-true herb! Garlic stimulates liver function, flushes out toxins, reduces free radicals that can cause cancer, boosts the immune system and acts as a germicide. In addition to helping stave off and treat viruses, tumors, parasites and fungus, garlic lowers high blood pressure and improves digestion. It is also often used as a natural flea preventive.

Like burdock, this is another good herb to add to your dog's meals several times a week. It can be fed fresh or as a powder. As with most herbs, more is not better—it has been suggested that prolonged use might cause anemia—so feed garlic in moderation.

Ginger (Zingiber officinale)

Ginger's nausea-relieving properties are well known, and it is often used as a remedy for vomiting and motion sickness. A dog who tends to be carsick might benefit from powdered gingerroot capsules given a half hour before the excursion. Because of its properties as a stomach soother, this herb also helps treat indigestion.

Hawthorn (Crataegus spp.)

Traditionally, hawthorn was used as an astringent to treat diarrhea, among other conditions. Today, we regard it primarily as a heart tonic, helping stimulate the circulatory system, normalize blood pressure and reduce arrhythmia. Its restorative effects on heart muscle make it a candidate for dogs with cardiovascular problems and congestive heart failure.

Licorice (Glycyrrhiza spp.)

This anti-inflammatory, antiarthritic, antiviral herb is called the "great detoxifier." It can help boost the adrenal and endocrine systems.

Because licorice soothes inflammation and mucous membranes, consider it for colitis, diverticular disease and gastritis. These same properties make it a good choice for coughs and respiratory ailments. This herb should be avoided in animals with heart problems, especially rapid heartbeats or high blood pressure.

Milk Thistle (Silybum marianum)

This herb, a member of the sunflower family, is synonymous with the liver. Charged with the demanding job of eliminating toxins from the body, the liver sometimes needs a helping hand during times of stress—for example, when a dog is given a potentially toxic drug or treatment such as chemotherapy, or after vaccination or anesthesia. Milk thistle helps safeguard the liver when toxicity is high. Most herbalists recommend giving this herb only when it is needed, not as a general liver tonic, because it can negatively affect liver function if given indiscriminately. Also, avoid this herb if your dog is pregnant.

Parsley (Petroselinum crispum)

Here's another great addition to your dog's food bowl. Parsley is a cancer inhibitor and tonic—meaning it helps boost the body's overall functioning, clearing the bloodstream and liver of toxins. As it does in humans, parsley can help improve bad breath in dogs.

Raspberry (Rubus idaeus)

This herb has always been regarded as a female tonic, strengthening the uterine walls and relaxing spasms. This is a popular supplement for bitches who are going to be bred, and is often used throughout their pregnancy to tone the uterus and encourage adequate milk production.

Herbal Resources

All You Ever Wanted to Know About Herbs for Pets by Mary L. Wulff-Tilford and Gregory L. Tilford (BowTie Press, $49.95). Perhaps the best book you can find on herbs and animals. Chock-full of lovely photographs and extensive information, this book describes each herb in detail, presenting common uses and caveats.

The Natural Remedy Book for Dogs & Cats by Diane Stein (The Crossing Press, $16.95). A wonderful compilation that mentions herbs and homeopathy, flower essences, essential oils and others. Organized by ailment, the book provides you with a range of detailed holistic options.

Natural Health Bible for Dogs & Cats: Your A-Z Guide to Over 200 Conditions, Herbs, Vitamins, and Supplements by Shawn Messonnier (Prima Publishing, $24.95).

Veterinary Botanical Medicine Association
334 Knollwood Lane
Woodstock, GA 30188
www.vbma.org

Slippery Elm (Ulmus fulva)

Herbalists know this tree bark to be a first-line treatment for diarrhea, colitis and most any inflammation of the intestinal tract. It soothes the mucous membranes of the intestines, as well as the respiratory and urinary tracts. This is the herb to try for dogs with sensitive stomachs, who have extreme reactions to even the slightest variation in diet.

Valerian (Valeriana officinalis)

Valerian is a natural sedative, reducing pain, muscle spasms and palpitations. It has been used for centuries for its tranquilizing properties, and small, frequent doses can help calm a panic-stricken or anxious dog. Try giving this herb before any stress-inducing situation—a visit to the vet, fireworks on the Fourth of July, a long road trip.

There is some evidence that valerian can help minimize seizures in epileptic animals. Giving too high a dosage may cause intestinal upset, and use of this herb is contraindicated in pregnant animals.

Yarrow (Achillea millefolium)

This common roadside flower has many qualities to recommend it. It is a good diuretic, helping the body flush out wastes and toxins. It reduces inflammation and has a healing effect on mucous membranes. Useful for treating fevers and infections, yarrow can also help in blood clotting.

AROMATHERAPY AND ESSENTIAL OILS

In order to understand what aromatherapy is, perhaps it's best to start with what it is not. Aromatherapy is definitely *not* lighting a cinnamon-scented candle or setting out a bowl of peach potpourri.

"A lot of people have a strong misconception about aromatherapy because of the cosmetic industry's focus on the fragrance aspect," says aromatherapist Kristen Leigh Bell, author of *Holistic Aromatherapy for Animals* and the founder of Aromaleigh, a company that makes essential oil blends for animals.

Aromatherapy is the use of essential oils—the concentrated, aromatic oils extracted from plants through distillation, most often by steam. One way to think of them is as the "blood" of a given plant, containing antiviral, antifungal, antibacterial qualities that help boost the immune system, oxygen absorption and overall health. To get an idea of how potent these oils are, consider how much of the plant is required to produce them: 220 pounds of lavender yield only seven pounds of lavender essential oil. With rose oil—the most expensive of the essential oils—it takes 2,000 pounds of rose petals to produce a mere ounce.

Although essential oils have been used medically in Europe for more than a century, many veterinarians in this country have never even heard of them, much less tried them.

"They're underutilized, and when they are used, oftentimes it's incorrectly," says Nancy Brandt, a holistic veterinarian from

Las Vegas, Nevada, who has used oils for everything from calming a stressed patient to treating cancerous tumors. "There's no training—that's a biggie."

Essential oils work on several different levels. Physically, essential oils can help alleviate medical conditions and traumas such as bruises, infections, motion sickness and fatigue, and offer antiviral, antifungal and antibacterial properties. Emotionally, they can help center an animal suffering from stress, anxiety, irritability and compulsive behavior. When inhaled, they affect the most primitive part of the brain—the limbic system, which controls feelings and emotions.

While essential oils can be inhaled (the "aroma" in "aromatherapy") that isn't the only way they can be administered. Using an electronic glass diffuser is particularly effective, as it will disperse the ionized oil into the air in a mist of suspended droplets that can then be absorbed through the nasal passages. When topical application is appropriate, practitioners often recommend dabbing the diluted oil behind the ears, where the dog cannot lick it. Some oils are safe to apply topically on larger areas of the skin to help treat everything from wounds to mange to skin irritations. And a handful of others, such as peppermint, can be taken internally—with appropriate care and supervision.

It's at about this point that virtually all holistic practitioners plug in the great big blinking "caution" sign.

While "people should not be afraid of essential oils, they also should not be frivolous," says Bell, who advises trying oils on yourself before thinking about using them on your dog. "I have seen many cases of toxicity, all caused by people thinking that 'natural' equals 'safe.' Essential oils, like any natural remedy, should be used with understanding, and always in moderation."

Some animals handle essential oils better than others. Cats, for example, have different metabolic processes, and the oils can so easily approach toxic levels in their bodies that they are to be used with extreme caution, if at all. While most dogs are not as sensitive, caveats still apply.

"Like chemotherapy, the stronger something works, the stronger its side effects can be," says veterinarian Susan Wynn. She has seen diluted tea-tree oil cause a dog to drop to the ground

WHAT ARE HYDROSOLS?

Hydrosols are a byproduct of the distillation process used to make essential oils. As the plant material is heated, steam rises, carrying essential oils with it to the top of the still, where they condense.

Meanwhile, the water-soluble parts of the plant, as well as certain essential-oil components, run down the sides and collect at the bottom. This fragrant water run-off is known as a hydrosol, and it is gentle enough to be used on babies, dogs and cats.

Jeanne Rose disagrees with taking an either-or approach to essential oils and hydrosols. Instead, she advocates using them together because they contain different parts of the plant and complement one another.

Finding hydrosols is a challenge, however, since not all essential oil suppliers carry them. The box on page 40 lists some suppliers.

and become very lethargic. Because she has concerns about the high potency of essential oils, no matter how diluted, Wynn recommends the use of their gentler cousins, hydrosols, instead (see the box above).

Wynn is skeptical of essential oils' inhalent effects.. She says she has yet to be convinced "that you can get these oils into the atmosphere in concentrations that are truly effective. I have some doubts about whether you can put enough in the air to cause major pharmacological changes."

When it comes to the safety of essential oils opinions vary, in particular along cultural lines. The French, for example, tend to use essential oils "neat," or undiluted, and are more comfortable with using them internally. The British, by comparison, are more conservative, using the oils for massage and topical application, and stressing the importance of diluting them in a carrier oil such as sweet almond or hazelnut. In part because of the language compatibility—it's easier to read case studies and research in our mother tongue—American vets tend to follow British methods. "I find that I get just as much of an effect with them diluted," says Brandt. She generally uses a dilution of 10 drops of carrier oil to one drop of essential oil.

Jeanne Rose, executive director of the San Francisco–based Aromatic Plant Project, who has been using essential oils for 30 years, agrees with erring on the side of caution. She never recommends using an oil undiluted, including even exceedingly safe oils such as lavender and chamomile. Keep in mind the size of your dog, she cautions. "One drop of oil on a Chihuahua is at least 10 times stronger" than that same drop on a big dog.

Another huge area of concern with essential oils is quality. Since there is no association or body that governs essential oil standards, "buyer beware" is an understatement. Essential oil labels can be information-challenged at best, and misleading at worst. The word "pure" on a label is meaningless, and it is difficult to tell if a particular oil has been adulterated with a cheaper oil or a nature-identical chemical, which is a synthetic version of a naturally occurring component of the oil. "Rose oil, for example, is very expensive, and a manufacturer might cut it with rose geranium or rosewood oil because they smell very similar," says Bell. While an experienced aromatherapist might be able to tell the difference at first sniff, you won't.

There are many grades of essential oils, and the vast majority of those sold commercially are too adulterated for therapeutic use. "For soap-making or fragrancing the home, I think the essential oils sold at health-food stores are fine—but not for external application to the delicate skin of a dog," says Rose. The very best essential oils often are handmade by quality-conscious small-scale producers.

Essential Oil Do's and Don'ts

- **Don't** mix oils without doing research, as some do not combine well. Instead, beginners should buy premade combinations, or blends, from a reputable source. Many practitioners believe most oils work best when used in combination, enabling them to work in synergy. If you want to use several individual oils topically, you can layer them separately; that is, you can apply one properly diluted oil, wait at least half an hour for it to evaporate, and then apply another.

THE HISTORY OF ESSENTIAL OILS

It's a powerful scene: Three Kings, visiting the Christ child shortly after his birth to pay homage, lay before him three precious gifts: gold, frankincense and myrrh.

Essential oils? Not quite, says Jeanne Rose. Those last two were likely infused oils, which use resins from plants and trees. Figuring prominently in ancient civilizations, from China to Egypt, infused oils were used by priests and healers to treat illness and infection. But it wasn't until about 500 years ago that essential oils began to be extracted through steam distillation.

French chemist Rene-Maurice Gattefosse—who coined the term "aromatherapy" in the early part of the 20th century—is considered the father of modern aromatherapy. In 1912, he burned his arm in a laboratory mishap and plunged it into a vat of lavender oil. It healed so quickly that he was prompted to explore essential oils, and helped introduce them to the modern world.

While essential oils were used in the United States in the early part of the 20th century, World War I brought that to an end, says Rose. The discovery of antibiotics heralded the biochemical revolution, and "essential oils went out the window." Today, as with many healing modalities of ancient provenance, they are being rediscovered.

- **Do** check contraindications for every essential oil. Some, such as birch, thuja and wintergreen, should never be used without professional supervision. Some cannot be used on pregnant or epileptic animals. Others can cause photosensitivity or skin reactions. Be very careful with dogs who have chronic, debilitating conditions such as cardiac and kidney problems. Consult a veterinarian or qualified practitioner when using them on very sick or weak animals, especially topically.

- **Don't** use essential oils near the eyes or mucous membranes. For oils that are safe to apply topically when diluted, behind the ears is a common application site— anywhere that a dog cannot reach to lick.

- **Don't** use water to wash oil away from an inappropriate area; it will only intensify the effects of the oil and drive it deeper into the skin. Instead, use another type of oil, such as vegetable oil, to dilute the essential oil. In a pinch, butter, whole milk or any type of fat or mayonnaise will do.

- **Don't** give essential oils internally unless you do so under the supervision and direction of an experienced practitioner.

An Essential Oil Starter Kit

Essential oils are as diverse as the plants from which they come. Here are some individual essential oils and ways in which they can be used. As with any holistic modality, seek out a professional before trying any of these oils on your dog.

Eucalyptus

A powerful expectorant, eucalyptus can be used for respiratory problems such as bronchitis and sinusitis. *Eucalyptus radiate* is an especially gentle cultivar, and Bell recommends it for use with animals.

Frankincense

This immune system booster has been used for anointing and healing for thousands of years. Top-

> **QUALITY CONTROL**
>
> Essential oils are called "volatile" oils because they evaporate so quickly. Poor-quality oils doctored with synthetics and chemicals, however, leave behind a residue. To test the quality of an essential oil, put a few drops on a coffee filter or piece of white paper and leave overnight. In the morning, if an oily stain remains, chances are your oil contains more than just the essentials.

ically, it can be used with care to treat external tumors and warts. Also consider it for dogs who will be exposed to stressful situations (such as dog shows and dog runs) where lots of unknown dogs—and diseases—congregate.

Essential Oil Resources

Books

Holistic Aromatherapy for Animals: A Comprehensive Guide to the Use of Essential Oils and Hydrosols with Animals by Kristen Leigh Bell (Findhorn, $14.95). The best book yet on the subject.

Veterinary Aromatherapy by Nelly Grosjean (C. W. Daniel Company, $15.95).

The Complete Book of Essential Oils and Aromatherapy by Valerie Ann Worwood (New World Library, $19.95). Not animal-specific, but an indispensable reference guide.

375 Essential Oils and Hydrosols by Jeanne Rose (Frog, $14.95). Also written for people, not animals, but worth the investment.

Essential Oils

Aromaleigh offers an entire canine aromatherapy line using hand-blended, therapeutic-grade oils. Available are blends that address everything from soothing ears to repelling ticks to relieving arthritic joints. You can download the company's Canine Catalog from www.aromaleigh.com, or call (877) 894-2283.

Helichrysum

Also called Immortelle, this essential oil is helpful for conditions that affect the nervous system and to help heal sites where nerve damage has occurred. In her book, Bell likens its odor to "squashed bugs." It is also useful for healing old scar tissue.

Lavender

A must-have, lavender is a calming agent, helping to soothe an animal both emotionally and physically. Exceedingly gentle, this oil can aid in healing skin wounds, especially burns and cuts.

Young Living Essential Oils can be purchased as single oils or blends at the company's website, www.youngliving.com, or call (800) 763-9963.

Other essential oil suppliers include:

Acqua Vita
85 Arundel Ave.
Toronto, Ontario, Canada M4K 3A3
(416) 405-8855
www.acqua-vita.com
A good source for hydrosols.

Nature's Gift
314 Old Hickory Blvd. East
Madison, TN 37115
(615) 612-4270
www.naturesgift.com

Prima Fleur
1525 East Francisco Blvd, Ste. 16
San Francisco, CA 94901
(415) 455-0957
www.primafleur.com
Also carries hydrosols.

Oregano

Its powerful antibacterial qualities make oregano an excellent choice for battling infections, including staph.

Lemon

An oil with cleansing properties that can help boost immune function, lemon can also be used to ward off insects.

Niaouli

Bell prefers this oil to its Australian cousin, tea tree, because niaouli is gentler and less prone to cause skin irritations. It's often used for skin allergies and for cleaning ears and treating ear infections.

Peppermint

This is a popular digestive aid that helps prevent motion sickness and nausea. It's one of the few oils that some practitioners feel comfortable recommending for internal use—with common sense, of course. For an upset stomach, Rose recommends diluting the peppermint essential oil in an equal amount of carrier oil, then dabbling it on a spot where the dog *will* lick. A mental picker-upper, peppermint is another good insect repellent.

Chapter 3

Homeopathy: When Less Is Definitely More

Homeopathy is the first modality you'll be reading about that requires a belief in the healing power of energy. Although our Western minds expect medical explanations to center around descriptions of chemical reactions and molecular trysts, this is not going to be an adequate framework for understanding how homeopathy works. Instead, we need to recognize that this kind of life-force energy exists, even if it is not readily quantifiable.

That's not as difficult an intellectual leap as it sounds. After all, we understand the technology that makes it possible for a radio to blare out the latest rap song, even if we cannot see radio waves. And we understand what happens when the frequency of a particular wave is not in tune, or balance, with its receptor—we get static.

One way to understand how homeopathy works is to think of each homeopathic remedy as a sort of tuning fork. If the right remedy is chosen, it will resonate with our body and help tune it back to the correct frequency. Once that happens, whatever our internal notes are—salsa or reggae or country—they can vibrate with clarity and purity . . . the musical version of health.

Homeopathy has always been very popular and widely used in Europe, from its highest-profile adherents, the British royal family, to "commoners" of all persuasions. Its history in the United States, however, hasn't been quite as smooth. "In the 1800s, homeopathy was one of the more dominant forms of medicine," says Richard Pitcairn of Eugene, Oregon, one of the country's foremost homeopathic veterinarians and the author of one of the first modern holistic dog-care guides, *Natural Health for Dogs & Cats.* "Twenty-five percent of medical doctors used it. The nation's first hospitals and the first medical association, the American Institute of Homeopathy, were founded by homeopaths."

But homeopathy was never universally popular among medical doctors, and by the mid-1800s, a new group sprung up with the precise purpose of discrediting it. It's an organization that survives and thrives today—the American Medical Association (AMA).

Despite the AMA's work to marginalize homeopathy among doctors, it is enjoying a resurgence today—a sort of mixed blessing for homeopaths. On the one hand, more and more people are discovering homeopathy and using it to heal themselves and their animals. On the other hand, many are using it incorrectly—or at least not in the way its founder intended when he pioneered this healing modality almost 200 years ago.

THE HISTORY OF HOMEOPATHY

Homeopathic concepts far predate Samuel Hahnemann, the German physician who is credited with creating modern homeopathy in the early 19th century. Its principles reach as far back as ancient Greece and the doctor Hippocrates, upon whose medical ethics the Hippocratic oath is based. But more than 2,000 years later, it was Hahnemann, disheartened by the brutish medical practices of his day, such as blood-letting and blistering, who developed the homeopathic system that we use, relatively unchanged, today.

Hahnemann's "aha!" moment in homeopathy came while translating a pharmacology textbook. Reading that cinchona bark (which is the source of quinine) was a cure for malaria specifically because of its bitter taste, he decided to test the theory for himself. After each dose of quinine, Hahnemann developed sweats and fever—basically, symptoms that mimicked malaria. Once the quinine wore off, so did the symptoms. In his search to debunk the bitterness theory, Hahnemann had stumbled on something much deeper.

From this experience, Hahnemann formulated the first of homeopathy's three fundamental principles:

The Law of Similars

Or, "Like cures like." In other words, the very thing that can cause certain symptoms may also be able to address the imbalance that created them—sort of the holistic equivalent of "the hair of the dog that bit you." If a lot of something can cause a disease's symptoms, Hahnemann theorized, then a small amount of that same substance can stimulate the body to heal that disease.

As he did with his own quinine experiment, Hahnemann used tests on healthy people—called "provings"—to find out what symptoms certain plants and substances induced. Then, homeopathic versions of those substances were used on sick individuals with similar symptoms.

"Hahnemann thought that when the patient is disturbed by disease and gets a remedy that does the same thing, that sort of overpowers disease," Pitcairn explains. "The correct remedy takes the place of the natural disease, and, having more influence, it stimulates a reaction that's stronger."

The Law of Infinitesimals

This second tenet of homeopathy says the more diluted a remedy, the more potent it is. This is what makes homeopathy so exceedingly safe to use. When a remedy is made, it is diluted, then "succussed"—basically, shaken vigorously—to release its energy. A remedy is diluted and succussed so many times that, ultimately, very little or none of the original material remains, except for its energy. One popular theory about how homeopathy works is that this trace amount of the substance gives the body a blueprint for how to heal itself.

One of the reasons traditional medicine has trouble accepting homeopathy is that this seems, at first glance, illogical. "If you think about a remedy as a physical substance, it's counterintuitive," Pitcairn agrees. But if you think of it as a homeopath does—that the more a substance's physical presence is reduced, the greater its energetic effects—you understand how less really can be more.

This correlation between dilution and potency needs to be taken into account when you select a remedy. A 6X remedy (which has been diluted six times, using one part of the substance and nine parts of the dilutent) is not as powerful as a remedy marked 30X (which has been diluted 30 times). Preparations marked with a "C" instead of an "X" are more powerful because they contain even less of the remedy—one part out of 100. Opinions on safe dosages vary: While Pitcairn recommends that potencies higher than 6X be used only by experienced homeopaths, other veterinarians feel 30C potencies can be safely used by laypeople.

This extreme dilution explains why homeopathy uses some remedies that, in their original form, are toxic. Poison ivy, for example, is the basis for the remedy called Rhus tox. Normally, that plant causes painful rash and itching. But when it is administered in homeopathic form—in minute, microscopic amounts—it can cure those same ailments.

THE "H" WORDS

Although they are often confused by people who are new to holistic medicine, herbalism and homeopathy are not the same thing. Some of the misunderstanding stems from the fact that many homeopathic remedies are based on plants that also are used by herbalists. Arnica, for example, is available as a topical herbal cream as well as a homeopathic remedy. But while you could use either preparation to achieve the same goal—say, treat a strained pastern on a limping dog—the way the herb and the homeopathic remedy work to achieve the same effect is very different. The herb works on a biochemical level, while the homeopathic remedy works on a deeper, more energetic level.

Reference Tomes

If you are serious about homeopathy, you will need a Materia Medica and a Repertory. A Materia Medica (Latin for "medical materials") lists each remedy alphabetically, reporting the symptoms (or "rubrics") that the remedy elicited in provings, as well as comments from the clinical experiences of the homeopaths involved in compiling the book. The Repertory indexes the Materia Medica by symptom, so that practitioners can see the possible remedies relating to a given symptom.

The Whole Individual

The third principle is that the whole individual must be considered. Homeopathy is highly individual, and when a practitioner prescribes a certain remedy, it is after careful analysis and observation of the patient. Factors such as activity level, affinity for cold or heat, degree of appetite or thirst, tendency toward motion or stillness, sleep patterns and the emotional state of the animal might all be considered when selecting the right remedy.

"In the allopathic model, the focus is on diagnosis," Pitcairn says. "The reason for diagnosis is that it puts you in a therapy category where there is a standard treatment protocol." But the homeopathic position "says that's not the right way to understand disease. Two people won't have the same symptoms, and so they have to be evaluated individually. It's an entirely different perspective."

The more individualized the diagnosis, the more accurately a remedy can be selected.

CLASSIC VERSUS "ALLOPATHIC" HOMEOPATHY

Walk through any health-food store or visit any holistic health site on the Web and you will find all sorts of so-called combination homeopathic remedies for virtually every ailment under the sun—from arthritis to cancer to skin disease. "A lot of companies know there is a big market for anything alternative. You can grab a bottle that says Arthritis Remedy, and it has 20 things with a low dosage," says Marcie Fallek, a holistic vet and homeopath who splits her practice between Manhattan and Fairfield, Connecticut. "It may help a little bit, temporarily—enough to get people interested. But ultimately it will confuse the body and cause more damage."

Classical homeopaths have a name for this buffet-style approach, says Pitcairn. "We call it allopathic homeopathy." It's an intentional oxymoron. "Most people are using homeopathy to counter symptoms," just as conventional vets and doctors use drugs to suppress the body's reaction to disease, he says. Neither approach deals with the underlying imbalance that brought forth the symptoms in the first place.

Pitcairn's position underscores the difference between classical homeopathy, which holds that homeopathy is all that is needed to restore the body to health, and more eclectic approaches that use homeopathic remedies in combination, as well as in tandem, with other holistic modalities.

Classical homeopaths use the remedies just as Hahnemann did—singly. Not only will classical homeopaths not use combinations, but they use homeopathy alone, their experience being that other healing modalities are not necessary if homeopathy is being applied correctly. While classical homeopaths will sometimes recommend improvements in diet, nutritional supplements, chiropractic, massage and flower essences, they have observed that other modalities—including traditional Chinese medicine and acupuncture—interfere with their homeopathic treatment, or at the very least make it difficult to evaluate how a remedy is working.

DO-IT-YOURSELF HOMEOPATHY

Does all this mean that you can't use homeopathy unless you're a veterinarian who has taken a 130-hour certification course? Or that you need to lug around a Materia Medica wherever you go?

Of course not, says Fallek. "Homeopathy is excellent for treating acute things. People can learn to do it on their own and they can empower themselves." To that end, Fallek points to what some homeopaths call "the Arnica experience." When the right remedy is used for the right acute condition—such as Arnica for a bruise to soft tissue—the results are fast and impressive. "Arnica has gotten more people into homeopathy than any other remedy," Fallek says.

For acute conditions only, Fallek recommends using a 30C potency of a remedy from once to every few hours, as needed. Even if you choose the wrong remedy, she says, with an otherwise healthy animal at a low dosage, "you're probably not going to do much harm."

"It's perfectly fine for people to use remedies for first aid," Pitcairn agrees, although he advocates using a lower-potency dose of 6X. "But if they are using it for chronic conditions, they're playing with fire." So, it's one thing to use Arnica for a bruise your dog got while cavorting during doggy play-group, but quite another to use it to treat arthritis.

Chronic conditions such as diabetes, hip dysplasia and cancer are not for the inexperienced to treat, and this is where dabbling can do great harm. Treating chronic conditions homeopathically without the supervision of a trained homeopath "will weaken the animal over time," Pitcairn says. While symptoms might disappear temporarily, "you will be suppressing the disease rather than curing it."

Pitcairn offers these characteristics of chronic disease: It is persistent, as in the case of allergies, skin and ear problems, hypothyroidism and inflammatory bowel disease. Symptoms keep coming back over and over again. And, as chronic diseases go on, they develop increased pathology, meaning the body starts to be transformed—the joints swell, the spine bends and hunches, the skin changes color.

While homeopathic remedies are available in liquids and pills, the most common form you'll find are sucrose pellets in little blue vials marketed by the Boiron company. When you turn the base of the container, hard little beads of the remedy drop into the clear plastic cap, which prevents them from being contaminated by your hands and other surfaces. Crush the beads in a clean envelope or with the back of a spoon, then slide the powder directly onto the dog's tongue or add it to a small amount of spring water or cow's milk and administer with a plastic syringe. It is extremely important to keep handling to a minimum and to always give remedies between meals.

Generally speaking, try only one remedy at a time. If you don't see positive results in a reasonable period of time, discontinue its use and try another remedy. (A reasonable period of time, when you're dealing with a first aid situation, is anywhere from five minutes to 15 minutes to an hour. For a chronic condition, a homeopath might wait a day to a week before assessing a remedy's results.) Once a remedy is showing results, discontinue its use, so that the original dose can continue to do its work unimpeded. Remember, the remedy is just a catalyst for the body to heal itself.

When in doubt, give less rather than more. Giving too high a dose can actually aggravate the condition you are trying to address. If a dose is too low, you can always increase it to a higher dilution.

GETTING STARTED

Although there are about a thousand homeopathic remedies, some are used more often. While a chronic condition requires a consultation with a trained homeopath, there are some common acute conditions for which you can use homeopathy yourself.

As with any other form of holistic healing, do not use homeopathy in place of consulting a veterinarian. And remember that the succinct explanations offered for each remedy belie the excruciating attention to detail that homeopathy requires. To truly find the exact remedy for your dog, her individual personality and state of health need to be scrutinized and then researched in a Materia Medica.

That said, the remedies listed here are basic, everyday remedies that you might call upon for simple acute conditions such as a bout of diarrhea or a wasp sting. Consider them a homeopathic starter kit.

Aconitum Napellus (Aconite, or monkshood)

This remedy is for conditions that come on suddenly and without warning, such as shock and fever. Aconite is also useful for emotional trauma, such as uncontrollable fear or panic. Use this remedy first to try and get the condition under control. You may then have to switch to another remedy.

Apis Mellifica (Honeybee venom)

This is the remedy used most often for allergic reactions, hives and swelling resulting from insect stings. (Except those from bees—in that case, the remedy Ledum is used.) Apis mel can also be used to treat conditions that involve inflammation and fluid retention, such as a hygroma on the joint.

Arnica Montana (Leopard's bane)

One of the most useful remedies for first aid, arnica is used for closed-tissue injuries such as sprains and soreness. It helps promote circulation of blood and lymph in the affected area, moving out liquid and toxins.

Although Arnica, which comes from the sunflower family, can be used in herbal form, it can cause internal bleeding if the quantities given are too high. This is why the homeopathic version is so often used; the minute amount of arnica it contains is very safe. Herbally, Arnica is available in cream form and can be applied topically to strains and fractures to promote healing.

Belladonna (Deadly nightshade)

Belladonna is the remedy used to combat fevers, ear infections and other conditions that make the body "hot." It's an option for treating heat and sunstroke, as well as mastitis in bitches. Belladonna is also used to help get sudden, aggressive behavior under control.

Bryonia Alba (Wild hop)

Bryonia is indicated for pain that grows worse with movement and ceases when the animal rests. It is also used for kennel cough when the hacking is prompted by movement.

Calendula Officinalis (Marigold)

Available as a cream (for topical application) or as a homeopathic remedy (for use internally), Calendula stimulates healing of wounds and cuts.

Carbo Vegetabilis (Vegetable charcoal)

Overweight, sedentary animals who are prone to collapse are candidates for this remedy. It helps with fatigue, can revive an unconscious animal, and is good for treating indigestion characterized by a lot of gas. It is also sometimes suggested for bloat, although veterinary attention is paramount.

Chamomilla (Chamomile)

This soothing remedy helps dissipate pain, especially in the mouth. Try it on teething puppies.

Cocculus (Indian cockle)

A wonderful remedy for the traveling dog who is prone to motion sickness. It also helps exhaustion and sleeplessness.

Colocynthis (Bitter apple)

There's probably no more frightening sudden-onset condition in dogs than bloat, in which the stomach expands and sometimes twists, creating a life-threatening situation. Seeking immediate veterinary assistance is crucial. En route, you can try this remedy. Another option is Nux moschata.

Drosera (Round-leafed sundew)

This is often the remedy of choice for dealing with kennel cough that is spasmodic and characterized by violent hacking, as if the dog has something caught in her throat.

Euphrasia (Eyebright)

The plant from which this remedy is derived is nicknamed eye-bright, referring to its use for centuries as a tonic for the eyes. Euphrasia works on eye irritations with burning, stinging tears. A possibility for conjunctivitis.

Gelsemium (Yellow jasmine)

Gelsemium works on paralysis, especially when it is brought on by fear. It is also useful for performance anxiety where stress slows the canine athlete.

Hepar Sulphuris Calcareum (Burned oyster shells with sulphur)

Hepar sulphur works to dispel early-stage infection, whether it's from a bite wound or an abscess. Consider it for infected anal glands, skin eruptions and pus-filled wounds that are not large enough to require stitches.

Hypericum Perforatum (St. John's wort)

This remedy addresses nerve damage and the shooting, radiating pain associated with it. Try it for painful injuries affecting the tail and paws, especially those caused by crushing and puncture wounds.

Ledum Palustre (Marsh tea, wild rosemary)

Ledum is traditionally used for punctures and bites—wounds that do not bleed. It may also be effective for abscesses and inflamed joints.

Mercurius Solubilis (Mercury, quicksilver)

Merc sol is useful for conditions that are expressed with acrid discharges, such as infected anal glands. It can also help in treating gingivitis and for bouts of liquidy, mucousy diarrhea.

Nux Vomica (Poison nut)

This remedy is often called upon to help treat anxious and nervous patients who get so worked up they give themselves a stomachache. Try it on dogs suffering from indigestion, constipation, flatulence, gastric upsets and vomiting due to nervousness or overeating.

Homeopathy Resources

The Academy of Veterinary Homeopathy
6400 East Independence Blvd.
Charlotte, NC 28212
(866) 652-1590
www.TheAVH.org

Richard Pitcairn's web site offers a list of recommended practitioners who have completed his professional course in homeopathy. www.drpitcairn.com

Books

Dr. Pitcairn's Complete Guide to Natural Health for Dogs & Cats by Richard Pitcairn and Susan Hubble Pitcairn (Rodale, $17.95). A trailblazing book, this perennial favorite includes nutrition information, approaches to common ailments and Pitcairn's "particular love," homeopathy.

Homeopathic Care for Cats and Dogs: Small Doses for Small Animals by Don Hamilton, DVM (North Atlantic Books, $25). An indispensable reference that not only outlines treatment options and dosages, but also explains the theories and philosophy behind homeopathy.

Homeopathic First Aid for Animals: Tales and Techniques from a Country Practitioner by Kaetheryn Walker (Healing Arts Press, $14.95). Written in the folksy style that its name suggests, this anecdote-filled guide is a refreshing departure from the more clinical books listed here.

Homoeopathic Medicine for Dogs: A Handbook for Vets and Pet Owners by Hans Gunter Wolff (The C.W. Daniel Co., $28.50).

Pulsatilla (Windflower)

This remedy is helpful for dogs who are clingy and sensitive, especially those prone to separation anxiety. It is commonly used with false pregnancy.

Another good reference book that presents homeopathic remedies in the context of the conditions they can be applied to.

Pocket Manual of Homeopathic Materia Medica and Repertory by William Boericke (Laurier Books, $25) is a tried-and-true edition of this important reference tool for selecting precisely the right remedy for a particular condition and individual. But there are many other editions of Materia Medica and Repertory; one that many vets use is *Synoptic Materia Medica* (Homeopathic Educational Services, $40) by Frans Vermeulen. For an animal-specific Materia Medica, consider *Veterinary Materia Medica and Clinical Repertory With a Materia Medica of the Nosodes* (Beekman Publishing, $19.95) by G. MacLeod.

The Veterinarians' Guide to Natural Remedies for Dogs by Martin Zucker (Three Rivers Press, $14.95). A bright, easily navigable compilation of advice from an assortment of holistic vets. In addition to homeopathy, nutritional and herbal options are offered.

Remedies

Homeopathic remedies are available at most health-food stores as well as online at sites such as www.a2z homeopathy.com and www.homeopathyovernight.com. Investing in a homeopathic first aid kit is also a good idea. Kits of various sizes are available from Washington Homeopathic Products (800-336-1695 or www.homeopathy works.com) and Hahnemann Laboratories (888-4-ARNICA or www.hahnemannlabs.com), among others.

Rhus Toxicodendron (Poison ivy)

Rhus tox treats the very same conditions that, in larger doses, it creates: rashes and hives, especially those that are derived from contact with an irritant, such as poison ivy.

Silicea (Silica, pure flint)

Silicea helps regenerate dead tissue and knit bones and tendons. It cleanses the body of congestion, infection and mucous. It can also help heal scar tissue.

Sulphur

Often used for skin problems, Sulphur can be considered for mange and allergic reactions that manifest themselves in itchy, angry-looking skin. This remedy is also used to treat coughs, infected ears, flatulence and diarrhea.

Thuja Occidentalis (Arbor vitae)

A remedy with antibacterial properties, Thuja is sometimes used to combat the side effects of overvaccination.

Urtica Urens (Stinging nettle)

This remedy is made from the stinging nettle plant, and that is precisely the condition it helps heal. Consider Urtica urens for an acute condition that has a burning appearance and scalding pain, such as burns and hives.

DECISIONS, DECISIONS, DECISIONS

Odds are that after reading this chapter, a part of you may feel more confused than when you began. When should you turn to homeopathy? What about the herbs mentioned in earlier chapters? If you've skipped ahead and looked at the later chapters, you're probably even more perplexed by the choices before you. What about flower essences? Are they better for your dog's condition than, say, essential oils? How about acupuncture?

In short, which modality should you pick?

The answer is, it depends—on the circumstances and on you. For example, when my dog gets diarrhea, I might dose her with the homeopathic remedy Nux vomica, or I might give her some tablets of slippery elm, a common herb used for intestinal upset. If we're going to visit a new dog run, I might add some extra garlic to her meal. (Garlic is a very useful herb with immune-boosting properties.)

There is no blueprint I read to arrive at those treatments or preventions—I added them to my holistic repertoire with time and experience. The guidance and input of your vet is important, as are her limitations—she will only be able to tell you what she knows about, and so you may have to go elsewhere for guidance if she has little holistic knowledge to offer.

There may be certain modalities that you just have an affinity for. Oftentimes, a certain approach will just "feel" right. Go with that. You have to start somewhere. Don't let the sheer number of options paralyze you into not starting at all.

Chapter 4

Traditional Chinese Medicine: East Finally Meets West

I'm thirsty. Guess it's time to dig a well.

That clever metaphor for Western medicine's approach to health comes from the *Yellow Emperor's Classic of Internal Medicine*, a medical treatise attributed to Huang Di, a quasi-mythical figure said to have founded China around 4,000 B.C.E. Whether he actually existed or not is less important than the legacy associated with that first medical textbook, the principles of a healing system that today we know as Traditional Chinese Medicine, or TCM.

There are many metaphors for how Western medicine and TCM differ, and all underscore the former's tendency to wait for disease to be manifested before addressing the body's weaknesses and imbalances. When it does, the focus in Western medicine is on the individual pieces rather than the whole — on the diseased body part, not the overall constitution that enabled the disease to take hold in the first place.

From a TCM perspective, the best time to think about satisfying our thirst, or bolstering our health, is not when things have become so dire that we find ourselves in a crisis. Since we know we will always need to drink, and we will always need to maintain our health, the time to address those issues is when we feel sated and well.

For those who are new to it, the exquisite common sense of TCM can sometimes be overshadowed by the intricacies and idiosyncrasies of this ancient healing system. Developed at a time when society was agrarian and humanity's connection to the earth was much stronger and clearer than it is today, TCM draws its logic and philosophy from the rhythms of the natural world. The body's interior landscape is described in terms of elements such as water and metal and fire. The interactions of organ systems are evaluated in terms such as dampness and windiness.

To a Western ear, this can sound, well, silly. How could it be that your dog's liver is chilly or that her kidneys have too much wind? What kind of a diagnosis is Liver Fire Flaming Upward?

The first step to understanding TCM is putting aside our Western cultural context. In this high-tech age, which encourages us to lock ourselves away from nature and disconnect from the earth, describing our bodies in such naturalistic terms may seem simplistic, odd and perhaps naïve. But there are parallels between TCM and the hard science veterinarians have been steeped in.

"When I teach vets to practice TCM, I do translate it," says veterinarian Robert Silver. "Words like 'heat' and 'dampness' and 'phlegm' do have counterparts. Heat could be inflammation or infection. Dampness could be a defect in fluid metabolism or a pathologic buildup of tissue fluids. And while 'wind' doesn't translate well, it can be what we would call shifting symptoms."

Despite its longevity, the basic principles of TCM are fuzzy to most conventionally oriented vets and dog owners. But ironically, most are very familiar with one of TCM's most popular modalities, acupuncture. And some vets practice it without a deep understanding of the philosophy behind it.

"You definitely get the best results if you use the entire TCM system, because it's another conceptual way of seeing things," says Cheryl Schwartz, a veterinarian based in San Diego, California, and the author of *Four Paws Five Directions: A Guide to Chinese*

Medicine for Cats and Dogs. Rather than just treating the signs or expression of a disease, using the TCM system as a whole enables a practitioner to identify and treat the underlying causes of disease. "In hip dysplasia, for example, unless you address the kidney, you may not get as good a response," says Schwartz, because of the complexity of energy exchange in the body from a TCM perspective. "You may also need to address how blood is moving." But even when used in a superficial, disconnected way, TCM in general and acupuncture in particular are still effective. That, Silver points out, is a testament to their incredible healing ability.

> **Traditional Chinese Medicine Resources**
>
> *Four Paws Five Directions: A Guide to Chinese Medicine for Cats and Dogs* by Cheryl Schwartz, DVM (Celestial Arts, $25.95). One of the few books that applies Traditional Chinese Medicine to animals, it is indispensable for understanding the theory and philosophy behind such treatments as acupuncture and Chinese herbs.
>
> *The Last Chance Dog and Other True Stories of Holistic Animal Healing* by Donna Kelleher (Scribner, $24). A veterinarian's journey into using holistic modalities, including TCM.

A true TCM practitioner is as much artist as scientist, looking over the canvas that is the patient for any sign of disharmony. But with this healing system, honed over the millennia to reflect the body's intrinsic truths and ancient patterns, the crudest painter or practitioner can get results, even if he can't tell the difference between magenta and maroon. "The powerful thing about TCM," Silver says, "is you can still do paint by numbers and get a beautiful picture."

THE PRINCIPLES OF TCM

"Traditional Chinese Medicine is an extended metaphor," explains Bruce Ferguson, a holistic veterinarian from Micanopy, Florida. So the key to understanding TCM is to set aside cultural biases and try to follow the symbolism, looking for the greater meaning and wisdom in what Ferguson rightly reminds us is "the longest-running intact medical system on the planet."

Traditional Chinese Medicine relies on several interconnected concepts that, like the functions of the body that TCM heals, have blurry margins and frequent overlaps—something that new comers might have a hard time with. "TCM uses very simple words for very complex ideas," says Schwartz, adding that they have been refined for generations. She encourages dog owners to take the time to understand TCM, realizing that, like any new subject, there will be a learning curve. "It's important to be educated in this different way of thinking, and you will get something with every layer," she says. "With knowledge, people become much more open to fixing their animals—and themselves."

Qi

Many traditions of healing are centered around the concept of a central life force—the energy that infuses us all. In TCM, this animating energy is called Qi or Chi (pronounced "chee").

Qi is all around us—it makes up the world and it flows through physical spaces, from our backyards to our bodies. The goal in TCM is to manage the flow of this energy, since its balance within our bodies is what gives rise to good health.

One helpful metaphor for Qi is water. Imagine a gently flowing stream, moving briskly enough that debris such as branches and leaves are swept along, but not with such force that boulders are unearthed or boaters are swept away on dangerous currents. When the water is blocked, think of the stagnation and soupiness of a swamp; when it is unchecked, think of the blunt force and destruction of a tidal wave. Both symbolize extreme imbalances of Qi.

Meridians

In Traditional Chinese Medicine, Qi is thought to move through the body along meridians—akin to rivers or streams, if you want to continue our metaphor. These meridians connect and govern different body parts. If the Qi in a meridian is blocked or unbalanced, that disturbance in the energy flow can cause disease or malfunction in the body system and organs affiliated with that meridian.

There are a dozen major meridians with corresponding organs in a dog's body, and each meridian has a sister meridian whose energy complements it. Along each meridian are acupressure points, or acupoints. They are sort of like docks along the river of Qi, allowing energy to exit or enter the meridian. Most acupoints are located in an area of the body's surface that has many nerve endings, and each point has electrical properties. A point's location may not be anywhere near the organ or body system to which it corresponds.

Acupoints have many different classifications. Among them are *accumulation points,* which is where Qi gathers and can be released. *Alarm points* can tell a practitioner whether the energy imbalance goes beyond the meridian and involves a particular organ. *Association points* work on an organ directly and can bring energy to it.

Yin and Yang

Just as protons and electrons make up an atom, yin and yang comprise Qi. And like those negatively and positively charged particles, yin and yang are opposites. Yin is the calm, yielding, female energy, embodying stillness, darkness, water and the moon. Yang is the insistent, unyielding, male energy, representing activity, brightness, fire and the sun.

Despite their polarity, yin and yang are interdependent. This reciprocal relationship is represented in the symbol for yin and yang—a circle that is half black and half white. In the center of the black portion is a small, self-contained white circle; in the center of the white portion is a small black circle. In this way, both yin and yang contain each other, and each is incomplete without the presence of the other.

The yin-yang concept infuses virtually all aspects of Traditional Chinese Medicine. Each meridian, for example, has yin and yang organs. The yin organs, such as the lungs and the liver, are dense, while the yang organs, including the stomach and small intestines, are hollow or cylinder-like.

Yin and yang are never static. In an organ, in a meridian, in the body itself, they are fluid and always shifting. The challenge for a practitioner is to identify imbalances of yin and yang and adjust them so the body can function more easily.

A TOUR OF THE MERIDIANS

Lung Meridian. This meridian governs respiration, which can be described in TCM terms as taking Qi from the air and distributing it throughout the body. This meridian also rules the skin and hair. It is associated with yin energy, the autumn season and the element metal. Total number of acupoints along this meridian: 11.

Large Intestine Meridian. Elimination is the focal function here, and expelled along with bodily material is sluggish Qi. Because this is a sister, or complementary, meridian to the lung meridian, the large intestine meridian has yang energy. Like the lung meridian, it is affiliated with autumn and metal. Total number of acupoints: 20.

Stomach Meridian. This meridian is the center of digestion, extracting Qi from food and sending it, with the help of the spleen, to all the body's outposts. This meridian governs the muscles and lymph. It is associated with yang energy, the late summer season and the element earth. Total number of acupoints: 45.

Spleen Meridian. The sister to the stomach meridian, the spleen meridian, along with its associated organ, the pancreas, regulates the blood and the immune system. It is associated with yin energy, the late summer season and the element earth. Total number of acupoints: 21.

Heart Meridian. The symbolism of this organ explains the influence of the heart meridian: It is the repository of Shen, or spirit, which can be affected by negative thoughts and emotions. This meridian controls the circulation of blood. It is associated with yin energy, the summer season and the element fire. Total number of acupoints: 9.

Small Intestine Meridian. The sister to the heart, the small intestine is the sorter, absorbing nutrients and energy that nourish the body while discarding the chaff. The small intestine's Solomon-like discernment makes it a good partner with the heart, which struggles to balance emotions and thoughts. It is associated with yang energy, the summer season and the element fire. Total number of acupoints: 19.

Bladder Meridian. This meridian is a portal to all the others, as points along it can be used to balance the entire meridian system.

It is associated with yang energy, the winter season and the element water. Total number of acupoints: 67.

Kidney Meridian. Just as Shen energy lives in the heart, Jing energy lives in the kidneys. It is a kind of reserve of vitality or aliveness. Original Jing is hereditary, but it can bolstered or depleted through nutrition and sexual practices. The kidney meridian governs the growth of bones, the teeth and the reproductive system. A sister to the bladder meridian, the kidney meridian is associated with yin energy, the winter season and the element water. Total number of acupoints: 27.

Pericardium Meridian. Since the heart is so sensitive to feelings and emotions, this thin membrane that surrounds it acts as a protector. It is associated with yin energy, the summer season and the element fire. Total number of acupoints: 9.

Triple Heater Meridian. There are no organs associated with this meridian, which is the sister to the pericardium. Instead, the triple heater helps regulate temperature and metabolism in the body's three compartments—roughly, the head, trunk and lower body. It is associated with yang energy, the summer season and the element fire. Total number of acupoints: 23.

Gall Bladder Meridian. This is the meridian that orchestrates the flow of Qi through the body, a process that can be affected by emotional as well as physical imbalances. It is associated with yang energy, the spring season and the element wood. Total number of acupoints: 44.

Liver Meridian. Like its sister, the gall bladder meridian, the liver regulates Qi flow, largely through metabolism. It is associated with yin energy, the spring season and the element wood. Total number of acupoints: 14.

In addition to these 12 major meridians, there are two meridians that are used in TCM treatments to help regulate Qi. They are:

Governing Vessel Meridian. This meridian works to balance the body's yang energy. Total number of acupoints: 26.

Conception Vessel Meridian. This meridian works to balance the body's yin energy. Total number of acupoints: 24.

Five Element Theory

Traditional Chinese Medicine sees a correlation between substances in the world of nature and the body's organ systems. The world encompasses five different elements, each with their own properties and propensities, each interrelated in an inevitable cycle: *metal, water, wood, fire* and *earth.*

In the world, as well as the body, TCM identifies two cycles in which the elements are transformed. In the Creation Cycle, or *Sheng,* fire burns to create ash, which makes up earth. Earth gives rise to geological formations, which contain metal. When metal is smelted, it gives off steam, which becomes water. Water, in turn, feeds trees, allowing them to create wood. And wood, when consumed, makes fire.

In the Control Cycle, or *Ko,* the elements are destroyed, not created. Fire melts metal. Metal chops wood. Wood falls and blocks earth. Earth makes a barricade and dams water. Water returns us to the beginning of the cycle by dousing fire.

While this sounds charmingly folksy, what does it have to do with Traditional Chinese Medicine? In a word, everything. The Five Elements are used in TCM to classify the organs and meridians, and are further associated with seasons of the year. Since the TCM practitioner knows what the progression of the elements is in each cycle, she can follow that same pattern to see how imbalances will be manifested, depending on the organs involved.

The Eight Principles

While there are several methods used in TCM diagnosis, the Eight Conditions, or Eight Principles, are an integral tool. Grouped in pairs, the Eight Principles are really four sets of opposites: *yin* and *yang, internal* and *external, cold* and *hot, deficiency* and *excess.*

In a sense, the last six principles are redundant, since the first two, yin and yang, encompass them all: yin is internal, cold and deficient, yang is external, hot and excessive. But when a TCM practitioner is diagnosing, he or she will use all of them to come up with as complete a picture as possible of how yin and yang are manifesting physically in your dog.

TIMING IS EVERYTHING

Traditional Chinese Medicine holds that each organ system has a two-hour period during the day when it performs at its best: This period is when Qi is at its strongest.

How does this apply to your dog and her health? Let's say there's a particular time of day when your dog is sluggish, or when she vomits or has difficulty getting around. A TCM practitioner would consider that in the context of which meridian is most active at that time in helping arrive at a diagnosis.

Organ	Time
Liver	1-3 a.m.
Lung	3-5 a.m.
Large intestine	5-7 a.m.
Stomach	7-9 a.m.
Spleen	9-11 a.m.
Heart	11 a.m.-1 p.m.
Small Intestine	1-3 p.m.
Bladder	3-5 p.m.
Kidney	5-7 p.m.
Pericardium	7-9 p.m.
Triple Heater	9-11 p.m.
Gallbladder	11 p.m.-1 a.m.

A TCM diagnosis is elaborate, and will involve everything from the practitioner observing your dog to asking lifestyle-oriented questions about his home life, sleeping patterns, food preferences, elimination habits and activity levels. A practitioner will listen to the dog's pulse and examine his tongue. The practitioner actually reads 12 pulses, each corresponding to a meridian; the rate and force of each pulse reflects the energy of the meridian. The tongue, too, reflects the internal conditions of the dog, and shape, color and coating tell the practitioner how certain organs are functioning.

ACUPUNCTURE

Homeopathic vet Richard Pitcairn has a theory for why acupuncture—inserting fine-gauge needles into the critical acupoints to help modulate the flow of Qi—has been so readily embraced by the medical mainstream. "They understand it because it uses needles," he says of conventional practitioners. "And they're familiar with needles."

It's a sardonic point, but a well-taken one. Of all the holistic therapies, acupuncture is probably the best known and most accepted by the medical establishment, both human and veterinary. Many conventional doctors and vets acknowledge the palliative benefits of acupuncture, and might refer their patients to an acupuncture practitioner to help manage pain.

"Acupuncture has evolved from an alternative to a complementary therapy," says veterinarian Allen M. Schoen of Sherman, Connecticut, co-editor of *Complementary and Alternative Veterinary Medicine: Principles and Practice*. "It's being integrated along with conventional medicine and surgery, mostly where medications are not working or are having side effects and where surgery is not a reasonable option or has not worked, or where a client prefers to try a more natural, noninvasive approach first."

Acupuncture's acceptance is due in large part to the fact that it can be understood within the framework of Western medicine. You don't have to buy into the concept of Qi to explain why acupuncture works, because it can be understood on a biochemical level instead of a purely energetic one.

The Western theory is that inserting the needles releases chemicals, including endorphins, that increase blood flow and stimulate the nervous system. "You can explain it scientifically in a way conventional vets can understand," says veterinarian Donna Kelleher of West Seattle, Washington, author of *The Last Chance Dog and Other True Stories of Holistic Animal Healing*. "Instead of saying the Qi is blocked, you can explain that you have this nerve that is firing wrong." Instead of discussing energy meridians, which are invisible and purely energetic, she continues, conventional vets look to their physical counterparts—the regions of nerve receptors called dermatomes.

Acupuncture (the name comes from the Latin *acus*, meaning "needle," and *pungere*, which means "to pierce") has been used on animals for millennia. Ancient records indicate that the modality was used on Indian elephants at least 3,000 years ago. And Chinese rock carvings from 200 B.C.E. show soldiers piercing their steeds with arrows to prime them for the rigors of battle.

In modern veterinary medicine, acupuncture is used to treat neurological problems such as epilepsy and gastrointestinal disorders such as irritable bowel syndrome. Hormonal imbalances, reproductive problems, allergies . . . the list is very long. Acupuncture is probably most often used to treat musculoskeletal conditions such as arthritis, lameness, hip dysplasia and slipped disks. It is also often used for behavioral problems such as compulsive licking (which results in open wounds called lick granulomas) and separation anxiety. Acupuncture also speeds healing, and can be used after surgery to help an animal recover more quickly.

As with anything in life, there are some risks to acupuncture. Although the needles used by practitioners are sterile and are not reused, there is always a small possibility of infection. Broken needles, while rare, do happen, and in a worst-case scenario might need to be surgically removed. Another possible problem could be inadvertently puncturing an organ or hitting a nerve.

Probably the biggest concern about acupuncture is whether or not the needles hurt. The answer is no. While your dog might feel a slight twinge when the needle is inserted, there is no discomfort after that point. In fact, many dogs find acupuncture treatments relaxing and restorative, and actually drift off to sleep during them. "Dogs tend to really love the needles," says Kelleher. "They bark to come in."

While acupuncture can show immediate results, it's important to give the treatments time to work. Figure on allowing for a minimum of seven or eight visits before drawing any conclusions about whether acupuncture is helping.

There's also a strong argument to be made for having acupuncture on your dog *before* problems become apparent, as a maintenance therapy. The more smoothly Qi flows, the better your dog's body functions and the less likely it is that imbalances will persist and become chronic, leading to illness and disease. Indeed, many racetrack horses get acupuncture as part of their regular health regimen to keep them functioning at peak performance. Perhaps when acupuncture is more broadly embraced as a healing tool, veterinarians will begin promoting it as a way of maintaining the well-being of your companion animal.

Conversely, as more veterinarians learn about acupuncture, perhaps they will cultivate a deeper, more intuitive understanding of it—a level of practice that goes beyond a "connect the dots" mentality.

"Acupuncture is an artful practice," Ferguson says. While canine acupuncture charts show the location of the acupoints, they are not fixed points in the constellation that is the body. "When you're ill, depending which point it is, it can migrate up to an inch or two. There's an art to finding those points—you have to cultivate a special feel in your fingers."

Acupuncture Variations

While needling is the traditional approach used in acupuncture, it is not the only one. "It's like making apple pie," says Jody Kincaid, a holistic veterinarian from Anthony, New Mexico. "Everyone has their own recipe."

Electroacupuncture. In traditional acupuncture, points are stimulated by twirling the needles in a certain direction. In this variation, acupuncture needles are inserted, then pulsed with electric current to provide stimulation. This technique might be used on dogs who are in severe pain or are paralyzed, since the electrical stimulation works on the acupoints in a more intense way.

Laser acupuncture. As its name suggests, infrared lasers are used to stimulate the acupuncture points. This form of acupuncture is often for animals whom vets describe as "fractious"—basically, those who are snappish and irritated at being touched, much less stuck with needles.

Aquapuncture. A safe, sterile liquid is injected into a meridian point and the pressure from the liquid stimulates the point in lieu of a needle. This is helpful for dogs who will not sit still long enough for a traditional acupuncture session. Some veterinarians use aquapuncture after a plain needle treatment to boost the

THE BUZZ ON
ELECTROACUPUNCTURE

Acupoints have an electrical charge—that's how practitioners can evaluate the Qi in any given meridian. In the 1950s, German doctor Reinhold Voll came up with the idea of measuring whether or not an acupoint needs stimulation. This form of electrodermal screening has come to be known as Electro Acupuncture according to Voll, or EAV.

"Voll discovered that an acupoint should have enough residual strength to resist a current for three seconds," says veterinarian Jody Kincaid, who uses EAV to evaluate what points on a patient need the most work. Using an ohmmeter, he can test a dog's acupoints to determine precisely which are weakest. He can also test various substances or remedies to see if the body needs that energy or not.

"You have to open up the energy channels," he says, stressing the importance of unblocking meridians in TCM. "Herbs and remedies will go in and release toxins, but if you haven't opened up channels for them to drain, they will go somewhere else."

Since its inception about 50 years ago, EAV has acquired new names, including electrodermal screening, meridian assessment, energy screening and bio resonance therapy.

effects. The liquids used can include vitamin B12 in saline, distilled water and electrolyte solutions.

Moxibustion. Mugwort *(Artemesia vulgaris)* is an herb known for its warming quality in Chinese medicine. It has the ability to speed up sluggish Qi and energize meridians. In moxibustion, mugwort is burned during the acupuncture procedure and put in contact with an acupoint. Sometimes this is done directly by placing a cone-shaped piece of moxa (pressed mugwort) on the point and allowing it to burn toward the skin. In indirect moxibustion, burning moxa can be passed over the needle to heat it. Regardless of which method is used, care must be taken not to inadvertently burn the patient.

Sonapuncture. This technique uses ultrasound to stimulate the acupoints, usually requiring only 10 to 30 seconds per point.

Gold Bead Implants

Some animals have chronic imbalances that require almost constant stimulation to keep their bodies in harmony. One possibility for them might be a permanent form of acupuncture called gold bead implantation.

Developed and perfected by Terry Durkes, a veterinarian from Marion, Indiana, this procedure involves implanting gold-plated beads that are about the size of poppy seeds and have a slight magnetic charge. Sometimes gold wire is also used. The beads are injected using a 14-gauge needle while the dog is anesthetized.

Like acupuncture itself, gold-bead implantation is very safe. Durkes says the biggest risk of the whole procedure is the anesthesia, and in more than 25 years he has had only one incident of a misplaced bead accidentally being inserted in a joint.

The implants are often used for musculoskeletal problems such as hip dysplasia, osteochondritis, arthritis and spondylosis of the back. Age has an important influence on effectiveness: Durkes says his success rate for hip dysplasia runs about 98 percent for dogs under seven years of age; that number goes down to 75 percent for 7- to 12-year-olds and 50 percent for 12- to 17-year-olds.

Another area where gold beads are used is in neurological disorders such as epilepsy and Wobbler's syndrome. Positioning the gold beads for these conditions is more complicated, however, and Durkes notes that the success rate is not as high as for skeletal problems such as dysplasia.

Using what is called a "French pulse technique," the vet-acupuncturist uses her own pulse to diagnose what points to stimulate with beads. When she is holding the bead-loaded syringe over the correct point, the practitioner will feel her pulse increase and get slightly more erratic.

Like acupuncture itself, no one can say definitely why gold-bead acupuncture works, but Durkes theorizes that the slightly charged beads neutralize negative conditions in the joint or area, possibly changing the pH of the nerve receptor sites and alleviating pain.

The implants should not be used when cancer, tumors or bone infections are present, because their weak positive charge can actually encourage growth.

Only vets certified in acupuncture can do gold bead implants, and even then it is no longer taught as part of the regular syllabus of The International Veterinary Acupuncture Society (IVAS). Instead, vet–acupuncturists who want to learn it must seek it out as continuing education. Durkes estimates he has taught fewer than 100 vets how to perform the procedure, so finding vets who can implant gold beads might be a challenge.

Acupuncture Resources

American Academy of Veterinary Acupuncture
P.O. Box 1532
Longmont, CO 80502-1532
(303) 772-6726
www.aava.org

The International Veterinary Acupuncture Society (IVAS)
P.O. Box 271395
Ft. Collins, CO 80527-1395
(970) 266-0666
www.ivas.org

ACUPRESSURE

Acupressure uses the same principles as acupuncture, except that fingers are used instead of needles—sort of "acupuncture lite." "The beauty of acupressure is the owner or guardian can do it themselves," explains Amy Snow, who (with Nancy Zidonis) is the author of *The Well-Connected Dog: A Guide to Canine Acupressure.*

"There are some animals who are so sensitive that all they need is acupressure," says Kelleher. "And sometimes animals are too refractory"—a nice way of saying impossible to manage— "to do acupuncture."

Financial considerations also come into the picture in choosing acupressure over acupuncture. Owners who cannot afford weekly acupuncture appointments can be taught the acupoints and can work on their dog at home, where the animal is likely to be more relaxed, anyway.

Snow became interested in canine acupressure about five years ago when her Golden Retriever was diagnosed, in her words, "with no hips." Opting for experimental surgery, she did acupressure on him before he went into the operating room and resumed it when he came out. A week later, "we strolled into the vet's office," Snow remembers. And the vet, focusing more on the patient's progress than the calendar page, exclaimed offhandedly, "Oh, is he here for his monthly check?"

"We know that acupressure can enhance and create an environment for healing," says Snow. "It helps bring more blood and Qi to an area that needs healing." For that reason, the list of conditions acupressure can alleviate is diverse, ranging from helping reduce pain in arthritic dogs to teaching amputees how to rebalance and reuse their bodies. "In senior citizen dogs, I see a tremendous response physically in terms of extending comfort," says Snow. "I'm not going to say we're going to cure a disease like spondylosis, but we can slow it and have the animal feel much more comfortable."

Like acupuncture, acupressure is often used for musculoskeletal conditions and other physical ailments. But Zidonis points out that it also has a place in helping an animal with emotional issues, such as fearfulness or grieving over the loss of a housemate. While she thinks acupressure needs to be combined with behavior modification and training to help a dog get over her emotional issues, "just the bonding effect of acupressure can be calming itself."

There are some caveats to doing acupressure on your dog, most of them relating to pregnant animals. Since a handful of points can induce premature labor, the conventional wisdom is to avoid acupressure entirely during pregnancy. Also, do not do acupressure on a dog who has just been exercised vigorously or who has just eaten a huge meal. Wait until the body has cooled down or the food has been digested, so the dog's energy is calm and diffused. Avoid acupressure if the dog is dealing with an infection or infectious disease. And, as always, if you suspect your dog is not well, have him checked by a vet first.

Acupressure Resources

The Well-Connected Dog: A Guide to Canine Acupressure by Amy Snow and Nancy Zidonis (Tallgrass Publishers, $25.95).

But generally speaking, with a young, healthy dog acupressure is a very safe procedure—even when performed by a novice who is just feeling her way. When it comes to balancing Qi, the body is very forgiving, says Kelleher. "When there's a deficiency, the body will feel that pressure and energy and will eat it up." But when a point is stimulated that doesn't need to be, the body just sort of yawns and rolls over. "Where there's excess, it kind of ignores that energy," she concludes. "The body is wonderful at regulating itself."

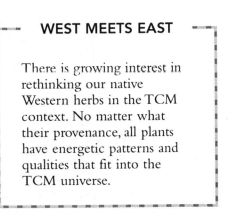

WEST MEETS EAST

There is growing interest in rethinking our native Western herbs in the TCM context. No matter what their provenance, all plants have energetic patterns and qualities that fit into the TCM universe.

And in the end, it isn't just the dog who benefits from an acupressure session. "There's such an energy exchange when a person is performing acupressure instead of needling," says Zidonis. "We don't know who heals who."

CHINESE HERBS

Acupuncture isn't the only way to balance and regulate Qi. Most ancient cultures used herbs as part of their folk medicine tradition, but the Chinese have taken millennia to develop and hone their use of medicinal plants—especially in the context of TCM philosophies such as the Eight Principles and the Five Elements—into a complex system of healing.

As a result, TCM assigns herbs different qualities. Some are hot or warm, others are cold or cool, still others are neutral. In this respect, they can be used to help regulate yin and yang and bring the body to equilibrium.

In addition to their thermal qualities, TCM recognizes that herbs have a direction—upward, downward or outward. Adding to the complexity, each herb is also classified by function—some herbs, for example, are sweating herbs, while others are harmonizing or tonifying.

Chinese Herb Resources

The American Association of Oriental Medicine's Complete Guide to Chinese Herbal Medicine: How to Treat Illness and Maintain Wellness with Chinese Herbs by David Molony et al. (Berkley Publishing Group, $13)

Chinese Natural Cures: Traditional Methods for Remedies and Preventions by Henry C. Lu (Black Dog & Leventhal, $24.98)

A Handbook of Chinese Healing Herbs by Daniel P. Reid (Shambhala Publications, $15)

The Way of Chinese Herbs by Michael Tierra (Pocket Books, $18)

When herbs are used in TCM, they are usually prescribed as part of a formula. A combination called *Gan Mao Ling,* for example, is used to ward off viral infections, and *Tang Kuei* is a blood tonic often used to bolster immunity and help during convalescence.

Silver helped develop the course curriculum for the International Veterinary Acupuncture Society's basic course in traditional Chinese veterinary herbal medicine and taught it for seven years. One reason Chinese herbs are not more commonly used, even by holistic vets, he says, is that they are perceived as foreign, literally as well as conceptually. "If we can't pronounce something, it's even harder for us to understand," he says. Add to that a medical community that is "chauvinistic" about research done in other countries, no matter how extensive or compelling. And some vets and owners are put off by trying Chinese herbs because they think it requires mastering the complexity of Traditional Chinese Medicine.

That last assumption is simply not true, says Silver. "You can use Chinese herbs as a symptomatic 'point and shoot'—you don't have to know a damn bit about yin and yang." And because most Chinese herbs are available as ready-made, or patent, formulas, concerns about dosage and the balancing effects between herbs have already been addressed by the formulators.

There is, however, a debate about the quality of some formulations imported from China. "The main concerns with patent [formulas] are adulteration with pharmaceuticals, like antihistamines, which is actually accepted in China, and the use of certain heavy metals, such as cinnabar or mercury, in some of their formulations," says Silver. "Also, poorer-quality formulas might use cheaper, less potent plant sources."

As a result, many practitioners use Chinese herb formulations that are made with plants grown and harvested in North America. Regardless of the source, be prepared for the bottom line: Chinese herbs can be expensive compared to their Western counterparts.

Chapter 5

Touching Therapies: A Look at Hands-On Healing

It's no surprise that most dogs love to be touched and petted. But what many of their human caretakers don't realize is that we can take that hands-on contact to much higher levels.

Studies in human infants show how important touch is for bonding between parents and their newborn children. Touching not only feels good, but it deepens our relationships and builds a sense of trust and well-being. It is no different with our animals.

Touch has a physical effect on the body, as well. Massage— that is, touching with intention—activates the parasympathetic nervous system, which triggers the body to relax and conserve its energy reserves.

We touch our animals all the time—an absentminded pat here, some distracted fur-stroking there. Although we might not be aware of how much physical contact we are making, we do know, perhaps unconsciously, that the contact makes both of us feel good. How much more effective, then, can we be if we are more purposeful when we touch our animals, using that healing art to address specific problems, whether emotional or physical?

This chapter looks at several kinds of touching therapies, from the very dramatic—the bone manipulations of chiropractic—to the very subtle—the gentle circular motions of a bodywork technique called TTouch.

CHIROPRACTIC

In 1983, when veterinarian Sharon Willoughby graduated from chiropractic school and became interested in using the spinal manipulation techniques she had learned on her animal patients, she got a uniform response: Unbridled laughter.

"It was really tough—everyone thought I was a quack," remembers Willoughby, who now lives in Wasilla, Alaska, where she has a small chiropractic-only practice that focuses on horses and sled dogs. "When I got out of chiropractic school, the chiropractors didn't want me and the vets didn't want me, either. But I kept on trying. The only way to make progress was persistence and education."

Today, of course, it's Willoughby who has had the last laugh. The organization she helped found, the American Veterinary Chiropractic Association, is the primary association certifying veterinarians and human chiropractors in animal chiropractic.

Chiropractic is based on the theory that the spine, with its interconnected bones and complex network of nerves, is one of the body's primary gateways to good health. When the spine develops subluxations, or displacements, of those bones, it can irritate nerves, which in turn can cause imbalances in the body. Through "adjustments," or manipulations of the spine, chiropractors gently push those bones back into place.

As with humans, chiropractic is useful for treating sports injuries incurred by jumping and running as in the sport of agility. Those kinds of activities put tremendous pressure on the skeletal system.

Constant corrections with a metal choke collar can also cause upper-cervical neck injuries and pain that can be addressed by chiropractic. Increasingly, the improper use of head halters is also leading to neck injuries. Dogs with lower back pain, especially

FIRM FOUNDATION

Dog breeders talk a lot about canine conformation. The phrase refers to a dog's physical structure, and how closely it conforms to the written standard for the breed. (You'll often see it misspelled, but "confirmation" is what you get when you make a hotel reservation.) No matter what kind of dog you have, being aware of his conformation, and its weak points, is crucial in preventing injuries.

For example, if you have a dog with straight shoulders— that is, the shoulder blade is more upright, rather than laying back at a more sloping angle to the ground—the dog's front end won't be able absorb shock very well. So, if you have a dog with straight shoulders who is doing agility, be mindful of the wear and tear you are putting on that weak front assembly. Every jump or leap shifts the dog's body weight on to those vulnerable shoulders, and the greater the impact, the greater the stress. Be judicious about how many jumps you direct her to do, and consider these structural weaknesses when asking her to do physically strenuous activities.

Dachshunds, whose elongated spines are particularly susceptible to disc herniation, may also benefit from chiropractic adjustments.

Most people take their dogs for chiropractic because the animal is in pain or has sustained some kind of joint or muscle injury. But as with humans, canine chiropractic can and should be used as preventive care, keeping a dog's skeletal system in balance to *avoid* stress and injury.

When Willoughby was in practice in Illinois, most of her chiropractic cases involved chronic problems such as disc disease, paralysis and lameness. "It's the whole concept of what health care is—most people only see it as taking care of disease, not maintaining health," she says. But the best defense is a good offense, and Willoughby encourages owners to bring their animals in for chiropractic maintenance before problems start. As with most things, the dog's individual circumstances will dictate frequency. Hard-core canine athletes who participate in physically demanding performance events such as agility or lure coursing might require monthly adjustments; a healthy middle-aged dog who gets adequate but not strenuous exercise might benefit from chiropractic twice a year.

This does not mean that the lazier your dog, the less likely he is to be a candidate for chiropractic. "Sometimes couch potatoes are the worst because they don't get any exercise at all," Willoughby warns. "They can injure themselves jumping on and off the couch."

The Chiropractic Controversy

Like many things holistic, chiropractic met with resistance and scorn in the human arena just a few decades ago. Dismissed as quackery by medical doctors, it existed on the sidelines up until recently. Now, chiropractic has become so commonly accepted that many HMOs include it as part of their insurance coverage.

Veterinary medicine, sadly, has yet to catch up. Most veterinarians do not have the opportunity to learn chiropractic care in veterinary school, and the American Veterinary Medical Association has refrained from taking a stand on chiropractic. Currently, the organization does not endorse or condemn it, but has convened a special committee to study chiropractic, as well as other forms of "alternative" medicine.

Most veterinarians who practice chiropractic are accredited by the American Veterinary Chiropractic Association (AVCA), which also certifies human chiropractors to treat animals. The difficulty for chiropractors who are not vets, however, is that many states prohibit them from working on animals unless the animal is referred by a veterinarian. In at least one state, New York, it is illegal for chiropractors to do any adjustments on animals, even if a veterinarian recommends it or supervises the procedure.

Daniel Kamen, a chiropractor from Illinois who is not a vet, has made a career of teaching chiropractic techniques for horses, cats and dogs to vets, human chiropractors and laypeople who attend his seminars and read his books, including *The Well Adjusted Dog*. And he has made a veritable sport of enraging state veterinary boards, some of which have plied him with lawsuits and injunctions because they contend that in his seminars he is teaching people to practice veterinary medicine without a license.

A TOUCHY SUBJECT

Who is the better chiropractic practitioner for your dog, a human chiropractor or a veterinarian? A human chiropractor may not have as in-depth an understanding of canine physiology as a vet, but is probably more experienced at performing manual manipulations—which can cause damage if not done correctly. A veterinarian with chiropractic certification may not perform anywhere near as many adjustments as a human chiropractor, but has that detailed knowledge of the canine body.

"It's been a sticking point forever," says Sharon Willoughby, who, as both a veterinarian and a chiropractor, can see both sides of the question. In her personal opinion, "I think the best chiropractors for animals are chiropractors, but where the chiropractor can really fall down is in knowing about the animals."

Ideally, Willoughby would like to see both working as a team. "The idea was to work together and help the animals, not sit around fighting about whose piece of the pie it is."

No matter who provides your dog with chiropractic care, make sure she or he is certified with the American Veterinary Chiropractic Association (AVCA). And your vet should always be the "gatekeeper" regarding any chiropractic treatment. If your dog goes to a human chiropractor to be adjusted, make sure your vet has examined the dog completely to rule out any underlying medical problems related to the spine or surrounding tissue that may be causing the pain, such as a tumor.

Practitioners such as Willoughby are understandably concerned about owners attempting chiropractic techniques on their own animals. "Unless you've got one-on-one training, a book or class doesn't do anything for you," she warns. "I think that with anything that you can help with, you can also do harm." In an animal with disc disease, for example, administering a chiropractic adjustment in the wrong place at the wrong time can result in permanent paralysis. Indeed, Willoughby argues that she would

CALLING CARDS

A practitioner's title tells you a lot about her level of training:

Animal Chiropractor: *a doctor of chiropractic who has been certified by the AVCA*

Veterinarian Certified in Animal Chiropractic: *a veterinarian who is AVCA-certified*

Veterinary Chiropractor: *a veterinarian who is also a doctor of chiropractic*

like to see more extensive training in chiropractic for veterinarians themselves—such as a three-year stint in college instead of the 180-hour certification courses that are commonly offered today.

Whether or not one agrees with Kamen's willingness to teach chiropractic to laypeople, his story underscores the stalemate that the veterinary community finds itself facing: unwilling to embrace complementary medicine at the same time that it refuses to enable others to fulfill a need for which there is a definite—and lucrative—demand.

A handful of veterinary schools have begun to offer chiropractic training to students, and it seems almost inevitable it will eventually be incorporated into the regular curriculum—if only because market forces call for it, and vets don't want to give up that economic pie slice to chiropractors, who are more than happy to take it.

Chiropractic Resources

American Veterinary Chiropractic Association (AVCA)
442154 E. 140 Rd.
Bluejacket, OK 74333
(918) 784-2231
www.animalchiropractic.org

THE ABCS OF VOM

Veterinary chiropractic has spawned at least one hybrid, a technique called Veterinary Orthopedic Manipulation, or VOM. Developed by former veterinarian William Inman, who for a time was affiliated with Kamen, VOM does not use manual adjustments to deal with subluxations.

"The only animals that are injured with chiropractic are injured with the manual technique," says Inman. Instead, his technique instead uses an accelerometer, or activator—a spring-loaded pushing device that is often used in human chiropractic.

A "chiropractic-like" therapy, and not technically chiropractic itself, VOM works on the premise that subluxations are not remedied by manipulating the bones of the spine back into place, but rather by releasing pressure on the nerves that run around and through the spinal column.

VOM uses the accelerometer first to test the animal to see if there are any reflexive responses, such as muscle jerks or winces, which would indicate there is a subluxation. If subluxations are found, they are treated by using the accelerometer to administer a gentle adjustment.

VOM Resources

VOM Technology/International Association of Veterinary Chiropractitioners (IAVCP)
7769 58th Avenue NE
Seattle, WA 98115
(206) 523-9917
www.vomtech.com

Inman's organization, the International Association of Veterinary Chiropractitioners (IAVCP), certifies both veterinarians and chiropractors in the VOM technique.

MASSAGE

Who doesn't love a massage? When done correctly, it feels good and leaves you with an overall sense of well-being and relaxation—whether you're a person or a Pomeranian.

But massage does more than just feel good. It aids in the circulation of lymph, helps oxygenate the body and releases muscle tension. Because it's so supportive of overall health and functioning, massage is also useful for animals who are suffering from a chronic illness such as heart disease or arthritis, or who are recovering from surgery or an injury. And with a healthy dog, regular sessions keep you in touch with the changes and conditions in his body, alerting you to problems before they progress too far.

"Even if at first it sounds complex, massage is very easily learned," says registered massage therapist Jean-Pierre Hourdebaigt of Wellington, Florida, who along with Shari L. Seymour is the author of *Canine Massage: A Practical Guide.* "It's just like driving a car—there are a few basic rules you need to know to do it safely."

Among the caveats: Be careful with areas that are inflamed, because applying friction can worsen the condition. Do not do massage if the dog has a viral infection. And avoid working on dogs with varicose veins.

"Beyond that, everyday touch can bring such comfort to an animal, especially an aging one," says Hourdebaigt. Humans also benefit from dropping their inhibition and letting their fingers go. "They get heat in their hands when they massage an animal," he says, "and it's like an awakening." The feeling often is mutual. Massage triggers the parasympathic response of the dog's nervous system, signaling the body to go into healing and repair mode. That calmness of the body enables nervous and abused animals to overcome their sensitivities and trust their human caretakers. "I've seen many animals who have been mistreated, and within three to five sessions they have switched their personas entirely around," says Hourdebaigt. "They are learning to trust."

"Any time you massage an animal, you will get bonding value," he continues. "And I think that connection with the animal is what attracts people to massage in the first place."

Unlike chiropractic, massage does not deal with a dog's bones. It focuses instead on the soft issues of the body, such as muscles. Always avoid massaging bone, or even close to it, as this is one area where you can do damage.

Canine massage therapists have an in-depth understanding of a dog's physiology, which enables them to pinpoint areas of stress and injury. In performance dogs, the feedback derived from massage can reveal whether the animal is being overtrained and can help prime her for an upcoming competition.

Some dogs are more sensitive than others to being touched and handled. Areas of concern vary from dog to dog. For one dog, paw touching can be very stressful; another might snap if you even brush against her hindquarters.

First and foremost, do not massage a dog you do not know, or even your own dog if she has behavioral issues that might prompt her to act aggressively toward you if you push too far into her space. Since massage is a relationship-building experience, the first requirement is a solid relationship. If you two don't have that, wait until it develops. If aggression is a concern, consult a behaviorist immediately.

For dogs who have issues about certain parts of their body but who you know will pose no danger to you, work to desensitize them to having that part of their body touched. If your dog is uncomfortable about having his paws touched, use a clicker to click and treat him each time he lets you touch his paw. (See Chapter 8 for a full description of how clicker training works.) Start off slowly, working up to longer periods of touching as the dog grows more comfortable.

The best way to create touch-tolerance in a dog is to instill it in puppyhood. Praise and reward your pup for letting you touch him all over. Make it into a game, and never use force. With lots of rewards and reinforcement, your puppy will carry these positive associations into adulthood.

Massage Mind-Set

Giving a massage is a gradual process, as is learning how to give one to your dog. Here are some tips that will benefit both of you.

Start slow. Despite your good intentions, your dog initially has no idea what you are up to, and he might need some time to realize that this is supposed to be a *pleasant* activity.

Especially for the first few sessions, it's important to approach your dog properly. Some dogs are intimidated when someone sits directly in front of them or drapes their body over them. Sitting next to your dog, facing in the same direction she does, is a non-threatening pose that most dogs will accept.

Let go of the misconception that the more pressure you apply, the more good you will do. Light stroking is just as valid a massage technique as deep muscle work. There's also a higher likelihood of success, because the gentler you are, the less chance you have of making your dog uncomfortable or concerned.

Set the mood—and the ritual. Because they are supposed to be relaxing (in theory, anyway), massages should be done in a quiet, traffic-free place. Close the door so other nosy household animals can't wander in and interrupt your flow. Think about how massages are given to humans—in a tranquil place, with dimmed lights and perhaps soft music playing. Replicate those conditions as best you can with your dog.

Find a position where your dog is comfortable—on a table-top, on your lap if it's a small dog, or on the floor. Since you want to establish a signal that says, "It's massage time," dedicate a special pillow or blanket to these sessions. When you take it out, the dog knows exactly what's coming. (If she turns and heads for the hills, it's time to re-evaluate just how good your massages feel to her.)

Learn to read your dog. Dogs can and do say "ouch," or "I've had enough." They just don't use words. If your dog is pulling away from you or yelping, or is tensed, or gets up to leave, that means she isn't enjoying the contact and you need to pull back. Signs of contentment should be just as obvious: leaning into you, falling asleep, licking, stretching and groaning (in pleasure, that is!).

Dogs, like humans, do not all enjoy the same things. "Some like light massage, some like it deep. Some dogs like long massages, others are ready to go after 10 minutes," Hourdebaigt says. It's up to you to figure out what your dog's pleasure is.

Instead of being silent through the massage—something you may do unconsciously, especially if you are concentrating deeply—talk to your dog in a soft, reassuring patter. This will help both of you relax even more.

Remember your dog's physical makeup. Always massage away from the extremities and toward the center of the body, so toxins don't get trapped and can be easily flushed out of the system. So, for example, if you are massaging a leg, work from the paw up to the thigh, not from the thigh down.

Also, since most dogs don't find it relaxing to have their fur ruffled, try to work in the same direction as the hair grows.

Don't assume the position. Dogs are individuals; they each have their preferences about what makes them comfortable. Instead of forcing a dog to lie on his side—something male dogs may hesitate to do, as it is a very vulnerable posture—work with the positions your dog is most comfortable in, whether standing, sitting or lying down. One of my dog's favorite massage positions is to plunk all 95 pounds of himself on my lap, with his back to me, as I sit cross-legged on the floor. I may need a massage afterward, but at least he's happy.

Learn to read yourself. Tense people shouldn't give massages. If you're feeling negative, you'll transmit that to your dog—which is just the opposite of the outcome you're looking for.

Wait for the right time. When you plan your massage sessions, remember that dogs have different rhythms and preferences than you do. Just because you are ready to give a massage doesn't mean it's a good time for your dog to receive one.

When I started giving massages to my dogs, I chose the evenings, after I had returned from a draining day at work and was settling down to watch TV. After all, that would have been the ideal time for *me* to get a massage. But the last thing my dogs wanted to do was to get down off the couch and have a massage. They live to curl up into little balls on the sofa at night, and would much rather snooze than shmooze.

Our massage sessions were short and sweet: The minute they got the opportunity, they hopped back up on the couch and curled up so tight that there was no opportunity to reach anything but an errant ear.

But one day I noticed that whenever I sat at my computer typing in the late morning, both dogs would invariably wander in, stand next to me in my chair, stare at the keyboard and then whine for me to give them a butt scratch or a prolonged petting. It took me months to figure out that they were trying to tell me, "If you want to touch and massage me, now's a good time." Immersed in commas and paragraphs, I just wasn't listening. Humans can be so dense that way.

HOT STUFF

Christine Zink, a Maryland-based veterinarian who specializes in sports medicine and is the author of *Peak Performance:
Coaching the Canine Athlete,* recommends combining heat
therapy with massage to help speed up the healing of an
injured muscle or joint.

Wet a hand towel with hot water and wring it dry, so
only the warm moisture remains. Place it on the affected
area, cover with a heating pad turned to the medium setting,
and keep wrapped for 10 minutes.

Remove the towel and heating pad and massage the tissue
right above and below the affected joint with the heel of
your palm.

Repeat the massage above and below the injured area, this
time using the balls of your three middle fingers instead of
your palm. Don't press any harder than you would on your
eyeball.

Next, massage the area over the joint by gently rubbing
the joint between the thumb and fingers—Zink likens this
to the finger-rubbing gesture that is the nonverbal shorthand
for "money." Then gently flex and extend the leg, without
forcing it. Finally, run the flat of your hand down the leg
once or twice in the direction of the hair.

Massage Menu

Here are some simple massage techniques you can use on a
healthy dog. As always, if the dog tells you to stop, please listen.

- **Effleurage.** This French word means "to skim." It
  refers to long, firm strokes made with the palm of the
  hand that glide along the dog with constant, though
  light, pressure. Always stroke toward the heart, not away
  from it. Effleurage is a good way to both start and end
  a massage, because its rhythmic, gentle waves are relaxing. Do these gliding strokes from head to tail, and to
  transition from one massage technique or body part to
  another.

HOLD THE MYO

If you've ever gone to a human massage therapist, you know that massage comes in all flavors, from Swedish to shiatsu. As canine massage gets more mainstream, practitioners are focusing more on nuanced techniques. Myofascial release—which uses skin lifts and rolls to manipulate the tough connective tissue layer known as the fascia—is a prime example.

The fascia is found in layers everywhere in the body, surrounding every muscle group and all the organs. "To do massage without myofascia is like serving dinner without salt and pepper," says Jean-Pierre Hourdebaigt, who is writing a book on the subject.

Myofascial release "is a very different approach than massage, and it doesn't look like much," he says. Hourdebaigt likens tensed fascia to a parking brake in a car. When it is locked up, it needs to be manually released. Myofascial release uses gentle, continuous stretching to relax fascia that have become bound or bunched, restoring range of motion and alleviating pain.

- **Kneading.** Think about how you knead a ball of dough—using your palm to apply pressure, lifting, then moving on to a nearby area to continue. You can apply this technique to large muscles. For smaller muscles use your fingertips, making small circles and pressing gently.

- **Skin lifting.** Use this on areas of the dog where there is loose skin, such as the neck or back. Using your thumb and forefinger, gently take a fold of skin and lift—not so much that you hurt the dog, but just enough to pull up and release.

- **Tail pulls.** Of all a dog's parts, the tail usually gets short shrift during a massage. Perhaps that's because since childhood we've been warned never to tug on a dog's tail. But done properly and gently, tail tugs can feel very good. First, be sure the dog has no injuries or weaknesses in her tail. Grip the tail at its base and gently squeeze it. Work your way down the tail, being careful not to apply too much pulling pressure, and squeezing as you grip.

Massage Resources

Dog Massage by Maryjean Ballner (St. Martin's Griffin, $11.95). Written with a folksy touch, a good beginner's book.

Canine Massage: A Practical Guide by Jean-Pierre Hourdebaigt and Shari L. Seymour (Howell Book House, $24.95). Lots of physiological information, as well as in-depth discussion of techniques and routines.

The Healing Touch: The Proven Massage Program for Cats and Dogs by Michael W. Fox (Newmarket Press, $12.95). One of the first on the subject.

- **Stretches.** If you have a performance dog, encouraging him to stretch before vigorous workouts can help extend his range of motion. Make sure the dog is warmed up before you do these exercises. Trotting him around in circles for five minutes or so should get him—and his muscles—warmed up. Then, using a piece of food as a lure, you can get him to lower his head between his front legs and stretch his neck outward and upward. Making sure he keeps his rear legs in place, get him to stretch to touch each flank so he can get his treat. One great all-over canine body stretch is the play bow (the dog's front legs are straight out and parallel to the ground; his rear and tail are up in the air). You can teach your dog how to do a play bow on command by holding a piece of food on the floor and making him bow to reach it.

After any strenuous exercise, make sure your dog gets a cooldown walk, just as racehorses do. A slow, steady walk for five minutes will help cool the body down and dispel lactic acid, which causes muscle stiffness.

TELLINGTON TTOUCH

Tellington TTouch is a system of bodywork created by animal expert Linda Tellington-Jones to help relax animals and modify their behavior by bringing them more in tune with their own bodies. Although TTouch obviously uses touch, it is not massage. Its goal is not simply to release muscle tension, but rather to stimulate new neural pathways, reawaken slumbering cells and prompt a dog to think instead of to simply react.

How can techniques such as skin-stimulating touches help awaken a dog's ability to learn and listen? Here's an analogy: Say you take the same route to work every day. It won't take but a few weeks before the ride is so predictable that you stop seeing all the houses and buildings that you pass every day. They are there, but not to you. You've worn too deep a groove in your routine.

But if every day you were required to take a different route to work, you would be roused from your complacency. You'd notice more things as you ride by; you'd be more present and alert during that commute. You'd start thinking about what streets you might take tomorrow, about the shade of yellow those people chose to paint that bungalow, about how funny the sycamore trees look when they lose their leaves.

Our body sense—or our dog's—is no different than that car ride. Because we are creatures of habit, we adopt certain body moves, certain stances, and habitually fall into them. To take this a step further, some healers suggest that all the traumatic experiences we go through are somehow stored on a cellular level, leading us to react unthinkingly and reflexively when those same situations present themselves again.

TTouch reprograms the dog's sense of his physical body—and the corresponding emotional and behavioral issues—through the following techniques.

Bodywork

Tellington's TTouches—gentle, connected circular movements all along a dog's body—help jump-start cellular activity and increase

COSMETIC SURGERY

This chapter discusses therapies that maintain equilibrium in a dog's skeletal structure, release tension in muscles and support overall body awareness. But there are some appearance-altering conventions in our dog culture that, while supported by tradition or functionality, aren't compatible with the idea of balance that is at the heart of a holistic approach.

Cosmetic surgeries such as docking (amputation of the tail) or cropping (surgical trimming of ear cartilage to make a folded ear stand upright) are discouraged (and sometimes illegal) in most of Europe. But in this country tails are routinely docked on dozens of breeds, including Australian Shepherds, Old English Sheepdogs, Rottweilers and English Springer Spaniels. Ears are cropped on American Staffordshire Terriers, Pit Bulls, Great Danes and Manchester Terriers, among others. Some breeds—such as Boxers, Doberman Pinschers and Schnauzers—get a double whammy, being both docked and cropped.

There's also a third procedure that is not as hotly debated, but still falls into the realm of cosmetic surgery: dewclaw removal. This fifth claw, sort of the doggie equivalent of a thumb, is located above the dog's pastern.

Proponents for these surgical procedures say they are needed as much for function as aesthetics. Docked tails are not as liable to be injured as long, thumping ones, the theory goes. Also, in breeds developed to guard or fight, short tails and docked ears make it more difficult for the dog to be grasped and held by an intruder or other dog. Docked ears benefit from increased air circulation and so are less prone to infections. And dewclaws can catch on shrubbery and even carpeting, resulting in tearing and repeat injuries.

Opponents of tail docking and ear cropping counter that not only are they painful procedures, but they can have both physical and psychological ramifications down the line. Some veterinarians suggest that removing a portion of the tail, which is an extension of the vertebrae, creates disharmony in the dog's skeletal structure.

awareness. The TTouches have different names, each one corresponding to the animal that best represents it, from the Raccoon Touch (which uses the finger tips) to the Llama Touch (using the back of the fingers).

Without the rest of his tail to balance him as he runs and maneuvers, a dog may rely on other parts of his body to compensate, thus straining them.

The same argument can be made for dewclaws, which catch on things precisely because that is their function. If you videotape a dog running full tilt in a field and slow down the tape at the point where he veers, you will see that at a certain moment he has his entire arm, from the elbow down, perpendicular to the ground to help him change direction. Without the dewclaw to grip the ground, the dog is again forced to redistribute that function—and impact—to other parts of the body that were not designed to absorb them.

Anatomical issues aside, dogs have an exquisite and elaborate communication system that uses all parts of their bodies. Tails and ears are important transmitters in this respect, and when they have been surgically altered, dogs cannot communicate their body language as clearly or subtly as they would intend, leading to all sorts of social misunderstandings.

Tail docking and ear cropping, while performed at a young age, are nonetheless traumatic. And holistic practitioners point out that negative emotions are felt so deeply by the body that they are stored in its cells, regardless of the age at which they were felt.

That said, ours is a complex society, weighted down with traditions and expectations that can seem insurmountable. If you own a breed that is traditionally docked or cropped, what are your options? Can you or should you refuse to do those procedures, and anger everyone else in your breed community? Should you continue to dock and crop while quietly working to change perceptions and norms? Or should you just walk away and find another breed where those issues don't exist?

A holistic approach doesn't exist in a vacuum; it is part of a complex whole. Asking these questions and considering these issues is important for arriving at an honest, thoughtful decision.

The basic TTouch, the Clouded Leopard Touch, uses the finger pads of all four fingers, moving the dog's skin in a circular clockwise motion for one and a quarter turns. Mastering the hand position and movement of the touches—four fingers

LOBE LOVE

One of my favorite Tellington-inspired moves is the Ear
T Touch. Holding the base of the dog's ear between thumb
and forefinger, you slide the ear leather between the two fingers using extremely light pressure. Working from different
angles, you cover the entire ear, so you have touched every
inch of it, thereby hitting all the various acupuncture points
in this nerve-packed part of the body.

In addition to helping calm nervous or hyper-alert dogs,
Ear T Touches can help reduce pain and shock. It's a must to
calm nervous Nellies in the vet's waiting room. Once at a
party, I started doing Ear T Touches on the host's Dachshund
mix, who was sitting in my lap. She was facing away from
me, but eventually all the conversation in the room stopped
as people stopped to comment on how "blissed out" she
looked!

together, thumb "grounding" the hand, wrist straight, gentle
pushing that moves skin but not the fingers themselves—is
important for the technique to work correctly.

Tellington uses her T Touches on all parts of an animal's body,
from the feet to the gums, to raise the animal's awareness and
help centering.

Other T Touch exercises, such as Leg Circles, require a dog to
move his body in ways he doesn't normally move and feel sensations he doesn't usually feel.

Groundwork

In addition to the T Touches, which are stationary exercises,
Tellington has developed a repertoire of leading and confidence-
building exercises to help a dog understand what it feels like to
use her body in different ways and overcome fears. By negotiat-
ing obstacles such as cavaletti (poles placed at even intervals on
the ground) and ladder walks, the dog learns to concentrate—
and succeed.

TTouch Resources

Getting in TTouch with Your Dog: A Gentle Approach to Influencing Behavior, Health and Performance by Linda Tellington-Jones (Trafalgar Square Publishing, $16.95).

Unleash Your Dog's Potential: In TTouch With Your Canine Friend (50-minute video, Trafalgar Square).

One of the oddest looking, but most successful tools in the TTouch repertoire is the Body Wrap. An ace bandage is wrapped around the dog in a certain pattern, looking vaguely mummy-like. The Wrap helps make the dog aware of his physical boundaries and raises his body awareness, lowering his apprehension of the world around him.

Chapter 6

Vibrational Therapies: Seeing Isn't Always Believing

If you are ever tempted to paint all holistic veterinarians with the same brush stroke, this chapter is a good place for a reality check. There are some modalities that are not used frequently by holistic veterinarians, but not because they are unsafe or hazardous or require years of training. In many cases, it's simply because their effects are so subtle. Flower essences, which fit neatly under the umbrella heading of "vibrational medicine," are a prime example.

Previous chapters looked at some modalities that are thought to work vibrationally by balancing and unblocking the body's energy flow, working on an energy level rather than a physical one, or a cellular level rather than a biochemical one. Some healing systems work both ways. Essential oils clearly have a physiological effect when ingested and applied topically, but they are also thought to work on a vibrational level, centering emotions and smoothing out energy. And homeopathy is a centuries-old science that seeks to heal the physical body with remedies that work on an energetic, or vibrational, plane.

But, unlike homeopathy, which is practiced by many holistic veterinarians, flower essences are nowhere near as accepted or as widely used. Perhaps that's because they are not part of a rigorously defined system and have not been studied as a science—two perks that homeopathy enjoys. Or maybe it's because their influence and results are mostly emotional, not physical.

Our culture's emphasis on physicality—on what we can see and touch and quantify—is a real obstacle when trying to understand and appreciate vibrational remedies, says Nancy Brandt, a holistic veterinarian who uses flower essences in her Las Vegas practice. "They're just very subtle and work on the emotional layer, which is the layer that needs to be addressed and is not recognized in Western medicine."

While it sounds extremely New Age, vibrational medicine can be explained using quantum physics. When talking about the universe and everything in it, quantum physics recognizes that matter is only a small sliver of the equation. Energy is also very real, and very powerful, whether it takes the form of light or sound or the splitting of an atom—or thoughts or feelings or emotions. We live not only in a physical world, but an energetic one, with energy fields that overlap and influence one another.

Conventional medicine, veterinary or otherwise, has been reluctant to look beyond the physical to consider other, energy-related causes of disease. But some veterinarians, such as Brandt, believe there is more to health than just the physical reality of membranes and arteries and tendons. The energy we absorb and radiate—which is intimately linked to our emotional lives—is also directly related to our health and well-being.

"To me, it just makes more sense that there's a vibratory nature to disease," says Brandt. "There are enough modalities out there that have been based on it for so long, and we have enough negative energy impacting us now, that we have to start thinking on that level—*before* it gets to cellular degeneration."

Energy isn't neatly packaged, though. In the vibrational model, our energy and that of our animals are interrelated, as interlocked as our lives. "Dogs are so emotionally connected with their person that even a small thing, like a fight, affects them so much," says veterinarian Donna Kelleher. "We have this energy

INTENT ON INTENTION

Conventional doctors believe that cures are biological processes, not spiritual or emotional ones. If a medicine is going to improve your health, that is based purely on chemistry.

With vibrational medicine, by contrast, the intent of the practitioner is considered a valid dimension of the treatment. The goodwill of the healer—the genuine desire to see the patient whole and restored to good health—counts. By focusing on the clarity and purity of your intention—what am I trying to do here? what am I really trying to address?—you not only affirm your desire to help your companion animal, but may be inspired to think even more deeply about the root cause of the symptoms you see.

My good friend Susan, who is a holistic practitioner, takes the concept of intention very seriously. Before she uses a product—whether it's a flower essence or an essential oil or the raw meat she feeds her animals—she personally visits or at least calls the person who prepares or manufactures it. Not everyone has good intentions or is motivated by the "right" things, and she wants to be sure they're on the same page as she is before administering any of their products to her animals.

While you may not go to those lengths, what you do want is to fix this basic intention in your mind: You want this remedy to do good.

Whether you want to think of it as just the power of positive thinking, or something significantly more, that's up to you. But it can't hurt to remind yourself of the focus and purity of your intentions before administering any holistic remedy.

that lives with us, and our animals' energy parallels that in order to maintain homeostasis." So if we experience stress and negativity in our personal lives, that can very well affect our animals and their health.

Kelleher says she sees this sometimes with chronically ill animals who literally take on their owners' issues and illnesses. "How many people do I see who have diabetes, and who say, 'Oh, my cat has diabetes, too.'"

Vibrational Resource

Energy Medicine: The Scientific Basis of Bioenergy Therapies by James L. Oschman (Churchill Livingstone, $39.95).

In some of her patients, Kelleher sees a direct correlation between the stresses and dysfunctions of the owners and their animals, who, no matter what modalities she tries, cannot return to health. "So sometimes I'll say, 'I don't think he's going to get better until you get better,'" she says of her conversations with those owners. "And finally, it hits home."

Still, many women and men of science are reluctant to make the intellectual leap required for using vibrational modalities. Others will not accept anything that cannot be quantified and explained through clinical studies.

But the good news is that, generally speaking, where your vet stops, you can pick up. All of the vibrational modalities described in this chapter are very noninvasive and nontoxic. With a few caveats—and what healing system doesn't have them?—they can be practiced safely and effectively by laypeople.

FLOWER ESSENCES

There is no "hard" scientific evidence to prove conclusively that flower essences can do what some holistic practitioners say they can—help balance emotions and create a sense of well-being. But just because there are no double-blind studies to explain the cellular interactions flower essences have with the body, and no accumulation of scientific papers detailing precisely how they work, doesn't mean that they *don't* work. Countless breeders, dog lovers and holistically minded vets have used flower essences on animals to help with stress, separation anxiety, head shyness and behavioral problems such as submissive urination and territoriality.

"I use them, really, because they work," says Anna Maria Scholey, a holistic veterinarian from Orcas Island, Washington. "It makes sense that they work with the body; everything has a frequency, and flower essences can rebalance it."

It's always prudent to be cautious about any holistic remedy, especially in terms of how it may interact with the body and any potential side effects. But the conventional wisdom about flower essences—even from allopathic practitioners—is that they are extremely safe. Although in rare cases certain reactive remedies (specifically, agrimony, centaury, cherry plum, crab apple, holly, impatiens, mustard, water violet and willow) can cause temporary but intense emotional releases that might intensify symptoms before helping heal them, flower essences are nontoxic and basically harmless. You cannot overdose your dog on them—unless you give such a vast quantity that your dog is affected by the alcohol in the tincture. As negative results go, the worst effect from using flower essences is to have no effect at all.

Basically, the only thing you have to lose is your skepticism.

How They Work

Flower essences started as a 19th century phenomenon, the inspiration of an English physician and biologist named Edward Bach. A pioneering homeopath, he began to explore the healing properties of flowers and trees, theorizing that each species had specific qualities that helped balance corresponding emotional states in humans and animals. Using his intuition to guide him, and testing the essences on himself to determine their properties, Bach identified 38 plants common to the English countryside that eventually formed a collection of essences called Bach Flower Essences.

Essences are prepared by taking the flowers or buds, placing them in pure water and exposing them to sunlight or boiling them, so that the flower's energy pattern is transferred to the water. This is then made into a tincture to stabilize it. Traditionally, some form of alcohol is used as a preservative, and the Bach remedies you will find in most health-food stores are brandy tinctures. But flower essences can be stabilized in nonalcoholic media as well, including glycerin and vinegar.

The theory behind flower essences is that they interact with the body on a cellular level, vibrationally centering a dog (or any other animal, as well as humans) and helping resolve emotional disharmony. For this reason, they are considered safer than herbs, which work on a chemical level. As with homeopathic remedies, think of a flower essence as sort of a tuning fork that helps the body find equilibrium.

STORING YOUR ESSENCES

Flower essences need to be kept in a dry place out of direct sunlight. And as convenient as it would be to tuck a bottle or two in the glove compartment of your car, remember that they should not be exposed to temperature extremes, especially heat. Room temperature is best.

If you store your flower essences in your kitchen or another activity-filled room of the house, be mindful of their vibratory nature and keep them away from sources of electrical or magnetic energy—including appliances such as microwaves or televisions.

The idea of flowers being potent sources of energy far predates Bach. The ancient Chinese discipline of *feng shui*, which seeks to balance the energy flow in our physical surroundings, discourages homeowners from displaying dried flowers because they radiate dead energy. (Fresh flowers, by contrast, are wonderful sponges that suck up negative energy, by *feng shui* standards.)

Bach's 38 original essences are hardly the only ones you can use. Since every plant is its own universe, with its own vibrational qualities and identity, virtually any flower can be made into an essence. There are several companies worldwide creating and marketing the essences of indigenous plants from Australia to New England.

How to Use Essences

Flower essences are best suited for addressing emotional and behavioral issues in an animal. The biggest factor in using them successfully is knowing your dog. The more you observe her, the better you can figure out what her specific issues are and what seems to be prompting them. And the better you will be at choosing the right essence from among hundreds of possibilities.

This sensitivity to your dog's behavior and reactions is also important in evaluating the results of an essence once you have administered it. If you are truly in tune with your dog, you will notice subtle but definite changes. If you haven't taken the time to really figure out the source of the problem, chances are you'll miss these nuances. Essences are not like great big mallets that hit your dog over the head and transform her in a couple of days; their effects are gradual and gentle, and often their most dramatic effects can be noticed only over a prolonged period of time.

Try one essence at a time, and see the results over a few days. When it comes to how much to give, the frequency of the dose is more important than the quantity. In other words, you'll probably see better results giving four drops four times a day (which is Scholey's recommended dose) rather than eight drops twice a day.

In selecting an essence, "The more specific you get, the better it works," says Scholey. For example, many people give Rescue Remedy in situations where an animal is panicked or nervous, such as an impending thunderstorm. While Rescue Remedy often helps address those acute reactions to the storm, Scholey says, it doesn't necessarily "get to the bottom of the fear" itself. For that, Scholey says, she might try mimulus, which is for fear of known things.

Like many practitioners, Scholey has favorite remedies that seem to produce consistently good results in animals with specific issues. Holly, for example, is the remedy she calls on for addressing aggression. For animals who take on the energy and problems of their owner—what Scholey calls "unhealthy energy transfer"—she uses pink yarrow (which is not one of the original Bach essences).

Scholey allows six to eight weeks of daily dosing to give flower essences ample time to do their work of rebalancing and recentering. If, after that period, you feel your dog hasn't progressed much, she suggests consulting a homeopath to address the deeper issues at hand through homeopathic remedies.

While flower essences are frequently used for behavioral problems, they are not a cure-all. If your dog shows signs of being a danger to himself and those around him, you need to consult with a veterinarian to first rule out a medical reason, and then an animal behaviorist (not just a "trainer"). Flower essences can help nudge an animal in the right direction behaviorally, but they are no substitute for proper professional help.

To get you started, here are brief summaries of each of Bach's essences. Remember, they are not the only essences out there, but they are the most commercially available. You'll find them at most health food stores, sold in little amber bottles that protect the essences from the damaging effects of light.

WHAT'S THE DIAGNOSIS?

The most basic way of deciding whether your dog needs the energy in a particular flower essence is to look at her emotional state and see how closely that essence's description corresponds.

But there are other ways of testing the body's energy fields to see if an essence—or any substance, whether it's an herb or a food—is needed.

Applied Kinesiology

Kinesiology is the study of movement. Applied kinesiology is a system developed by American chiropractor George Goodhart that involves testing isolated muscles to communicate with the body to find out what energy it needs and what it doesn't. Theoretically, if your body is in contact with a substance or energy that is not helpful or needed, it will demonstrate a weak muscle response; if the substance would be helpful, the muscle will stay strong and resist pressure exerted on it.

In humans, muscle testing works like this: You hold your arm out perpendicular to your body, either next to or in front of you. In the hand of your extended arm, you hold the object in question—say, a vial of the flower essence mimulus. The tester pushes down on your wrist and gauges the response. If your muscles give way easily, that is a "no" response and the remedy is not needed. If your arm muscles resist and stay in place, the answer is "yes" and the remedy is needed.

Rescue Remedy

Technically, this isn't an essence. It's a mixture of five flower essences that Bach thought worked together well for cases of extreme stress (rock rose, star of Bethlehem, impatiens, cherry plum and clematis, all of which are detailed later in this chapter). But Rescue Remedy is the most popular of Bach's creations. Consider Rescue Remedy for a dog who has an extreme fear, anxiety or stress response.

Many people find Rescue Remedy to be most effective when it is used in conjunction with another, primary essence. In this respect, Rescue Remedy acts almost as an amplifier of the other essence.

Since that arm-stretching, vial-holding scenario doesn't work for dogs, they require a surrogate for muscle testing. Using the same mimulus example, you would hold your testing arm out and then, placing the essence in the palm of your other hand, you put that hand on the dog. You've now created a circuit between you and the dog, and the dog's responses can be tested through you.

Bionetics

Think of this as the high-tech version of applied kinesiology. Instead of using muscle resistance, practitioners rely on computerized testing systems that measure energy through acupuncture points.

The system Brandt uses is called Meridian Stress Assessment (MSA); other systems include Bio Energetic Stress Test (BEST). Using a stylus or probe, the practitioner tests various acupuncture meridians on the skin and notes the level of electromagnetic energy. A computer program then pinpoints the specific essence or group of essences needed to correct any imbalances.

"You don't get to ask many questions of an animal," says Brandt about why she uses this diagnostic aid. "We humans can go ahead and assume one thing about the way an animal feels, but sometimes the animal is way off somewhere else."

Unlike the other remedies, Rescue Remedy is available in a cream form for use topically on burns, cuts, rashes and other external traumas.

Agrimony

"Never let them see you sweat" is fine as a motto for a deodorant company, but some animals can take this desire not to show pain or discomfort to unhealthy levels. Agrimony is for the stoics among our animal friends, as well as the ones who are so out of touch with their feelings that they suppress their anxieties with over-the-top friendliness.

Consider this essence for a dog who is too eager to please, to the point where he ignores his own needs and well-being.

Aspen

Fear comes in many forms, and aspen is called for when it is so generalized that its source is unknown. Animals can have panic attacks, just as humans do—look for panting, pacing, trembling and circling.

Consider this essence for a dog who gets nervous and wide-eyed for no apparent reason, or who mistrusts others.

Beech

This is the remedy for animals who cannot handle change well, or are easily annoyed by the behaviors and eccentricities of others in the household. It tones down irritability and helps open them up to being more flexible and tolerant.

Consider this essence for a dog who grumbles at or rebuffs a newcomer to the household, whether animal or human.

Centaury

If there were an essence assigned to address wimpiness, centaury might very well be it. This is for animals who are so unsure about their own identity—and so unwilling to assert their needs and desires—that they kowtow to and obey those more powerful than they, even though it's not in their best interests.

Consider this essence for "sidekick" animals who are forever doing the bidding of a more powerful animal in the household, or for runts of the litter who need to learn how to stand up for themselves.

Cerato

If an animal has leadership issues, this is the essence you might try. Cerato aids animals in finding confidence and assuredness, and weans them from finding self-worth by relying on others. This essence remedies self-doubt and urges the animal to trust her own instincts and opinions.

Consider this essence for a dog who will not participate in an engaging activity—such as playing with other dogs—because it takes her away from you. You might also try it on an aging dog whose behavior is becoming more juvenile and dependent.

Cherry Plum

Sometimes animals act out in a frenzy for what seems like no reason at all. Cherry plum addresses this core of unpredictability, whether it manifests itself as an unprovoked attack or a panicked escape attempt. This total and utter surrender to fear is what cherry plum remedies.

Consider this essence for a dog who loses self-control easily or reacts violently to normal events, such as being put into a crate. It might also be appropriate for an abused animal who retains panic-provoking memories that are easily triggered, or one whose phobias generate extreme fear and panic.

Chestnut Bud

Getting stuck in bad habits and chronic patterns happens to animals as well as humans. This essence opens up the ability to learn from the past and to reprogram behavior that has become ingrained and reflexive.

Consider this essence for a dog who refuses to learn how to be house-trained, or who has a mental block about performing a particular command correctly. It is also useful for puppies who are lagging behind their littermates developmentally.

Chicory

Excessive neediness is what this essence addresses, helping an animal become more self-sufficient and less clingy. This essence is also useful for animals who are overprotective of their humans, sometimes allowing this let-me-take-care-of-you impulse to manifest itself in aggression and dominant behavior. Because it is motivated by insecurity and selfishness, over-the-top possessiveness is another characteristic that can be remedied by chicory.

Consider this essence for a dog who is glued to your side all the time, interprets any person's overtures to you as a threat, or exhibits inappropriate guarding behaviors. It can also be useful for dogs who are too territorial, barking at every passerby or every leaf that blows up the driveway.

Clematis

This is the essence for animals who have trouble being "in the moment," who are absentminded or seem to be daydreaming. This sense of being out of touch goes beyond a lack of focus or easy distraction; it is a kind of turning inward to the animal's inner landscape, abandoning what is going on in the real world.

Consider this essence for dogs who become so disengaged that they fall asleep, or who lose focus during training.

Crab Apple

Animals with poor hygiene can benefit from this essence, which has a cleansing effect. It is also useful in helping stop obsessive grooming behaviors, or unwise dietary habits such as coprophagy (stool eating) and soil or rock eating.

Consider this essence for a dog who is a compulsive licker, has been exposed to environmental toxins or is recovering from an infection.

Elm

This is the essence for animals who think they can never measure up or are overwhelmed by expectations. They feel a responsibility to carry out certain roles, but on some level don't feel that they have the experience or ability to do so successfully.

Consider this essence for a normally confident and capable dog who is confronted with any high-pressure situation— bitches with demanding litters, search-and-rescue dogs at a disaster scene, service dogs who have been assigned a new partner.

Gentian

Sometimes, life metes out so many setbacks that we have to struggle to find the inspiration to try again. Gentian helps lift this pessimism and listlessness, and imparts a sense of optimism.

Consider this essence for a dog who has been repeatedly returned to a shelter and who despairs of ever finding a forever home, or who has lost a beloved owner or companion.

Gorse

Although it addresses issues that are similar to gentian, gorse is for animals who have taken their despondency a step further: They have lost any hope at all and have become numb. They have reached the point of not caring whether they live or die, and the vacant, blank look in their eyes will communicate this to you.

Consider this essence for a dog who has been abandoned by the only caretaker that he knows or, for whatever reason, has just given up.

Heather

Some animals are look-at-me types, always wanting to be in the limelight, at the expense of their relationships with others. Heather helps get this egomania under control, so that the dog can become aware of the fact that a relationship is a two-way street.

Consider this essence for a dog who is constantly pawing at her owner or barking for attention. Such a dog may manifest signs of separation anxiety, but not because she misses her owners. It's the attention from someone, anyone, that she craves.

Holly

Think about the leaves of this evergreen bush, which can poke and pinch. This is precisely the temperament that holly addresses, helping to dispel jealousy and intense dislike. Vine, which curbs dominance, is often used in conjunction with holly.

Consider this essence for the dog who holds grudges, and whose actions seem motivated by out-and-out dislike or envy. Or for dogs who are suspicious of a new member of the pack.

Honeysuckle

Adjustment is a part of life, and this essence can ease a transition for an animal who is having trouble coping with new circumstances—or is pining for the ones left behind. Pick a flower from this vigorous vine and pull its stamen in just the right way, and you are rewarded with a drop of hidden nectar. This is the lesson honeysuckle imparts: Every new relationship and life stage has a sweetness to it, if only we are willing to work to find it.

Consider this essence for a dog who has a hard time adjusting to new circumstances, seems unable to get settled in and is homesick for what she has left behind.

Hornbeam

This is the essence that imparts oomph—that surge of energy that gets an animal moving again after a hiatus or convalescence. It also addresses mental inertia—the kind of lethargy and laziness that can lead to procrastination and balking at pursuing interesting activities.

Consider this essence for the unresponsive dog who'd rather snooze than take an invigorating walk, or who needs a boost after a debilitating illness such as parvo or distemper.

Impatiens

The common name for this popular shade-loving annual says it all: Impatiens is for the impatient. This essence creates focus and gives the animal the single-mindedness not to be distracted by every little thing going on around him.

Consider this essence for dog who cannot concentrate in obedience class, or who has difficulty hearing his owner's commands because there is something more interesting to smell on the ground.

Larch

This is the confidence-building essence. If it had a sound track, it would be that old ditty about the ant and the rubber-tree plant. This is the essence that reaffirms our belief in our ability to rise to the occasion. It helps us say, "Yes, I can do that," and then gives us the confidence to go ahead and give it our best effort, without self-doubt getting in the way.

Consider this essence for a dog who is so hampered by lack of self-esteem that he won't try new things for fear he will fail or make a mistake.

Mimulus

Traditionally, this essence addresses fears that are specific: fear of men, or water, or being petted from above. Whatever the worry, mimulus centers a dog enough to confront this fear.

Consider this essence for a shy dog who is afraid of being handled or approached, or who has had a traumatic experience that has left her afraid of a specific thing.

Mustard

This essence is the antidote for deep depression—the kind that manifests itself in a pervasive gloominess without a clear cause or provocation. Think of the Christian parable of the mustard seed—how the smallest of all seeds can grow into the tallest of trees, no matter how impossible it seems. This essence promises that same truth: Trusting in the smallest grain of hope will eventually lead to growth and renewal.

Consider this essence for the dog who seems deeply depressed for no identifiable reason.

Oak

In ancient times, the oak was a symbol of strength and resilience. Those are admirable qualities, but there can be a downside to stoicism: Always having to be the strong one means that an animal might not acknowledge her weakened state and so will not take the time to heal, rest and recuperate.

Consider this essence for a convalescing dog who will not stay still, pulls at stitches and pushes to walk and play even as he approaches the point of exhaustion and collapse. It's also for the dog who ignores and works through clear pain signals that his body is sending.

Olive

Rejuvenation is what this essence accomplishes, helping animals who have been pushed to their physical or mental limit to rebound. This is the remedy for sheer exhaustion.

Consider this essence for a dog who has a physically or emotionally demanding job, whether it is working livestock or searching for a missing person.

Pine

There's a reason why household cleaners are often pine-scented: it's a deep cleanser, and so too is its essence. Pine addresses the negative emotion of guilt, although it may be hard to tell if your dog is experiencing this emotion, as opposed to fear or submission.

Consider this essence for a dog who appears to be acting out of a sense of guilt or shame, or who may be picking up on your own negativity. Try it on puppies who are being housebroken, to screen out messages of negativity.

Red Chestnut

This is the essence for worriers—for those animals who are always anticipating what can go wrong next. Their overriding motivations are fear and concern over loss of control, and this often manifests itself in overprotectiveness.

Consider this essence for a dog with separation anxiety who frets while you are out of sight and is only calmed by your return.

Rock Rose

Terror is the emotion that this essence addresses. No matter what provokes this reaction—and there is usually a specific trigger for it—rock rose can help panicked animals find a center of calm within themselves.

Consider this essence for a dog who is profoundly afraid of a certain event or person—fireworks or someone who resembles an abusive previous owner, for example—and who is made hysterical at the prospect of confronting that fear object.

Rock Water

Suppleness and flexibility are important adaptive qualities. Without them, animals "snap" like a dry tree limb when pressure is applied. Rock water addresses this inability to go with the flow, both physically and emotionally. It remedies rigidity, and helps foster spontaneity and relaxation.

Consider this essence for a dog whose muscles are stiff and unyielding, who bridles at a change of routine, diet or environment, or who refuses to learn new behaviors. It can also help a status-obsessed dog who is overly dominant and territorial because he refuses to make concessions to others with whom he must share his space.

Scleranthus

We all know people—and animals—who suffer from mood swings: happy and content one minute, sulking and bitter the next. Scleranthus helps smooth out this erratic behavior, fostering emotional balance and steadiness. It also addresses indecision—animals who cannot settle down because they are torn between too many options, or who drive their owners crazy because they cannot figure out what they want.

Consider this essence for a dog who has an unpredictable temperament or who has dramatic ups and downs as a result of hormone changes. Because scleranthus restores equilibrium, it may also be useful in preventing the inner-ear imbalance that causes motion sickness.

Star of Bethlehem

The one word to remember with this essence is shock. It is called for in any situation where circumstances have unfolded so quickly, unexpectedly and traumatically that the animal is immobilized.

Consider this essence for a dog who has experienced trauma, whether physical or emotional—new mothers, or dogs who have lost their owners, experienced intense physical pain or undergone anesthesia.

Sweet Chestnut

Sometimes, animals experience so much pain and anguish that acquiescence and even death would be preferable to fighting a losing battle. Sweet chestnut restores the will to persevere and keep trying in the face of seemingly insurmountable obstacles. Remedying sheer exhaustion—both physical and mental—it reignites the hope of a light at the end of the tunnel.

Consider this essence for a dog who has been viciously or chronically abused, who has spent time in the spirit-breaking environment of a puppy mill or who grieves the loss of an owner or companion. Physically, this remedy is often used for animals who are prone to that terrifying and seemingly unpredictable intestinal condition, bloat.

Vervain

This is the essence for Type A personalities—always raring to go, constantly needing to be in motion, fixated on where they are going instead of where they currently are. (Is it a coincidence that the word "verve" is hidden in this flower name?) Vervain helps these overenthusiastic animals curb their excitability.

Consider this essence for a dog who is naturally exuberant, often to the point of seeming high strung or hyperactive.

Vine

If Lucy, the overbearing character in the *Peanuts* comic strips, needed an essence, this would be it. Vine is for bullies, dominant and domineering types who like things to be their way or else.

Consider this essence for a dog who rides roughshod over less dominant members of the household, who seeks to accomplish things through sheer force of will and who is overly concerned with defending his turf.

Walnut

Life is all about change and that is a good thing, because change brings with it growth and maturity. But letting go of the familiar can be difficult and discomfiting. Walnut is the essence that helps us weather these natural and normal changes, helping us adjust as we embrace them.

Consider this essence for a dog who is going through a transition: changing owners or homes, welcoming a new family member, giving birth or being boarded for the first time.

Water Violet

Some animals are loners, seemingly uninterested in interacting with other animals or even the humans who love them. They may prefer to suffer pain silently and by themselves, and may recoil from being petted or caressed. Water violet helps foster better connections, making an aloof and self-sufficient animal more willing to give of himself.

Consider this essence for a dog who has difficulty bonding to a new owner, or who perhaps started off living sequestered from humans and so learned not to become too emotionally invested.

White Chestnut

This is the remedy for restlessness. It also helps an animal quiet his mind and relinquish obsessive and preoccupying thoughts that can lead to destructive habits and repetitive behaviors. This remedy also helps an animal let go of old training patterns and embrace new ones.

Consider this essence for a dog who needs to break chronic habits such as obsessive chewing or self-mutilation, or stop any old behaviors that are no longer productive. Try this essence with an insomniac dog, or with one who cannot seem to settle down and rest.

Wild Oat

This is the essence to give to an animal who does not seem to be striving to reach her full potential and is somehow blocked from achieving what her humans know she is capable of. Known as the pathfinder essence, wild oat helps dispel that lack of connection and gives a sense of direction.

Consider this essence for a dog who just can't seem to find his niche or who is leaving behind a career—such as a long, successful stint as a show dog or a search and rescue dog—that provided a large chunk of his identity.

Wild Rose

This essence combats apathy. It restores a love of life, an interest in and willingness to engage in the outside world.

Consider this essence for a dog who seems indifferent to what goes on around her or for an older dog who is grumpy after a new puppy is introduced into the household. Wild rose is also suitable for dogs who are recovering from a chronic illness or who seem to be in a depression that is worsening for no discernible reason.

Flower Essence Resources

If you are interested in learning more about Bach remedies, Nelson Bach USA, which has the rights to make and market Bach flower essences in the United States, is a prime resource. At the company's website, www.nelsonbach.com (800-334-0843), you can learn about training courses and seminars offered about the essences, as well as buy reference charts, videotapes and the essences themselves.

The UK-based Dr. Edward Bach Foundation offers a distance-learning program for those who are interested in a correspondence course. Visit www.bachcentre.com/found/dlp.htm for more details (The Bach Centre, Mount Vernon, Bakers Lane, Sotwell, Oxon, OX10 0PZ, UK, Telephone 44 (0) 1491 834678).

The Essences

The three-dozen-odd essences identified by Bach are not the only ones available to you as you explore the healing power of flowers. In theory, every flower and plant has special healing properties. Many practitioners suggest using essences made from flowers in your geographic area. So if you are in the Pacific Northwest, for example, you might explore the essences made by the Alaskan Flower Essence Project (www.alaskanessences.com, 800-545-9309). Flower Essence Services (FES) sells remedies from flowers grown in California's Sierra Nevada mountains (www.fesflowers.com, 800-548-0075 or 530-265-0258). Essences from Down Under are available from Australian Bush Flower Essences (www.ausflowers.com.au, 45 Booralie Road, Terrey Hills, NSW, 2084, Australia, International Telephone 61 2 9450 1388).

Green Hope Farm in Meriden, New Hampshire, offers a whole line of flower essences using plants that are from faraway locales such as Bermuda, as well as old-fashioned garden favorites. The homegrown company uses red shiso (a mint plant from Japan) and vinegar to stabilize the essences, instead of alcohol, and offers a whole line of essences especially for dogs and cats. Included in its Animal Wellness Collection are 22 combination remedies, including Grief & Loss, Healthy Coat, Jealousy and Senior Citizen. Visit www.greenhopeessences.com or call (603) 469-3662.

Other flower-essence makers include Living Essences of Australia (www.livingessences.com.au, P.O. Box 355, Scarborough, WA 601, Australia), Master's Flower Essences (www.mastersessences.com, 800-347-3639 or 530-478-7655), Pegasus Products (www.pegasusproducts.com, 800-527-6104 or 970-667-3019) and Perelandra (www.perelandra-ltd.com, 800-960-8806 or 540-937-2153).

Online Resources

Yahoo.com has a discussion group for seemingly every subject imaginable, and flower essences are no exception. You can sign up for the 500-member "talkbach" e-mail list at groups.yahoo.com/group/talkbach.

Books

There are several good books that offer an in-depth look at flower essences and how they can be used with animals. Be careful not to confuse the first two—they have identical titles.

Bach Flower Remedies for Animals by Helen Graham and Gregory Vlamis (Findhorn Press, $12.95). If you can have only one reference book on hand for flower essences, this is a good one. Each essence is described fully and clearly, and species-specific details are included under each heading. Indispensable.

Bach Flower Remedies for Animals by Stefan Ball and Judy Howard (C.W. Daniel Company, $24.95). Organized somewhat differently that the other books mentioned here, this British import offers more case studies.

Flower Essences for Animals by Lila Devi (Beyond Words Publishing, $14.95). The book profiles essences from California-based Master's Flower Essences, which Devi founded in 1977.

Treating Animal Illnesses and Emotional States With Flower Essence Remedies by Jessica Bear and Tricia Lewis (Richman Rose Publishing, $12.95). Good descriptions of each essence, and a very useful index of ailments that points to all the prospective remedies.

Willow

Some animals (like some people) always seem as if they have gotten up on the wrong side of the bed. They're grumpy, sulky and oftentimes, if they feel they have not gotten their way, spiteful. Or they may simply be oversensitive, taking everything personally and overreacting.

Consider this essence for a dog who seems to retaliate by destroying something in the house or withholding affection. It is also a choice for a dog who needs to overcome resentment about the way he has been treated in the past.

BIOMAGNETIC THERAPY

In childhood, many of us noodled around with magnets in earth science class or played with toys like Wooly Willy, whose bald head and face could suddenly sprout a Mohawk or a handlebar moustache when iron filings were dragged in place with a magnetic pencil.

Perhaps because we've been familiar with the seemingly magical energy of magnets since a tender age, many people are more open to this form of vibrational healing. Indeed, magnetic therapy is used relatively frequently by holistic veterinarians and there are a variety of bio-magnetic products available for dogs, from mattress pads to blankets. The theory is that magnets can enhance circulation and oxygenation, but the exact explanation of how they work is still up for debate.

Veterinarian Roger De Haan uses magnets in a number of ways in his practice. "I've used it on cancer and some infections and immune problems," he says. But, like many of us who see the television infomercials selling magnetic belts for backaches, he's used magnets "primarily for pain and inflammation—especially in animals who have arthritis or disc problems."

Popular in the time of the ancient Greeks, today magnetic therapy is commonplace in countries such as Japan, where it's used for everything from arthritis to migraines. In this country, magnets have pockets of popularity, particularly among professional athletes, whether they're golfers or racehorses.

Magnets are either unipolar (that is, they are negatively charged, or have North Pole polarity, on one side and positively charged, or have South Pole polarity, on the other) or are bipolar (they alternate north-south polarity on the same surface). Unipolar magnets have a greater penetration, and so are more often used therapeutically.

Magnetic Therapy Resources

Magnet Therapy: The Pain Cure Alternative by Ronald M. Lawrence, MD, PhD, Paul J. Rosch, MD, FACP and Judith Plowden (Prima Publishing, $15.95).

"With cancer, pain or inflammation, you want to use a negative, or North Pole, polarity," De Haan explains. Using positively charged magnets in this case may worsen the situation, since they stimulate growth and development and can actually encourage a cancer to spread. "I almost always use North Pole polarity," says De Haan, "because 99 times out of 100, that's what most areas of the body require."

While De Haan characterizes magnetic therapy as "pretty safe," there is, he points out, "a right way and a wrong way to do things. And, as with any modality, it's always best to have some basic understanding of what you're doing."

In the case of an older dog who is very toxic, "sticking a magnet on him for two days can create an over-detox," he explains. "Magnetism realigns the polarity, and you can end up getting an animal feeling bad because he's detoxing too fast."

As a general guideline, De Haan's suggested minimum is 15 minutes. Leaving a magnet on for any less time will yield no results. Leaving it on for too long could lead to a "reverse rebound," in which you undo all the progress you've made. Generally, most practitioners recommend a starting point of two to three hours a day, with a gradual increase depending on the individual dog. Do not use magnets with dogs who are pregnant. Dogs who are older or very ill should be treated under the guidance of a professional. And since the quality and construction of magnets vary, this will affect the outcome of treatment, as will placement of the magnets. A holistic vet who works with magnetic therapy can tutor you on all these things.

De Haan says he almost always uses magnets in conjunction with other therapies, such as chiropractic and acupuncture. "I can't say I'm only going to do the magnets," he says, "because healing depends on synergy. Each modality is doing different things—all of which increase the chances of healing."

REIKI

Perhaps the best way to understand what reiki means is to simply translate it from the Japanese. "Rei" is often interpreted to mean "universal"; "ki" is the life force that animates us all. Basically, what reiki does is deliver the healing force of the universe through the laying on of hands.

Founded by Dr. Mikao Usui (who is said to have received this healing energy while meditating on Mount Kurama, a holy mountain in Japan), reiki is not so much taught as the stewardship of channeling it is transferred. After being "attuned" by a reiki master who, in turn, was attuned by someone else (the chain, or lineage, can be traced back to Usui himself), a reiki practitioner can now be a conduit for the energy.

There are three levels of reiki attunement. In the first, a person is attuned to give hands-on healing. After her second attunement, she can do long-distance healing, and after the third attunement she is a reiki master and can begin to give attunements herself.

In a reiki session, the practitioner connects with the universal life force and then channels it through her hands to the being she is working with—who can just as easily be a hamster as a human. Working on various points on the body that correspond to its seven chakras, or energetic pathways, the practitioner channels this universal energy, which she benefits from as well. On the most pragmatic level, reiki is said to reduce stress and increase relaxation. From a metaphysical point of view, it clears the chakras of blockages caused by negative thoughts, as the energy goes to where the body needs it and will benefit from it.

Reiki is said to speed healing, and in those with physical injuries, dramatic, if brief, irritations may occur as toxins leave the body rapidly.

The vast majority of holistic vets do not offer reiki, for a variety of reasons. Brandt says that it is so readily available from other sources—including owners themselves—that the demand isn't that great. And, practically speaking, "it's time-consuming," adds Scholey, who is a reiki master. She does it in the down time during an acupuncture session. "Once I put the needles in, I have to wait about 20 minutes, so there's the time to do it then."

That said, Scholey thinks reiki is a wonderful adjunct to any holistic modality, and she thinks it amplifies the good results of her acupuncture treatments. "All it does is open the body to receive the energy of the universe," she says. "Your intention is to heal, and everyone has the innate ability to do that to a lesser or greater degree. I think it augments other systems, and I don't think it's going to do any harm."

Chapter 7

Vaccination: Too Much of a Good Thing?

Regardless of how long you've been a "dog person," chances are that through the years you've received one unchanging and unqualified message about vaccines: That they are necessary and good, and that you are irresponsible if you do not take your dog to the veterinarian every year for that annual battery of booster shots.

Without fail, most veterinary practices send out reminder notices and postcards exhorting you to do just that. You go, you pay and you depart, usually not knowing much about what was in that syringe. All you know is you're relieved, secure in the knowledge that you've protected your beloved companion from some of the most virulent and lethal diseases on the planet.

But life isn't usually that simple, and vaccines are no exception.

The first thing to realize is that, despite the near icon status we give them in our dogs' health regime, vaccines are not 100 percent effective. Vaccinated dogs can and do contract the diseases against which they have been immunized. In fact, vaccines aren't expected to be infallible: According to the United States Department of Agriculture, a vaccine can be licensed for the prevention of disease if only 80 percent of the animals vaccinated in a clinical challenge trial were disease-free.

As with nutrition, veterinary attitudes about vaccination are molded in large part by the industry that supplies them. Most veterinarians inoculate dogs every year because that is what the vaccine companies recommend, plain and simple. Federal regulations require vaccine companies to conduct trials to prove the minimum duration of a vaccine, but not the maximum.

When it comes to annual shots, many dog owners figure it can't hurt. While a very small percentage of dogs have an immediate and potentially fatal allergic reaction to vaccines—called anaphylaxis, it can include breathing difficulty, collapse and even death—the vast majority of dogs just go on with their lives, perhaps a little lethargic and feverish for a day or two, or with some swelling at the injection site, but seemingly fine.

Or so you think. But the effects of vaccination and overvaccination can be subtle and can appear months, even years, after the vaccines have been given. Repeated challenges to your dog's immune system—which is precisely what vaccines are—can eventually turn into a real health crisis.

To understand why, think about what's really in a vaccine. That syringe doesn't contain jack-booted antibodies that spread out into your dog's system, ready to combat disease. In fact, quite the opposite: The vaccine contains either weakened ("attenuated") or inactivated infectious agents that *cause* the disease. Vaccines work by tricking the immune system into thinking it has been infected, thereby stimulating it to create antibodies to fight the disease. If all goes well, your dog develops an immunologic memory of the altered disease agents he has fought, and will be able to fight the real thing if he's exposed to it later. So immunity is created by your dog himself—provided his immune system is up to the challenge.

The problem is that the immune system is not an invincible BattleBot. It can weaken, especially when assuaged from all sides. Poor nutrition, environmental toxins, emotional stress from a change in lifestyle, hormonal fluctuations such as estrus or pregnancy—these can all affect the immune system, making it vulnerable. Also, most vaccines are injected directly into the body, bypassing front-line defense mechanisms such as antibodies in the saliva and mucous membranes.

All this isn't to say that vaccines are bad. They are important, powerful tools in any veterinarian's arsenal. But precisely because they are so powerful, they must be deployed with care and consideration.

Since attitudes about vaccines and their potentially harmful side effects are changing, there is a wide spectrum of opinion among veterinarians on this subject. Some believe in vaccinating year in and year out. Others have switched to vaccinating adult dogs every three years, as several university teaching hospitals are now suggesting. Still others rely on titers, which are blood tests that can help pinpoint immunity levels. And some holistically oriented vets choose not to vaccinate altogether unless it is mandated by law.

"All right then," you think, tapping your foot impatiently, "what should I do? What is the right solution?"

If you've read this far into this book, you know that that question needs to be rephrased. The better question is, What is the right solution for *my dog?* There are many elements that factor into how you want to approach vaccinating, including your dog's age, emotional and physical health, diet, previous vaccination history and her social life—how often she interacts with unknown dogs outside your home. Geography is important, too: Some diseases that are common in one region of the country may be virtually unheard of in others; also, local laws mandate the frequency of immunization for diseases such as rabies. Finally, you'll need to decide how much risk you are willing to take in terms of how far you want to stray from what are considered traditional veterinary guidelines.

As with anything involving your dog's care, educate yourself about the potential risks and benefits, then weigh them with the help of your vet to come to the best decision for your dog.

THE EFFECTS OF OVERVACCINATION

If you choose not to vaccinate and your animal is exposed to a particular disease-causing agent, there are three possible outcomes:

- Your dog will not contract the disease
- Your dog will contract a mild form of the disease, which you may not even notice
- Your dog will contract the disease in its full-blown form

It's the last possibility that frightens us into the when-in-doubt-vaccinate way of thinking. But what we often don't think about are the risks of vaccinating. While there are few controlled studies that draw a direct correlation between vaccination and disease, many prominent veterinarians point to overwhelming anecdotal and experiential evidence that vaccines can damage the very immune system they are meant to enhance.

In many ways, this parallels the current situation in human medicine, where suspicions of a link between vaccination and autism in children have yet to be proven, but are being widely explored.

"Vaccine reactions are underreported in animals, just as they are in people," says W. Jean Dodds of Santa Monica, California, a veterinarian and hematological expert who has written and lectured extensively on the impact overvaccination has on the immune system. "Vets don't think about reporting it because they're not concentrating on adverse reactions," which sometimes become apparent years after the fact.

Dodds theorizes that overvaccination can trigger diseases in certain breeds that are predisposed to them, from epilepsy to hypothyroidism. Also, because vaccines can overload the immune system, that weakness can invite all sorts of immune-mediated conditions. In a kind of biological domino effect, the immune system begins to falter or even turn on itself, causing hypersensitivity and immune-mediated disease. While the list of possible physical conditions is huge, from allergies to arthritis to cancer, the adverse reactions don't stop there. Some holistic vets attribute increased aggression and behavioral changes to the rabies vaccine.

In the late 1880s, a homeopathic veterinarian named J. Compton Burnett coined a term for these chronic physical and emotional changes caused by excessive vaccines: vaccinosis. While many conventional vets think vaccinosis is rare, that may be because vaccinosis is not one particular condition, but rather an undermining of what homeopaths call an animal's "vital force." Once that has been compromised, the door is open to all kinds of health issues. And because many conventional vets aren't looking for a connection between vaccinations and other health problems, they tend to treat those diseases or disorders as isolated occurrences, instead of symptoms of an overtaxed immune system.

Some of the biggest culprits in overvaccination are combination vaccines, the so-called 5-in-1 or 6-in-1 shots that many vets give seemingly without a second thought. It's one thing to give a puppy or dog five or six different challenges to his immune system; it's another to give them *all at once*. Many veterinarians—holistic and allopathic—are now recommending that each vaccination be given separately, and with a suitable time interval between each one. Think long and hard not only about what vaccines to give, but how and when to give them.

PUPPIES AND VACCINES

Nature, in her wisdom, gives puppies special tools to combat disease. They are called maternal antibodies, and they are passed to the wriggly puppies from the mother's first milk, called colostrum.

When a puppy has maternal antibodies in her system and a vaccine is introduced, the result isn't double your pleasure—immunity doesn't increase. Instead, the naturally occurring antibodies and the artificially introduced vaccine virus can cancel each other out, leaving this new soul more susceptible to killer puppy diseases such as parvovirus. While most puppy vaccines these days are "high titer"—that is, they contain enough antigens to be effective even if maternal antibodies destroy some of them—there is still some risk. The best prevention is not exposing very young puppies to probable sources of disease—including your vet's office. For a new litter of puppies, there is wisdom in the old-fashioned doctor's house call.

The general rule is that maternal antibodies wear off somewhere between nine and 14 weeks old. (Precisely when varies from puppy to puppy. A particularly pushy fellow who outnurses his littermates, for example, will acquire more maternal antibodies.) This immunologic gap—the time between the ebb of maternal immunity and the puppy's own immune system getting strong enough to fend off disease—is when puppies are most at risk. For that reason, many vets counsel their clients not to take their puppy to places where large groups of dogs congregate until they reach the 16-week mark.

If you want to give your puppy the fewest vaccines possible while providing reasonable protection against the diseases she's likely to encounter, Dodds' recommended protocol is one place to start. She stresses that this is her personal opinion, and that other veterinarians may advocate different schedules. She notes that she does not vaccinate for Bordetella, coronavirus, leptospirosis or Lyme unless those diseases are endemic in the area where the dog lives. After one year, she recommends titering for parvovirus and distemper, and vaccinating for rabies to the minimum required by your local law.

AGE OF PUPPY	VACCINE
9 weeks	MLV Distemper/Parvovirus only (such as Intervet Progard Puppy)
12 weeks	MLV Distemper/Parvovirus only (such as Intervet Progard Puppy)
16 to 20 weeks	MLV Distemper/Parvovirus only (such as Intervet Progard Puppy)
24 weeks or older (if allowed by law)	Killed rabies vaccine
1 year (booster)	MLV Distemper/Parvovirus only
1 year (give 3 to 4 weeks *apart from* Distemper/Parvo booster)	Killed 3-year rabies vaccine

TITERING

Most vets agree on this point: If an adult dog has achieved immunity to a particular disease, it is unnecessary to revaccinate. But the point many disagree on is: How do you measure immunity?

The standard most vets use is a blood test called a titer. Titering measures how much immunity an animal has to a particular disease. The problem is, there are different types of immunity—that is, there are three kinds of reactions the immune system can have to a specific immunologic threat.

One kind of immunity, called humoral or antibody-mediated immunity, measures B cells, which create the antibodies that fight the disease in question. (The word "humoral" comes from the archaic name—humors—for body fluids, such as lymph and blood, which is where the antibodies are released.) The second type, cell-mediated immunity, relies on T cells to attack the pathogens directly. The third is secretory immunity, associated with the body secretions such as saliva and mucous that provide the first line of defense against infection.

All three kinds of immunity are needed to fight a disease effectively. Titers, however, can only measure humoral immunity. While there are tests that can determine cell-mediated immunity, they are not routinely available and are too expensive to be considered for regular use.

Veterinarians who rely on titers to gauge immunity levels are going on the assumption that if a dog has acquired humoral immunity to a disease, he has probably acquired cell-mediated and secretory immunity as well. Experts such as Dodds say that humoral, cell-mediated and secretory immunity go hand in hand, and that titers are a valuable tool in measuring an animal's ability to resist disease. But others are less inclined to make that leap.

With some diseases, such as distemper, parvovirus and rabies, the dog soon develops immunologic memory of how to combat the disease. Titers are therefore fairly reliable indicators of a dog's immunity to these diseases.

But with other diseases the vaccines offer short-lived immunity, or the exact level or type of antibodies that indicate immunity has not been determined. In those cases, titering is used primarily to test for exposure to the disease agent rather than to indicate levels of protection. These diseases include leptospirosis, coronavirus, hepatitis virus, Bordetella (part of the kennel cough complex) and Lyme disease.

WHICH VACCINES AND WHY?

There are about 18 diseases your dog could be vaccinated against. While almost no vet vaccinates for all of them, it's not unlikely that a conventional veterinarian will want to inoculate your dog for close to half—or at least discuss the possibility with you.

As you stand in the exam room listening to the vet tick off a laundry list of shots he's about to give, it's inevitable that you'll be overwhelmed, especially if you don't do your homework. And most people don't. A 1997 study from the University of Tennessee College of Veterinary Medicine found that most dog owners had no idea what was in the vaccines they were giving their dogs.

Each vaccine is different, and it's up to you to decide which ones—if any—you want administered to your dog, and how often.

The vaccine descriptions that follow have been written with both conventional and holistic viewpoints in mind. For the most part, they represent a middle ground between vaccinating to the hilt and not vaccinating at all.

As with all crucial medical decisions, it's important to arrive at a final plan with the input of your vet. Sad but true, money is a compelling motivation for some vets: The more shots he gives, and the more frequently, the greater the revenue for his practice. If it turns out that you and your vet have different philosophies regarding vaccination and how much is enough, you always have the option of seeking out another veterinarian whose views may be more compatible with your own.

Consider the facts, then find your own personal comfort zone.

Parvovirus

Canine parvovirus first appeared in the late 1970s and today it has displaced distemper as arguably the biggest threat among the infectious diseases for which vaccinations are given. It attacks the lining of the small intestine and heart, causing bloody diarrhea, vomiting, loss of appetite, dehydration and sometimes death from heart failure. Although adults dogs can contract this highly contagious disease, puppies and juveniles are most susceptible. The treatment is basically supportive: intravenous fluids to rehydrate the dog and antibiotics to fight secondary infections that commonly crop up.

Parvovirus is airborne, and can be tracked into the house on clothing or shoes. That's why breeders who have prospective buyers over to meet their puppies may require them to remove their shoes or step in some bleach, and wash their hands.

Immunity from the parvovirus vaccine is thought to be long-lived. Veterinarian Ronald Schultz of the School of Veterinary Medicine at the University of Wisconsin-Madison has said that after a vaccination series with an MLV (modified live virus) vaccine given at two, three and four months, followed by a booster at one year, dogs develop lifelong immunity to parvovirus. After that, you need not continue to vaccinate annually, opting instead to titer for immunity levels every year.

Distemper

As with parvovirus, this disease generally strikes puppies more often than adult dogs. At first, distemper causes gastrointestinal disorders and respiratory problems. Long-term effects include neurological complications such as seizures and facial tics. Although not as common as it once was, distemper is still routinely vaccinated against, especially in puppies.

Maternal immunity can interfere with the vaccine, which is why a series of distemper shots is recommended. Immunity is also known to have a long duration.

Schultz recommends the same vaccine schedule for distemper as he does for parvovirus. After the proper puppy and one year booster shots, immunity should be lifelong.

Rabies

Almost everyone knows about this disease, which conjures up images of a wide-eyed, crazed animal foaming at the mouth. Transmitted through the saliva from a bite, rabies attacks the neurological system. If the disease is not caught in its earliest stages, it is fatal for animals and humans alike. Accurate diagnosis can only be obtained through an analysis of brain tissue, which means death for any animal who has bitten a human and is suspected to be rabid.

Like parvovirus and distemper, most animals develop a lifetime immunity to rabies rather early, and today incidents of rabid animals are rare and are often geographically isolated. Still, the disease is considered a risk to the human population, and every state mandates that dogs be vaccinated against it, although the requirements vary from state to state. That legal reality tempers any discussion about whether or not to vaccinate for rabies.

Only a handful of states require the rabies vaccine to be administered annually; many states allow residents to use a three-year vaccine.

Are there some folks out there who are not vaccinating their dogs for rabies, despite what the law requires? Undoubtedly. But that is not a decision most veterinarians will endorse—unless your dog has had a documented adverse reaction to prior vaccination or has a chronic disease, and has titers showing adequate protection against rabies. If that's the case, your veterinarian needs to write a letter of explanation and you can apply to the appropriate state agency for a waiver.

Bordetella

A lot of organisms can cause tracheobronchitis, also known as kennel cough, in dogs. Bordetella is probably the biggest culprit. Most often, the vaccine is intranasal (given through the nose) because that stimulates local immunity in the dog's nasal passages and airways. Immunity is thought to be short-lived, and the intranasal vaccine must be repeated yearly. The killed vaccine is available as a traditional injection, although most vets recommend it be repeated every six months.

As its common name suggests, kennel cough is a possibility any time a large group of dogs are housed together in close quarters. While severe cases of Bordetella can progress into pneumonia, it is generally not thought to be a life-threatening disease. And, as with many other diseases, there are several strains to contend with, meaning that even if your dog gets the vaccine, he can still contract kennel cough.

Many vets do not administer the Bordetella vaccine unless your dog will be exposed to large groups of dogs, such as at dog shows or boarding kennels. Some vaccine critics, however, contend that conditions at those events and facilities are already so stressful that the last thing a dog needs is yet another strain on his immune system.

Coronavirus

Coronavirus infections produce mild symptoms similar to parvovirus, such as diarrhea and vomiting, but not nearly so severe. The concern is not so much with coronavirus alone, but with the possibility that it might occur with parvovirus, making for a deadly combination. Vets are divided on whether to take the chance on this immunologic one-two punch. But, noting that reported cases of coronavirus are rare, many vets choose not to give the vaccine.

Adenovirus 2

Adenovirus causes respiratory infections, and the vaccine also prevents canine hepatitis (adenovirus 1). While many conventional vets consider this a core vaccine, others feel that the incidence of canine hepatitis is now so infrequent that it does not pose a significant risk.

Parainfluenza

This very contagious respiratory disease causes kennel cough, which is not life-threatening, although secondary infections are possible. Although most vets do not consider this a must-have, it is usually a component of most combination vaccines (those that include antigens for multiple diseases in one inoculation). To avoid the parainfluenza vaccine, then, means avoiding combination (also called polyvalent) vaccines.

Leptospirosis

This bacterial disease is mainly transmitted through the urine of infected animals, which include rodents, foxes, raccoons and squirrels, as well as livestock such as pigs and cattle. Leptospirosis is also a zoonotic disease, meaning it is transmissible to humans. The spiral-shaped bacteria for which the disease is named need a specific environment in which to thrive: moisture (such as the stagnant water in pools or ponds) and moderate temperatures (77°F is ideal). For this reason, outbreaks are usually seen in the spring and fall.

Dogs who contract leptospirosis can exhibit lethargy, muscle pain, weakness, fever, loss of appetite and excessive drinking and/or urinating. It's precisely because the flu-like symptoms are so general that owners often delay taking their dog to the vet until the disease has progressed to the point of liver damage or kidney failure. If caught early, leptospirosis can be cured with a simple course of antibiotics and intravenous fluids to help with hydration.

ASK YOURSELF

As you think about the vaccination approach you want to take, here are some questions to ask yourself.

Is my dog healthy? Read the fine print on any vaccine and you will come across this caveat: Vaccines are to be used on healthy animals only. A dog who is recovering from a serious illness—or battling one—or who has been recently stressed from a move or change in lifestyle or spay/neuter surgery already has pressure on his immune system. If your dog is dealing with a short-term condition or a chronic disease, you and your vet need to determine whether his immune system can handle the extra stress.

Also think about other stresses on your dog. If she is fed a natural, preservative-free diet and if you don't use pesticides or other toxins around the house or yard, chances are her immune system is strong and vibrant enough to deal with a vaccine. Then again, she's probably also strong enough to deal with most diseases herself. That's up to you to decide.

Will my dog ever be exposed to this disease? Most veterinarians make a distinction between core vaccines such as distemper and parvovirus that they believe every dog should have, and others where individual situations often determine whether they will be administered. If, for example, your dog never attends events where there are large groups of other dogs—such as a dog show—is there any good reason to give the Bordetella vaccine?

How old is my dog? If your dog is 10 or more years old, has been vaccinated annually for much of his life and never leaves the house except to venture into a small backyard where there are no other animals or to socialize with other healthy dogs, you and your vet might conclude that the risk of ill effects from

To complicate things even further, there are many subspecies of leptospirosis. The combination vaccine given to many puppies as part of their 5-in-1 or 6-in-1 shot covers the *icterohaemorrhagiae* and *canicola* strains, which are less prevalent today. It does not, however, prevent against two newer strains, *grippotyphosa* and *pomona,* although a new vaccine has come on the market to address those. *Leptospira hadjo* is yet another newly encountered pathological strain, and at this writing there is no vaccine to combat it.

vaccination outweigh the benefits of inoculating an older dog whose possible exposure to infection is limited. At some point, the risk of negative reactions to the vaccine outstrips the risk of getting the disease.

What breed is my dog? Some breeds are at particular risk for adverse reactions to vaccines because of hereditary immune sensitivities. Among them are Great Danes, Weimaraners and Akitas. With any breed, consult with the breeders, if you know them, to find out the immunologic histories of your dog's parents and extended family.

What can I live with? Your decisions regarding vaccines depend a lot on how far you are willing to stray from conventional veterinary norms. If you have had a dog who had an adverse vaccine reaction, or whose chronic health problems you now think trace back to repeated vaccination, it will be easier to just say no.

Recognize, too, that choosing not to vaccinate doesn't mean fewer trips to the vet—in most cases, it means more. If you don't want to reflexively vaccinate, you will still have to pay for titering to measure immunity levels, and those tests typically cost more than the shots. Also plan on regular vet visits to monitor your dog's health. This applies not just for vaccines, but in other cases where you depart from "conventional protocol." Say, for example, you live in a part of the country where heartworm is not common and where long, cold winters keep the mosquito population inactive for all but the summer months. Even if you feed your dog mosquito-repelling herbs, a prudent approach would be to visit the vet for periodic blood tests to make sure he has not been infected.

Concern about this bacterial infection varies, depending on geography. In some areas of the country it is rare, so local vets do not automatically vaccinate against it. Elsewhere, particularly the Northeast, recent outbreaks have prompted vets to take a more aggressive approach. To further complicate matters, some strains may be common in one area but not in another.

Generally, if you don't live in an area where leptospirosis is found, most vets will recommend that you skip this vaccination, largely because the vaccine itself tends to cause more adverse

ASK YOUR VET

Use these questions as a starting point for talking to your veterinarian about vaccination.

Are you using combination vaccines? Many vets use multivalent or polyvalent vaccines, which combine several disease-preventing antigens in one shot. The popular DHLPP shot, for example, contains distemper, hepatitis, leptospirosis, parainfluenza and parvovirus—quite an immunologic wallop.

Insist instead on monovalent, or single-antigen shots, whenever possible. If your vet says that's not possible, ask him to explain why. Sometimes a monovalent vaccine is not available, or if it is, ordering it for just one patient is not economically feasible for the vet (vaccines are usually sold in 10- to 25-dose lots). If that's the case, you may want to look for a vet who uses monovalent vaccines regularly in his practice.

What vaccination schedule do you recommend? This decision is truly a balancing act: You need to weigh the risks of your dog getting a particular disease against the risks of damaging her immune system by overwhelming it with too much, too soon. Giving your dog breathing room between vaccines—especially rabies—is important; and you need to work with your vet to come up with a safe and appropriate timetable.

Are you using a modified live virus (MLV) vaccine? Vaccines must walk a biological tightrope: They have to be strong enough to provoke immunity in the animal, but not so strong that they actually cause the disease.

Modified live virus, or MLV, vaccines are made from live viruses that have been treated so that they lose their ability to cause disease. They are more potent—the protection they provide is generally

reactions than most (there is some evidence that this is particularly true in the toy breeds).

Those who live in areas where leptospirosis is a risk have a tougher time deciding on a course of action. Since immunity is short-lived, titering is not usually done and frequent boosters are recommended by the vaccine companies to keep immunity high.

If you do decide to vaccinate for leptospirosis, insist that the vaccine be given separately, a couple of weeks after other inoculations, and *never* as part of a combination vaccine. And make sure the strains your dog is getting are the ones prevalent in your area.

more complete and lasts longer—but they are more powerful and always replicate in the dog, potentially overwhelming his immune system. They can also be shed into the environment.

Killed, or inactivated vaccines, are an alternative. They are made of virus particles that have been killed by various means. Unlike MLV vaccines, they cannot revert to a virulent form, creating the disease itself, or cause the disease to be shed into the environment. For this reason, all rabies vaccines are killed vaccines. While killed vaccines are not as complete or as potent as MLV vaccines (and are not available for every disease), Dodds believes they pose less risk of damage to the immune system. Critics say killed vaccines are undesirable because they may have to be administered more frequently to get the same level of immunity as an MLV vaccine. They also say the killed vaccine contains adjuvants (substances added to enhance the immune response to the vaccine), which can cause allergic reactions. It's a risk you'll have to weigh.

What dose are you using? Most vaccine manufacturers recommend the same dosage whether your dog is a Chihuahua or a Great Dane. But some holistic vets, such as Dodds, take issue with this one-size-fits-all mentality, arguing that the size of the dose should fit the size of the dog.

Also, ask specifically about the rabies vaccine, which is available in a one-year vaccine or a three-year vaccine. Although rabies vaccination of dogs is mandated by law, requirements for the frequency of vaccination vary from state to state. If you live in a part of the country where the three-year vaccine is permitted, make sure your vet is using that one instead of annual rabies boosters.

Lyme Disease

This tick-borne bacterial disease causes lameness, joint pain and swelling, fever, lethargy, loss of appetite and, eventually, kidney failure. As with leptospirosis, Lyme disease is not prevalent in many parts of the country and geography is a huge consideration. Some vets have expressed concern with the vaccine, which is relatively new, because it can cause false-positive readings on the Lyme disease blood test. There is also concern about potential side effects from the vaccine, including antigen-antibody-mediated arthritic signs in previously exposed animals and organ failure. Most vets do not recommend the vaccine unless you live in an area where Lyme disease is endemic. Even then, weigh the pros and cons.

Giardia

This protozoan parasite lives in a dog's intestines and can cause loss of appetite, weight loss, diarrhea and slimy stools—but usually only in immuno-compromised or debilitated individuals. In some areas of the country, about a third of the dogs and cats are thought to have been exposed to this common parasite, which can be transmitted to humans, but many are able to deal with the bug on their own and do not exhibit symptoms. Most vets do not recommend the giardia vaccine.

NOSODES

If you read the earlier chapter on homeopathy, you know that the theory behind that system of healing is "Like cures like." And nosodes, the homeopathic alternative to vaccines, are no different. They are remedies made from the disease itself, using a sample of tissue, blood, urine or scab from an infected animal.

Vaccines, by contrast, are made of agents that cause the disease itself. They work by causing biochemical changes in the body. Since homeopathic remedies are repeatedly diluted and shaken to the point where there is barely a physical trace of the substance left—only its energy—nosodes do not work on the same level as vaccines.

Most conventional vets consider nosodes to be ineffective, because they do not produce measurable antibodies. And even among holistic vets, nosodes are a controversial subject. A great many are not convinced that nosodes can single-handedly protect against disease. So far there is no clinical evidence that they can.

Some holistic vets recommend administering a nosode a good while before giving a vaccination, so the immune system is naturally primed to deal with the challenge ahead. But Richard Pitcairn, who has used nosodes in his practice for 20 years, strenuously disagrees, saying it's harmful to do both. In homeopathic terms, what the nosode does is find the disturbance or weakness in an animal's vital force, and then "plugs the hole temporarily"

HOMEOPATHIC HINT

The homeopathic remedy Thuja is considered the "anti-vaccine" remedy because it can help with the after-effects of vaccination. Some homeopathically oriented vets advocate administering a dose of Thuja 30C after a vaccination. (With rabies, Lyssin 30C is often given instead.) But others disagree, saying vaccine reactions can be so varied and complex that Thuja may not be the remedy of choice. As with most gray areas, consult your vet.

---

so the animal gets ill with the nosode instead of the disease. Following up with a vaccine, Pitcairn warns, can actually aggravate the situation.

Sound complicated? It is. Pitcairn points out that nosodes should not be used on chronically ill animals, and the timing with which they are administered is crucial. "It's not as simple as substituting a nosode for a vaccine," he says. Which is why it's important to seek out a veterinarian who truly understands homeopathy before making any decisions about nosodes.

REPORT CARDS

If the veterinary community in general and the vaccine companies in particular are to address concerns about the effects of over-vaccination, they first have to acknowledge that they exist. And the reality is that most adverse vaccine reactions go unreported.

If you do use a particular vaccine, be sure to note the name of the manufacturer and the vaccine, the serial number and the expiration date, in case there is an adverse reaction. If that happens, you or your vet should report it to:

- U.S. Pharmacopeia, a private group that operates the Veterinary Practitioners' Reporting Program, which is endorsed by the American Veterinary Medical Association (AVMA). After your vet files a report, the results are shared with the manufacturer, the appropriate federal agency and the AVMA. Contact them at www.usp.org or (800) 487-7776.

- The United States Department of Agriculture's Center for Veterinary Biologics is charged with overseeing compliance with the Virus–Serum–Toxin Act. You can file an "adverse event report" with the Center for Veterinary Biologics by calling its hotline at (800) 752-6255.
- The manufacturer.

HEARTWORM PREVENTIVES

Heartworm medication is not a vaccine—quite the opposite. The monthly pills destroy heartworm larvae in the bloodstream before they can travel to the heart and develop into adults. So in reality, heartworm medication is a diluted version of the drug used to treat the disease. The full treatment itself is considered so toxic that many dogs do not survive it. As a result, heartworm medication can have side effects, such as vomiting, diarrhea and even seizures.

Certain Collie breeds also have a sensitivity to ivermectin, which is used in some heartworm preventives.

As with most immunologic concerns addressed in this chapter, there are no guarantees—there is no sure-fire way to make sure your dog does not get heartworm if he is not on the medication. Many owners add garlic to their dog's diet to boost the immune system and repel the mosquitoes that carry the disease, but studies have never been done on the effectiveness of this practice. Some holistic vets believe natural wormers such as black walnut hull and the appropriately named wormwood are effective at preventing and treating heartworm; others warn that their efficacy is not proven. It's also important to remember that both are powerful and potentially toxic herbs and should only be used under the supervision of a vet or qualified herbalist.

Since heartworm is transmitted by mosquitoes, which deposit the worm larvae into the bloodstream, keeping your dog bite-free is best. Investing in a device such as the Mosquito Magnet (www.mosquitomagnet.com), which lures mosquitoes with carbon dioxide and then traps them, is a pricey but chemical-free way of eliminating the pests. Spraying your property with a natural repellent—such as Mosquito Barrier (www.garlicbarrier.com), which is made of liquid garlic—is another option.

THINKING OUTSIDE THE BOX

Although they might be inclined to take a more minimalist approach to vaccinations, some dog owners wind up vaccinating their animal because they are forced to. If you plan to travel across the border to Canada, for example, proof of rabies vaccination is required. Producing a titer report is just not going to cut it. Since the law is the law, there is pretty much no way around it, short of leaving your dog home.

Boarding kennels, however, are another story. Long before you go on your trip, call the kennel to ask if they will accept a titer report from your veterinarian. Also ask them if they will waive the common requirement of Bordetella vaccine if you will write them a letter stating that the dog has not been exposed to large groups of dogs or a kennel in the previous month. They may still require proof of vaccination, but it's worth a try. (Titering for Bordetella, while available, is relatively expensive.)

If the answer is no, rethink why you are leaving your dog in a kennel in the first place. For dogs who live in the house (hopefully, all of them, since that's where they belong) being kenneled in a cement-floored chain-link run is a stressful change, to say the least.

The optimal solution is to leave your dog in a home setting—yours or someone else's. Pet-sitting services are springing up all over the country, and for good reason. Licensed and bonded animal lovers can visit your home to walk and feed your animals if you are away on an overnight trip. For more extended absences, many will take your dog into their own home. Often, the cost is comparable to what you will pay a boarding kennel.

It's a good idea to hire a sitter beforehand for a test run, to get your dog accustomed to him or her. Pick a day when you need to stay late at the office and have the sitter come in for a midday walk and play session.

For information about pet sitters in your area, contact:

Pet Sitters International
201 East King Street
King, NC 27021-9161
(336) 983-9222
www.petsit.com

National Association of Professional Pet Sitters
17000 Commerce Parkway, Suite C
Mt. Laurel, NJ 08054

Since heartworm is a concern only when mosquitoes are, some dog owners opt not to give heartworm medication, instead monitoring their dogs with periodic blood tests to make sure they have not been infected. The larvae take six months to develop into adults and begin damaging the pulmonary arteries; some vets believe that gives them ample time to get an infection under control before it becomes too serious. Others are concerned about the toxicity of the treatment.

If you live in a part of the country where heartworm is endemic and you decide to give your dog heartworm medication, talk to your vet about discontinuing the medication during colder months when there are no mosquitoes. Also discuss dosage. Some vets believe the medications may be just as effective given every other month or calibrated to take into account your dog's size and weight.

Chapter 8

Relationships: Dominion Doesn't Cut It Anymore

For most of my childhood, my mother was not open to the idea of adding a dog to our household. As a result, my earliest canine companions were imaginary ones.

In anticipation of the arrival of a flesh-and-blood dog, I borrowed library books about training and read them voraciously. One of them, whose title I have forgotten, starred a dog named Dammit. That wasn't the dog's given name, the book explained. It was just that her refusal to listen had prompted the harried owner to follow every command with that expletive. He used it so much, apparently, that the dog thought her name was Dammit.

And so, eventually, it was.

Three decades later, I still remember that dog's name, and not just for the cheap joke it provided. It spoke of frustration and anger on the part of the trainer, and resistance on the part of the dog. While in the end Dammit may have turned out to be a very

145

AN HISTORICAL PERSPECTIVE

Fido wasn't always a latchkey dog. Historians will tell you that the Industrial Revolution of the mid-19th century marked the start of a social fault line between our home and work lives. As factories and urban centers siphoned away the workforce, and cottage industries dwindled, a permanent and pervasive wedge was driven between the private and public. Earning a living meant leaving our homes, and the fabric of our society was rewoven—or, some would argue, torn.

Today, in modern American society, the roles that dogs fulfilled in pre-industrial times—as four-legged partners who worked and herded stock, hunted game and fowl, trotted alongside coaches, carted heavy loads—have all but disappeared. In some respects, that's a good thing, says psychologist and animal-behavior consultant Larry Lachman of Carmel, California, author of *Dogs on the Couch,* because it doesn't "perpetuate the utilitarian view of animals as property, not beings."

But our canine companions paid dearly for that shift from an agrarian society to an industrial one. Most urban and suburban dogs sit at home all day, awaiting the arrival of 9-to-5-ers who are often too tired to provide much more than a pat on the head and a square meal. Sequestered behind stockade fences or picture windows, they're deprived of rich daily interactions with humans and other animals.

"Today dogs are suffering from what kids have been suffering from for the last 30 years," says Lachman of this latchkey syndrome. "If you work eight to ten hours a day and you sleep eight to ten hours a day, that leaves four to eight hours of intermittent contact. Enough for a goldfish, maybe, but not a dog."

Dog trainers and behaviorists are seeing the trickle-down effects of that kind of isolation in a company-craving pack animal

successful obedience dog, I always wondered if she was a happy one.

What does training have to do with health care for your dog? From a holistic point of view, everything. We humans talk a lot about the importance of the body-mind connection. Why is it any different for dogs? Dogs have emotional lives and needs, and one of the primary ways they express them is through their relationship with their caretakers.

like the dog: separation anxiety, urinating and defecating in the house, chewing and scratching household objects, nuisance barking, fearfulness and fear-provoked aggression—the list goes on and on.

Despite the nostalgic soft-drink ads featuring the loyal dog in the back of the pickup truck (a very unsafe way for your dog to travel, by the way), today's America is not terribly dog-friendly. With the exception of service dogs, canines are not permitted in most restaurants, malls, banks, recreational areas and parks. And breed-specific legislation has made many innocent animals the target of media-hyped stereotypes.

Still, there is hope that the future holds an appropriate place for our canine companions—preferably, at our sides and snoozing at our feet. At the height of the dot-com frenzy, bringing your dog to the office was considered a perk of the new economy. In existence for a handful of years, Take Your Dog to Work Day, created by Pet Sitters International (www.petsit.com, 201 East King St., King, NC, 27021-9161, (336) 983-9222), has made some corporate inroads. And as companies recognize the cost and productivity savings offered by the home office, some dogs can hope to be reintegrated back into our daily lives, where they belong in the first place.

Meanwhile, dogs need and want human interaction, and it is up to us to provide it for them, despite busy schedules and conflicting demands. Additionally, many breeds of dogs are hardwired to want to perform specific tasks. The committed caretaker will go out of her way to find avenues that let a dog do the things he was born to do. The Appendix offers many suggestions for sports you and your dog can participate in.

As with everything to do with your dog, you make a conscious decision about the training methods you use. You decide whether your approach will be mostly positive or mostly negative, or somewhere in between. And the methods you use shape your relationship more than you know.

As recently as 15 years ago, the cutting edge of dog training involved compulsory tactics—basically, making a dog do what her human wanted through punishment and aversives such as corrective jerks and "pops" administered by a choke collar, and throw chains that startled a dog into learning the Come command. Many times, these trainers used techniques that reinforced the supposed dominance of the handler—among them the alpha roll, where the dog or puppy is rolled on his back and held there until he submits and stops struggling. Food or other rewards were not used because they were considered bribery; the dog was to comply just for the sheer joy of wanting to please the handler.

In recent years, positive reinforcement has slowly but steadily displaced training methods based on compulsion and force. Instead of training a dog to avoid punishment (such as a corrective jerk of the collar), positive reinforcement motivates the dog by rewarding him for doing something right.

A positive approach is not only kinder, it's more effective. What behaviorists call positive punishment—the dog does something wrong, and as a consequence something bad happens—just doesn't produce results as quickly or effortlessly as positive reinforcement. (Negative punishment, by contrast, is used all the time by positive trainers, since it's defined as discouraging a behavior by taking away something pleasant. When a dog refuses to listen to his owner in the dog park, for example, he will have to leave the park—kind of the canine equivalent of a time-out.) Dogs are self-interested creatures, just as we all are. In many ways, positive training follows a capitalist model: The harder the dog works, the more he earns—a veritable canine entrepreneur.

"Dogs forget punishment-based behavior, and that's biologically appropriate," says Karen Pryor of Waltham, Massachusetts, whose book *Don't Shoot the Dog: The New Art of Teaching and Training*, ignited interest in positive reinforcement techniques in the mid-1980s. "If we went around being afraid of every bush because there was a bear behind the first bush we encountered, we wouldn't get very far. Punishment is designed to fade."

Positive reinforcement, however, lingers. Dogs—and people—remember when and why good things happened to them, especially if there's a chance they might happen again. This is why, to use a favorite example of reward-based trainers, folks will put their last quarter into a Las Vegas slot machine. One day it just might pay out.

Some traditional trainers are very hostile to the idea of positive training, as if somehow it threatens their supremacy in the relationship. And in a way, it does. Positive training puts the dog in a position where she can make choices based on her own self-interest. ("If I choose to do it, I will get that cookie!") It encourages the dog to think. It makes the dog feel empowered within the relationship.

As we know in our human interactions, encouraging that kind of freedom is the key to a balanced and healthy relationship. Being a control freak is not. Oftentimes, when we permit the dog to take the lead in determining the pace and direction of the training session, our egos feel threatened. Somehow, because we are not the boss and the dog is not asked to respond like a robot, we aren't "in control."

When humans are in those kinds of constricting, critical and overwhelming relationships, many times they leave. Dogs don't have the option to do that physically (although, given the opportunity, they just might try). But they can "leave" the training session emotionally and spiritually by letting go of their joy and will to please and by just going through the motions.

The bottom line is that positive training will give you better, more consistent results than a training methodology based solely on punishment. It will make training *fun*, for both you and your dog. And isn't that the whole point?

CLICKER TRAINING

These days, many positive trainers use a technique called clicker training. Based on operant conditioning techniques developed to train dolphins, clicker training uses a sound marker—the quick click from a small plastic box about the size of a domino—to help the dog understand exactly what she is being rewarded for.

Although clicker training is currently trendy, it's hardly new. Long before clickers found their way into obedience classes, they were used to train animals who couldn't be reached—literally and figuratively—by traditional, physical means, such as marine mammals and zoo animals.

"Clicker training really isn't a training method. What it is, is a communication system that works in both directions," says Pryor, whose work with dolphins started her on a career as one of the world's most famous clicker trainers. "The dog realizes right away that what he is doing makes you click. This is exciting for the dog. Instead of being knocked around by his environment and the world, he has some control. The dog is in charge of what's happening. He likes this—we all do."

What clicker training does is literally have you accentuate the positive. Instead of pointing out what your dog does wrong, it tells her what she's done right. "It brings you more than a better bond," says Pryor. "It gives you mutual understanding. It teaches you to watch your dog in a different way—instead of watching for something wrong, you're always looking for good news. It really changes the way the dog can reach you. But more importantly, it changes you for the better."

Seven Steps to Clicking

1. **Buy a clicker.** Actually, more than one, since you want to keep these cheap plastic tools handy in places where you're likely to train. (Minimally, I have one in the kitchen, one near the computer, one in the car and one in my handbag.)

2. **Teach the dog that a click equals a treat.** Spend five minutes clicking and treating. You click, you give the dog a treat. You click again, treat again. No rat-a-tat-tat clicks. The rule is *every single* click gets a treat. Let the dog finish each treat before you move on to the next click. After a couple of sessions, the dog will soon understand that whenever she hears that click, food is coming. And she'll get *very* excited when you pick up the clicker.

3. **Teach (the better word is "capture") a new behavior to your dog.** Let's say you want to teach her to sit. You grab your clicker and a box of treats, and sit on the couch in front of the television. Your dog hangs

around expectantly, waiting for you to click. She tries a couple of things—she nudges your hand, she whines, she paces. At some point, inevitably, she will sit. And just as she does, right before her rear is about an inch above the ground, ready to plant itself, you click and give her a treat. *Don't say anything,* just click and treat.

Your dog is thrilled, but clueless. Again, she restlessly paces, paws, whines. Finally, again, in total exasperation, she will sit. And, using the same flawless timing, you will click just as she is in the process of sitting, just before her haunches touch the ground. Repeat, repeat, repeat, until you see the light bulb go on over her head. Eventually, in a flood of understanding, your dog will understand the connection between the click and the sit.

And, as Martha Stewart likes to say, that is a good thing.

4. **Repeat the exercise in subsequent sessions.** Simply wait wordlessly for your dog to sit before you click. Soon, she will be sitting constantly, because she has figured out that the more she sits, the more you click. At that point, she understands what you want from her.

5. **Give the behavior a name.** During all this, I know you have been itching to say something. *Now* that your dog understands why she has been clicked, you can. Tell your girl Sit, and when she does—and only then—does she get the click and treat. If she sits on her own accord, without you using the command, and looks expectantly at you, she gets nothing. At this point, you are clicking only for the behavior if it is verbally requested from you.

6. **Fade the reward.** Once your dog knows the command, and the behavior, and is performing it reliably, the clicker has done its job. The dog now understands the behavior the clicker was marking, and the verbal command you have given that behavior. So you begin to fade the clicker—to gradually stop using it each time to mark the behavior. You might start clicking for every

PURELY POSITIVE: IS IT POSSIBLE?

Trainers disagree about whether it is possible to be a purely positive trainer—that is, to *only* use positive reinforcement, with no corrections. "I think a lot people do half clicker training—they click for what they like and still correct for mistakes," says Karen Pryor. "But if you don't restrict yourself to showing the dog what to do—if you use what's called 'free shaping,' allowing the dog to develop the behaviors from scratch without using hints—you train in a way that actually teaches the dog to think." While that approach may be time-consuming, says Pryor, its results are extremely powerful and long lasting.

If corrections have any place in your training methodology, they should be done with forethought and understanding, not as an unthinking reaction or reflex. So many times, we react with a jerk of the leash or a harsh command not because we truly intended it, but precisely because we did not.

"We have a very punishment-oriented society, and we are very compulsive about repeating legacies," says Jean Donaldson, director for the Academy of Dog Trainers at the San Francisco ASPCA and the author of several animal-behavior books. "If you look at our law institutions, our religions, our major societal bodies, it's all about avoiding punishment. We're a very stick-oriented society—we drive the speed limit because we don't want to get a ticket. We don't reward people for getting it right; we don't have that as a construct."

Choosing not to use physical punishment isn't just kinder, says Larry Lachman. It's more effective. "Studies have shown both with animals and people that punishment doesn't eliminate behavior, just suppresses it."

What Lachman calls "ear-pinching, hang-em-choke-em-shock-em, Marquis de Sade, Hulk Hogan jujitsu techniques" such as ear pinches, throw chains, choke and prong collars, alpha rolls, and electric shock collars may get you fast, if temporary, results in the short term. But at what price?

third or fourth sit, then every tenth sit, and so on. This is called "variable reinforcement," and it's explained by the earlier example (on page 148) of the slot machine; if your dog is not sure when she will get a click and treat for her correct performance, she will treat each sit as a potential for a payoff.

7. **Capture another behavior.** Indeed, the more behavior you click for, the better, because it teaches your dog that there are many ways for her to make you click. Yawns, sneezes, stretches, yips, barks, tail chasing—they're all opportunities for you to click, capture and put on cue, a cute behavior in the making.

Piece by Piece

You can use a clicker to help your dog overcome fear and learn complex behaviors by breaking things down into small pieces and clicking for each piece.

Let's say you've introduced your dog to the canine sport of agility and he loves it, but you've hit a brick wall with the seesaw. He hates the loud noise it makes as it hits the ground and doesn't want to go *near* it, much less *on* it. So at first, you click him just for looking at it. Then for several sessions, you click him for going toward it. Then you click him for putting just one foot on it while you lure him toward it with some food. Then you click for two feet on the seesaw, then for all four, and so on. Eventually, by breaking up the seesaw exercise into tiny steps and clicking each one, you will get your dog across it. And chances are, if given a choice of a whole ring full of agility equipment, he'll gravitate toward the seesaw because he associates it with such positive things.

Remember, however, that *the click ends the behavior.* Once you click, that means the dog has done the right thing and can claim his treat. So if you click him for putting his paw on the seesaw and he jumps right off and runs to you when hears the click, that's fine. Next time, he will need to put two paws on the teeter-totter to trigger a click. Slowly but surely, he will get there.

Quick Clicks

Here are some important things to remember about the clicker.

The clicker is a marker. What the clicker says to your dog is, "Yes! That! The thing you did right then! That's why you are getting a treat!" It enables you to pinpoint a specific behavior. The nanosecond you click—*that* is the behavior being rewarded.

HEAD CASES

Some dogs are pullers. That's not a terminal condition; it can be remedied by consistent training. It's simply a matter of teaching your dog, "If you pull, I stop moving. If you give me slack in the leash, I click the clicker."

But there will be times when your dog is unable to walk nicely on a loose leash because the stimuli around him are so overwhelming. Instead of resorting to a choke or prong collar to control him, consider a head collar such as a Halti or Gentle Leader.

Head collars work on much the same principle as a bridle on a horse. A nylon strap loops over the dog's nose and secures behind the ears, and the leash is attached under the nose loop, just beneath the jaw. When gentle pressure is applied, the halter pulls the dog's head down and prevents her from moving or lunging forward. "If you control the head, you control the horse," the old saying goes, and the head halter proves it true for dogs, as well.

But, like any good tool, head halters can be abused. Pressure applied to the halter must be slow and steady, *never* quick and abrupt. Issuing sharp and severe corrections with the halter can result in serious neck injury to your dog. Always be mindful of this when walking him on a head halter.

There is no doubt in the dog's mind about what he did right. For this reason, the timing of the click is crucial.

Let's say you are starting to teach the command "Watch me." The instant the dog makes eye contact with you, you click and then treat. But if your timing is off by even a second, you will be clicking the dog for looking *away* from you, not *at* you.

If your timing is lousy enough, you can teach your dog incorrect behaviors. So to correct your slow trigger-finger, get a human partner and work on clicking her for specific actions. That way, you build your timing skills, but not at the expense of your dog's confidence.

The clicker is a contract. The deal you make with the dog is: Every time you hear a click, you will get a treat. That means even if you make a mistake and click the wrong behavior or if your timing is off. It's better for your dog to think that she got clicked for doing the wrong thing than think the clicker is unreliable.

Every click is an IOU. Be sure to honor your debts.

The clicker is a constant. Unlike your voice, a clicker sounds the same every time you use it. It has no emotion attached to it. It may take a while, and he may not understand why he's being clicked, but eventually your dog will figure things out and run through his repertoire of clicker-learned behaviors in the hopes of inducing a click.

The clicker is a motivator. The whole point of clicker training is that you don't make the dog do something; you wait until he does it, then click. This makes the dog think it's *his* idea, not yours, that somehow he is in control too, that *he* is making *you* click. The clicker makes the dog an active participant in the training process, and the resulting enthusiasm level is awesome.

Best of all, clicker training encourages a dog to *think*. There is nothing more amazing—or rewarding—than watching the wheels turn as your dog works to solve problems: "What is she clicking for now?"

The clicker is a nuanced training tool. Using a clicker enables you to teach things you couldn't possibly do with a traditional approach. How else, for example, would you teach a dog to do something as subtle as holding up her tail just so?

The clicker also lets you polish the behaviors you have already taught. Using the Sit example we've been following so far, let's say your dog has caught on really quickly and now sits whenever you tell her. But you are planning on embarking on an Obedience career with her, where sloppy sits are penalized. So you decide to raise the bar and click and reward only Obedience-style, straight sits. Soon, if you do not click them, those sloppy sits will be a thing of the past—a process trainers aptly call "extinction."

The clicker builds muscle memory. Think about how traditional trainers teach a dog to sit on command. They press up on the dog's chest (or pull up on his collar) and push down on his rump. This is why "trained" dogs will often have to be kick-started into offering a behavior; they are prompted to sit, for example, by the owner leaning over and reaching for their collar. The dog remembers on a physical level what comes next—the collar gets pulled up, my butt gets pushed down—and he reacts.

But in a clicker training session, you don't have to touch, or even go near, the dog to get him to sit. He does it all on his own because he remembers what it feels like to move into that sit position, without anyone guiding him.

The clicker is a mind-set. The more you use it, the more instinctive it will be, and the more opportunities you will find to communicate with your dog. If traditional training is the equivalent of rote memorization of your multiplication tables—how fondly do you remember those drills?—clicker training is sort of like doggie Montessori, emphasizing creativity and individuality.

Many trainers start clicking puppies in the whelping box—as soon as they can accept food and interact with them. The earlier your dog understands the power and promise of the clicker, the more enthusiastic a student she will be.

"Clicker training becomes an addictive sport for dogs, akin to crossword puzzles for me," says Pryor. "And they are operating in a state of elation that you don't see in traditionally trained dogs."

Clicker Myths

Often, people who don't like clickers don't really understand how they work. Here are some common misconceptions you may hear.

The clicker is a "remote control." Nothing could be further from the truth. The clicker is only used as a tool to help teach your dog precisely what you want, or to help refine a behavior. Once a behavior is learned and named, the clicker is no longer needed.

My voice is just as good. In truth, it usually isn't. It is hard to have the same consistent tone every time you give a verbal marker praising a dog's behavior. And whether you choose to use "Yes!" or "Good boy!" words take time coming out of your mouth. It's hard to have accurate timing, and even harder for the dog to figure out just what you are praising. With the clicker's unchanging sound and split-second timing, you can more accurately pinpoint the behavior you are trying to teach.

Like it or not, your voice has an emotional effect on your dog, good and bad. And sometimes that can interfere with training. One of my dogs, for example, has a habit of holding her ears plastered to the side of her head—something that definitely is a drawback when she's in the show ring or posing for a picture. So I tried to teach her the command "Pretty ears." If I used my voice as a marker instead of the clicker, she would cock her ear the minute a word of praise came out of my mouth. Pretty soon, she thought "Pretty ears" meant one ear cocked forward and the other on the side of her head. She even moved them around, like someone with a TV antenna looking for better reception. The clicker—with its quick, unequivocal sound—eliminated this confusion.

I don't have enough hands. True, clicker training involves adding another piece of equipment to your repertoire. And sometimes juggling all the trappings—bait bag, leash, squeaky toys, food—can be a challenge. But most clickers have little tabs so you can add a rubber band and let them dangle from your wrist. There are also retractable clicker holders that clip to your belt or waistband for easy access.

My dog will get confused when she hears other people clicking their own dogs. Anyone who has clicker-trained a dog for any period of time knows that dogs quickly learn to discriminate their clicks from those given for others. Dogs do get excited when they see you or someone else take out a clicker, but it's not because they're confused. Rather, they're excited at the prospect of training with it. How could that kind of enthusiasm be a bad thing?

I don't want to be dependent on a piece of equipment. That's like saying you don't want to be a gardener because you may not always have a trowel handy. If you don't have a clicker, you can always improvise: You can use a ballpoint pen to make a click sound or even cluck with your tongue. The most important thing about clicker training is not the clicker itself, but the

Clicker Resources

Until recently, it was impossible to find a clicker at a pet supply store. Now some of the big chains, such as PetCo, are stocking them. One quick and convenient source for these cheap plastic noisemakers is www.sitstay.com. The Nebraska-based site sells clickers singly or (your best investment) in quantities of 50 or more. They also sell clicker books and equipment such as wrist coils and retractable clicker holders.

Karen Pryor's site, www.clickertraining.com, offers many resources, from a Clicker Gear store to clicker games you can play with your pooch.

ClickerSolutions is an e-mail list dedicated to discussing and promoting positive reinforcement. To subscribe, go to www.clickersolutions.com.

There are many very good clicker books on the market, some written for very specific audiences.

Don't Shoot the Dog! by Karen Pryor (Bantam, $13.95) is considered a classic. It explains the principles of positive reinforcement, and how they work on animals and humans alike. Karen Pryor is arguably the clicker-training queen, having first used the technique to train dolphins. *Getting Started: Clicker Training for Dogs*, also by Karen Pryor (Sunshine Books, $14.95), is dog-specific and very readable. In *Click to Win! For the Show Ring* (Sunshine Books, $24.95), Pryor has written a book for the conformation crowd. It covers all the nuances of the show ring, from stacking to gaiting, from a clicker-training perspective.

Clicking With Your Dog by Peggy Tillman (Sunshine Books, $24.95) is a step-by-step guide to more than 100 clicker-trained

working relationship it represents. A clicker-trained dog is an active participant in the training process, which encourages her to be creative and think for herself.

As you explore clicker training, you will come across some people who don't believe in it. Worse, they'll object to you using it, for a host of reasons. Keep in mind that many obedience trainers have been training with their own methods for years, even decades. They may never embrace clicker training, and that's OK.

behaviors, from "Don't jump on guests" to "Pick up your toys."

Quick Clicks, 40 Fast and Fun Behaviors to Train With a Clicker (Legacy-By-Mail, $19.95) by Cheryl Smith and Mandy Book offers a good introduction to the concepts behind clicker training and easy-to-follow instructions for training.

Take A Bow . . . Wow! Fun and Functional Dog Tricks by Virginia Broitman and Sherri Lippman ($24.95) is a half-hour video. It gives quick, informative lessons on how to teach fun tricks such as "take a bow" and "ring the bell." A good choice for kid trainers.

Clicker Training for Obedience by Morgan Spector (Sunshine Books, $29.95) is very much geared toward those who want to do competitive Obedience. This book breaks each exercise down into exhaustive detail and explains how to use a clicker to achieve it.

Two indispensable books for the "training and behavior" sec tion of your library are *The Culture Clash* (James & Kenneth Publishers, $17.95) and *Dogs Are From Neptune* (Lasar Multimedia Productions, $16.95), both by Jean Donaldson. With a commonsense approach, Donaldson explores such top- ics as socialization, aggression, fear and overall training. A clicker proponent, Donaldson has great respect for the fact that dogs are just that—dogs—and need to be understood in the context of their own "culture."

Clicker training is not the only positive training method out there, and just because a trainer does not use a clicker does not mean they train primarily with punishment or force.

Before joining any training class, sit in on a session *without* your dog, to make sure you're comfortable with the philosophy and tone of the class. Even if clickers are not used, is the empha- sis on rewarding the good behavior, not punishing the bad?

FINDING "THE BUTTON"

Every dog is an individual, and there will be different things that turn him on and motivate him. Food is a common reward in training, but it is by no means the only one. *A reward is anything the dog thinks is fun or valuable.*

It could be tugging on a rope, or chasing the dot of a pen light around the floor.

It could be a squeaky toy, or a funny sound you make.

It could be a pat on the head.

It could be jealousy. I have one dog who's a "Why would I belong to any club that would have me as a member?" type. But if he is made to sit in a crate while I work with another dog, *then* he's eager to work with me.

Sit down and make a list of the things your dog loves, in descending order of desire. If you list food, try to break that up into categories. There are some things a dog will not do for a boring, rock-hard Milkbone that he might very well do for a luscious McNugget.

Remember, you need to be interesting to your dog, and so do your rewards. Mix them up, be creative. If you always keep your dog guessing, he won't have time to be bored.

THE BREED'S THE THING

Many of the most popular breeds in this country, such as Labrador Retrievers and Golden Retrievers, are sporting dogs. Bred to hunt with humans, these dogs have been selected over

THE NEXT LEVEL

All training is based on a relationship. But the expansiveness of that relationship will determine whether your exchanges will go beyond, "I say, you do." Suzanne Clothier's book *Bones Would Rain From the Sky: Deepening Our Relationship with Dogs* (Warner Books, $25.00) probably comes closest to defining the emotional and spiritual connection we feel with our dogs—and helping us hold the mirror to ourselves to discover what we do to jeopardize it.

the centuries, in large part, for their ability to obey the commands of their owners without hesitation or thought. Generally, their temperaments are tough enough to handle the corrections and demands of a traditional, punishment-dependent handler. Give them a jerk of the collar and they come back for more—albeit with a slink rather than a bound.

Contrast a sporting dog like a Golden Retriever with a hound like the Afghan Hound. Hounds are bred to have a totally different mind-set than sporting dogs. They are expected to be independent achievers, chasing and tracking fast and often large and dangerous game over great distances. They do not have the time nor the inclination to check in with their human handlers. If they did, it would severely impede not only their success, but possibly their survival. (Imagine the Rhodesian Ridgeback turning from the snarling lion he is holding at bay to ask, "Hey, mom, what next?")

When it comes to training, it is crucial to take into account the breed you are working with. This applies just as much with mixed breeds. If you know, or can guess, the combination of breeds that went into making your one-of-a-kind All-American dog, you can better anticipate the training challenges ahead.

Independent and intelligent breeds such as hounds, terriers and many of the nonsporting dogs do not do well with drill-based training. They do not see the point of repeating an exercise 10 times in a row when they executed it perfectly the first time. And they do marvelously with positive training because they see the point of it. There is something in it for them, and that something may not have a lot to do with pleasing you—at least not initially. And you should learn to be OK with that. Your desires are not at the center of the universe, and you should be thankful that your dog is teaching you that lesson.

TRAINING MAXIMS TO REMEMBER

Consistency counts. Dogs aren't stupid. Quite the contrary, if they see a fault line in your behavior, they will exploit it. To be fair to them and preserve your own sanity, decide what the rules are and then stick to them. If sleeping in the bed is off limits, then

BODY ENGLISH

Dogs have a language all their own, and it only takes a little effort for us humans to become fluent.

It's amazing how first-time dog owners can misinterpret what their animals are "saying" to others of the same species. I remember a woman at a dog park who was aghast that her puppy was rolling around with and nipping another pup of the same size and age; any experienced dog person could see that they were just playing. Dogs use their mouths in ways we humans might initially find confusing or frightening. It does us no good to anthropomorphize our dogs—that is, to interpret their behavior in human terms.

With dogs, as with humans, it's not so much what you say but how you say it, using your body as your "voice." Growling is not always bad, for example. Some dogs at play are very vocal—if they are making deep noises as they play-bow and wriggle their bodies, chances are they are just being exuberantly friendly. Conversely, tail wagging is not always a green light. A dog who feels threatened might hold his tail stiffly and slowly wag it back and forth—not a good thing.

Like any communication system, the more intently you observe canine body language, the better you'll understand it. Watching a dog's posture, ear position and tail set, the position of the lips and how much of the gums are exposed, can tell you volumes about how she's feeling.

In her slim but information-packed book *On Talking Terms With Dogs: Calming Signals* (Legacy by Mail, $9.95), Norwegian behaviorist Turid Rugaas identifies body postures that dogs assume to calm themselves and others. Most dogs, after all, don't want conflict if they can avoid it, and they have evolved a whole

it's truly off limits. If you get lonely one night when your husband is away on a business trip and make a "just this once" exception, the dog can't be blamed for believing the exception is now the rule.

Nothing in life is free. One of the reasons people don't train as much as they should is they find it hard to carve out the time each day. So why not just use the opportunities already built into your schedule? Instead of plunking the food bowl down in front of your dog, make him earn it. Ask him to do a heel around the kitchen and sit nicely before you release him to chow down. He system of cues that say, "I'm not a threat." For example, socially conversant dogs never approach a strange canine in a straight line—a very dominant and challenging act. Instead, they approach in an arc, to show they are not threatening and don't want to engage the other dog head on.

How is this applicable to your relationship with your dog? Well, if you are training your dog to do an obedience "come to front," and your dog returns to you following a course that looks more like a parabola than a straight line, you might want to rethink the signals *you're* sending to her.

Many other behaviors that dog owners think are just evidence of goofing off—like sniffing, yawning and turning away—can also be signals from the dog that she's stressed out and just wants the overwhelming situation to go away.

Once you know these calming signals, you can not only reassess the situation to find out the cause of your dog's stress, but also send out calming signals yourself. Blinking your eyes, licking your lips and yawning at your dog communicate that everything's OK and there's nothing to be worried about.

For the flip side of the equation—understanding how dogs interpret our body language—consult *The Other End of the Leash* by Patricia McConnell (Ballantine Books, $25.95). An animal behaviorist with a gentle sense of humor, McConnell points out how we humans unwittingly sabotage our canine relationships by using gestures and signs that are hard-wired for primates but not canines. For example, a chimp understands the affection implicit in a hug; in dog-speak, that's on a par with kicking sand on your beach blanket.

might be antsy at first, but if you don't give in, he eventually will settle down and start working for his supper.

Habits aren't broken, they're replaced. This is why cigarette smokers turn to sucking lollipops or scarfing down Oreos when they quit. They need to do something, *anything*, to keep their hands busy.

So if your dog does something annoying, it's not enough just to tell her to stop, because that doesn't supply a specific replacement behavior. Give her one. When she tries to jump on people,

WIDENING THE CIRCLE

Now that you have all these clicker tricks, what do you do with them?

One wonderful way to share your dog with others is therapy dog work. "Therapy dog" is a general phrase for those dogs—no matter what the breed or mixture of breeds—who have been certified as friendly and well-behaved enough to visit various groups or organizations, such as hospitals and nursing homes. These dogs are not necessarily used in therapy in a clinical way (although some are), and are not service dogs. They're simply dogs who come, visit and interact with people who can benefit from their presence. Studies have shown that the simple act of petting a dog measurably helps lower blood pressure, and interacting with animals is an all-around stress reliever.

There are many therapy dog organizations across the country, each with different requirements for certification and participation. But at the very minimum, all require your dog to pass a behavior test, oftentimes modeled on the American Kennel Club's Canine Good Citizen test (see the Appendix for more on the CGC test), and to be comfortable with objects they may encounter in an institutional setting, such as crutches and wheelchairs. You will need to provide proof that your dog's vaccinations or titers are up-to-date. When you become a member, you will be covered by the group's umbrella insurance policy—an important legal consideration.

Most therapy dog programs allow autonomy; once you are registered with a group, you can pretty much set your own schedule and pace. Perhaps you'll find a local dog club that makes therapy visits. Or maybe you'd rather establish a relationship with a local institution on your own, working independently, just you and your dog.

Consider your comfort level and your dog's personality when choosing your therapy location. If your dog is very calm and gentle and getting on in years, maybe a nursing home would be a good bet. If he is good with loud noises and sudden movements, consider a day center for the mentally retarded. If he's not a jumper and is gentle with children, visiting a pediatrics ward at a local hospital would be an option. Choose an environment that plays to your dog's strengths.

Use your imagination when planning your therapy visits. You can dress your dog up in a costume, or bring along his "baby album." Using your new clicker skills, you can teach him some tricks to wow onlookers. Try to make your visits as interactive as possible, so everyone—you, the dog and the people you are visiting—can get the most out of the experience.

Many therapy dog organizations offer titles that recognize a dog's extended therapy work. Therapy Dogs International, for example, bestows the TDIA title (Therapy Dogs International Active) on a dog who has completed 50 visits, and the TDIAOV (Therapy Dogs International Active Outstanding Volunteer) for an additional 100 documented visits.

But more than any string of letters or official accolades, the most important thing dogs and their humans get out of therapy work are the visits themselves.

Therapy Dogs: Training Your Dog to Reach Others by K. Diamond Davis (Dogwise Publishing, $19.95).

Wanted! Animal Volunteers by Mary Burch, PhD (Howell Book House, $16.99).

If you can't find a local therapy dog organization, here are two national groups:

Delta Society Pet Partners Program
289 Perimeter Road East
Renton, WA 98055-1329
(425) 226-7357
www.deltasociety.org

Therapy Dogs International
88 Bartley Road
Flanders, NJ 07836
(973) 252-9800
www.tdi-dog.org

tell her to sit. If your dog has a habit of growling at passersby, teach him the "Watch me" command—and ask him to do that instead. Click and reward your dog profusely for giving you the good behavior instead of the annoying one. Soon your jumper will fold into a smart Sit whenever guests walk through the door, and your growler will be looking at you when that jogger draws near.

Once you've gone around the block, you can't go back to holding hands. Another way of saying this is: Once a bad habit is established, the dog will always remember how rewarding it was. But if he's never given the opportunity to create that habit in the first place, he doesn't even know what he's missing. If you don't want a dog who digs up the yard, don't give him the opportunity to wander around out there unattended. If you don't want your new puppy making housebreaking errors on the new Persian rug, don't allow him to roam around out of sight, especially during prime pee times—after he's eaten, had water, played or woken up.

Sometimes it's two steps forward, one step back. Dogs backslide. We all do. They learn something one day, then don't quite remember it when you hit them with a pop quiz a day later. Having to reteach something to your dog isn't the end of the world. Remember that dogs do not generalize well: If your dog follows your "Sit" command perfectly in your living room, chances are he'll need a refresher course when he's brought to a different, more distracting environment, such as the park. That's normal.

Less is more. Resist the very human urge to finish what you started, to keep the successes coming one after another. Try to think of each training session as just one piece in a large patch-work. There really is no beginning or end. Although it can be difficult to stop before you want to, end each session on a high note. If the dog has one wonderful, awesome moment of under-standing, congratulate him, praise him and stop right there.

Keep this in mind at training classes, as well. I find that my dogs do not do well in hour-long obedience classes. They turn off like clockwork after about 45 minutes. It takes great discipline to say at 40 minutes, "OK, my dog has had enough—I'm calling it a day." But plowing ahead with the alternative—staying for the remaining 20 minutes so you can be like everyone else, and turning off and boring your dog in the process—means you have probably under-mined most of the good work you did in the first 40 minutes.

Chapter 9

Animal Communication: Exploring the Unspoken

Skeptics, I'll leave the porch light on for you. Animal communication—or "interspecies telepathic communication," as it has come to be called—is one subject you may take awhile to embrace, if at all.

Depending on what your thinking is, you may perceive animal communicators as charlatans who bilk people of their cash while pretending to commune with cats and canaries, or you may think the idea of being able to transmit ideas between you and your animal is something normal and natural that you do every day without thinking about it or giving it a fancy name.

Most of us—myself included—probably fall somewhere in the middle. We've tried communicators and have been surprised at the concrete advice and helpful insights they've given about our animals. But at the same time, we just don't quite know if we buy into this Doctor Doolittle stuff, or, at the very least, doubt we could ever cultivate the ability to do it ourselves.

While animal communication is not exactly in the mainstream, it has grown in visibility over the last several years. In bookstores, step-by-step books on how to talk to your companion animals share the shelves alongside traditional training tomes. Following the lead of some television networks, which have had success with shows featuring mediums such as John Edward, Animal Planet is currently airing *The Pet Psychic,* which follows the telepathic tête-à-têtes of animal communicator Sonya Fitzpatrick. And seminars on how to learn to communicate with your dog are available all over the country, offering instruction from beginner to advanced levels.

Penelope Smith of Point Reyes, California, half-jokingly calls herself the grandmother of animal communication—she's been doing it professionally for more than 30 years. No longer available for individual consultations, Smith instead spends her time teaching this skill to others. Like most animal communicators, she has an unruffled, undefensive attitude about communication, approaching it from the opposite direction of naysayers and disbelievers: She thinks the fact that we *don't* acknowledge our deep connection with animals is what's really weird, not the fact that she suggests we should try.

"What does having four legs and fur have to do with it?" Smith asks rhetorically, pointing out that most children, with their innocence and openness, don't consider the idea of talking to animals to be odd at all. "This is a skill that we all have that has been dulled because of our cultural conditioning. It's so veiled for people because they have not been encouraged."

For those who struggle with the possibility that humans can chat wordlessly with our animal friends, whether they are spiders or spaniels, Smith reminds us that just because something is not seen or heard does not mean it's not real. "When people first came across radio waves, I'm sure others scoffed and said they didn't really exist," she says. Similarly, thoughts and feelings aren't tangible or provable using the scientific method, but we all have them and we know they exist.

What people really want is proof that thoughts can be sent back and forth, like a mental conversation. For that, says Smith, you should try it for yourself. "Once you see the product of a communication with an animal, you can see something happening here. You will see results when people use their skills well."

To say that the veterinary establishment as a whole doesn't put much stock in animal communicators is a pretty gigantic understatement. The general assessment is that animal communicators are very skilled—at reading humans, not animals. The belief is that through the normal course of conversation and interaction, communicators collect information that will let them make believable, if general, comments about the animals they are supposed to be talking to.

But there are some veterinarians who are open to the idea, if only because they have seen unexplainable results and are willing to push the scientific envelope a little further than their more conventionally minded colleagues. "Based on quantum physics, the possibility of telepathic communication, of nonverbal communication with other species, is possible," says Sherman, Connecticut, veterinarian Allen M. Schoen, author of *Kindred Spirits: How the Remarkable Bond Between Humans and Animals Can Change the Way We Live.* On the one hand, Schoen says, he'd like to see communication definitely proven through controlled studies; on the other hand, he's seen enough work by communicators that suggests there has to be something more than chicanery going on. "As a scientist, if you see reality that doesn't fit into the scientific framework that you have, you don't simply say, 'No, it can't be.'"

You also don't ignore other explanations. One central question that Schoen and other scientists have about animal communicators—or, for that matter, mediums, who say they can speak to those who have "crossed over"—is: Who exactly are they talking to? Schoen says he still wonders whether communicators are simply reading the minds of the humans involved.

Still, the central idea behind animal communication is valid on other levels. Even if you don't believe we can "talk" to our dogs in telepathic conversations, there are very tangible signs that our animals are talking to us physically.

"We're all animal communicators," says Schoen. "We're communicating with animals all the time, and they're communicating with us all the time—through body language, smells and senses.

They're perceiving us very carefully—they're just not doing it in English." As a culture and a species, says Schoen, our glaring fault is that we are ethnocentric. "We expect all species to learn English as a second language, when instead we need to learn horse or dog or cat."

Even if you ultimately don't conclude that your animal can have a psychic conversation with you, one thing you can take away from this chapter is that our dogs do communicate with us—all day, every day—in ways both obvious and subtle. Taking the focus off ourselves and putting it on them for a few minutes each day can tell us volumes about what they are thinking and feeling, even if that information doesn't arrive as a little voice whispering in our head.

HOW ANIMAL COMMUNICATION WORKS

Telepathy literally means "feeling over distance." So for a communicator to have a conversation, the animal doesn't need to be in the same room or even the same city. As a result, many communicators do their consultations over the phone.

That fact puzzles and even annoys some people, who seem to feel that the communicator's physical contact with the animal is the only way a connection can be made. For many, the distance contributes to the idea that the process is a shady one. But if you think about it, having a long-distance consultation only eliminates some obvious cues for the communicator to pick up on—like your body language, not to mention your dog's.

Most communicators set a timer at the beginning of your conversation so that they can bill you for the exact length of the session. The common protocol is that you call the communicator on your dime, and if you decide to go beyond the agreed time, you simply tell the communicator how many additional minutes you'd like. Rates vary widely across the country, but $1 a minute is an average.

Before they begin, most communicators will want the name of the dog, her age and breed, so they can make sure they are connecting with the right animal. Some request photos of the animal, others don't need them.

While your dog is "talking" to the communicator, you won't necessarily see any behaviors that indicate focus on his part. He probably won't wrinkle his brow and look thoughtful, or make noises, or wag his tail. He might just keep on doing what he normally does—sniffing around the room, curling up on the couch, taking a nice long stretch before he goes into the kitchen for a slurp of water.

What exactly does the communicator understand during these sessions? It all depends on the person and how they receive information. "You can get colors, tastes, verbal messages—which I considered thoughts translated into words—and you can get physical sensations," says Smith. "They run the gamut. If you get really good at it, you can feel what the animal feels."

It's also important to remember that the way a communicator translates your dog's message has a lot to do with his or her perspective. Communicators are simply conduits, or filters, for what animals have to say. So as each communicator converts the animal's message, she uses her own words and metaphors and idioms. To some extent, her personality and world view become part of the message you get, if only because she is translating based on her own points of reference.

Communication is messy, no matter what species is talking. Think about all the misunderstandings you have every day with your spouse or children or co-workers. You *thought* you were being clear and that everyone was on the same page, but in the end everyone seemed to hear something different—or perhaps only the part they wanted to hear. Even when it comes to a basic communication skill that we use every day—the spoken word—the very nature of communication leaves ample room for misinterpretation.

Talking with animals is just as inexact, communicators say. Sometimes animals are cryptic and don't feel like explaining themselves. Sometimes they are more forthcoming, depending on their mood. And, to some extent, the communicator's personality determines how much your dog is willing to talk and how much information he will give. In your own life there are people to whom you could talk for hours, pouring out every intimate detail and heartfelt secret; there are others with whom a conversation about the weather is a tedious, tooth-pulling experience. Animals are no different. Some will like some communicators better than others, and be more or less cooperative.

"You don't seem like a dog person," a communicator told me my dog, Blitz, said to her. He was right: She really was more a cat person. And the tone of their conversation—what little conversation he was willing to make with her—bordered on the dismissive. Hey, every dog has his day.

THINGS TO KEEP IN MIND

If you decide to seek out an animal communicator, here are a few points to remember.

Have a game plan. Animal communication may be entertaining, but it's also expensive. To get the most out of your session, have a list of questions ready; the more specific, the better. The claim, after all, is that communicators can not only tell you what your dog wants, but also get your point of view across to your dog. This is your opportunity to lobby for changes you'd like to see and areas you want improved.

Some general areas to explore are:

- Health: Does he feel well? Does anything hurt? Does he know what is causing his allergies?
- Nutrition: Does he like his diet? Are there any minerals or nutrients he isn't getting enough of?
- Behavior: Why does he hate Aunt Flora? What can you do to convince him to stop waking you at 3 a.m.?

If there are some big changes coming up in your household, a consultation with the communicator *before* they happen can get your dog prepared—and enlist his cooperation.

All communicators are not equal. Animal communication is a skill, honed through years of practice and study. You don't expect all car mechanics to have the same level of expertise, which is why when you find a good one, you keep going back. It's very much the same with animal communicators: Some are very skilled and come back with specific information that is right on. Others are more circumspect, making vague statements.

Schoen groups communicators into three categories:

- Those who are very gifted and sincere and are skilled enough to get concrete information that can be of benefit to you and your dog.
- Those who have good intentions and are well-meaning but aren't savvy or secure enough to get much helpful information, if any.
- Opportunists who market themselves masterfully, charge a fortune and wind up giving all their colleagues a bad name.

Obviously, you want to find a communicator in the first category. That might take some trial and error. Animal communicators are just people, and people come with baggage. We all go through bad stages in life, and a person's issues and obsessions can cloud a reading, skewing its focus and interpretation. But, like that perfect auto mechanic, once you find the right communicator, you're a client for life.

Animal communicators are not veterinarians. Many people seek out communicators because they have a medical or behavioral problem with their dog that no one can seem to fix. That's fine, but it's crucial to remember that communicators are in no way a substitute for competent professional care. They should not be your primary source for diagnosis and treatment. If your animal has a life-threatening condition, or if his behavior is a physical threat to others, you need to be consulting a vet or qualified behaviorist.

That said, many common physical problems in our companion animals are emotionally based, and a communicator can often help get to the root of it. Lick granulomas—oozing sores caused by compulsive licking—are a good example. After your vet rules out a physical cause such as a skin condition, and before you pursue a costly and drastic course of action such as mood-altering drugs, you might decide to have a session with a communicator to see if your dog can tell you why he's so intent on self-mutilation.

Think of the experience as a buffet. Some fundamentalist Christians are very uncomfortable with the idea of animal communication because they interpret it as a violation of the biblical injunction not to "conjure spirits." Even if your personal belief system doesn't preclude animal communication, you may find that communicators will take you further than you want to go in terms of metaphysics and beliefs. Many communicators say they can talk to deceased animals and will talk about past lives—both your dog's and yours.

If you are uncomfortable with this kind of information, ask the communicator to focus on the here and now of what your animal is saying.

WHAT DOES IT TAKE?

The whole point of animal communication, say those who do it, is that it is very democratic. Everyone is capable of it, if they only tried. The problem is, our society is not wired to nourish or even accept such abilities. So, animal communicators say, it's not that communicating with our dogs is difficult. It's communicating with them within the framework of our own culture that causes all the obstacles.

Here are some qualities you'll need to cultivate as you get ready to explore animal communication for yourself.

Stillness

Think about that quintessential American vacation spot, Disney World. Despite the idea that vacations are supposed to be restorative and relaxing, you couldn't dream up a more demanding, inflexible or heavily programmed resort. In our adrenaline-addicted culture, the focus is on doing, not being. We are valued by the things we accomplish, the quantity of items we can check off our to-do list. Downtime is not only undervalued, in some respects it's disdained, as if it suggests weakness on the part of anyone who craves it.

Against this cacophonous background of accomplishing and striving and tallying and maneuvering and rushing, it's a wonder we hear anything from others of our own species, much less from a Cocker Spaniel or a Great Dane. While he makes for great cable TV viewing, Mr. Ed is not a paradigm of animal communication. If you are waiting around to hear your Maltese speak in full declarative sentences, you will be waiting a long time. Animal communication is far more subtle than that.

OPEN OR SHUT CASE?

It's perfectly fine to be skeptical about whether or not animals can talk to us, communicators say, and you should expect some proof, some signs that the communication is working. "Instead of standing outside, the really best thing is for people to get direct exposure, so people can see the byproducts of that communication," says Penelope Smith.

But while skepticism is normal and even welcomed by competent communicators, cynicism is not. The difference between the two is that while the skeptic says, "Show me, prove it," the cynic says, "Don't even bother, my mind is made up."

The total cynic is about as discerning as the individual who believes in animal communication blindly without expecting any proof or validation. Your mind doesn't have to be wide open to the possibility, but it at least has to be ajar.

The first step for most of us is to find some time to sit with our animals and just *be*. Easier said than done, because even when you find the time to do that, you still have to contend with your racing brain. Stillness is not just a physical state; it's a spiritual and emotional one, too. And it's pretty hard to hear a whisper when a mariachi band is playing in your head.

Patience

The ability to communicate telepathically is a skill, say practitioners, and it must be developed and honed. You wouldn't think of taking on Serena or Venus Williams if you'd never had a tennis lesson, and you wouldn't expect to make a hole-in-one if you'd never swung a golf club. Because our culture values the material over the spiritual, a lot of our intuitive skills have grown rusty. All the things that can get you outside of your own head—meditation, yoga, long walks—are part of priming yourself to listen.

The ability to communicate telepathically, say those that do it, doesn't work like a spigot. You can't just turn it on and off. Instead, it's more like a lake that starts from a trickle, building slowly and surely. Part of the process is not just wanting to listen, but removing the habits and obstacles that are in the way.

A BEGINNER'S TALE

Animal communication has a kind of mystique surrounding it. There's a sense that this is an esoteric talent, available only to a handful of peasant-skirt-wearing incense-burning insiders. Gretchen Kunz, a newbie communicator from Brooklyn, New York, is a case in point: She's only been doing it for a couple of years, after a visit to a communicator piqued her interest.

"I had a cat who was very ill and I was trying to figure out what to do," she explains. A new-age-type friend suggested she contact an animal communicator. "I thought it was kind of wacky, but I was desperate. I found the session really comforting, even if I wasn't entirely sure I believed in it."

After a few sessions, Kunz decided that her very sick cat was ready to let go, and she euthanized her with the deep conviction that she was doing the right thing. As she acquired more cats, Kunz got "more and more fascinated" with telepathic communication, something that the communicator told her she was already doing with her cats. "I've always been very perceptive about animals, and I was intuitively getting a lot of stuff," Kunz remembers. "But I wasn't necessarily classifying that as animal communication. I was thinking, 'Oh, I'm looking at their behavior and figuring it out.'"

Respect

At other times, in other ages, animals played a hugely different role in our culture and our lives. Native Americans, for example, revere animals as sentient beings and spiritual guides. But with the age of scientific advancement came the view that animals are objects—things to own, things to flaunt, things to use to achieve a material end. To speak with an animal, communicators say, you need to acknowledge her for what she is: another being who is different but certainly no less than you, who has the capacity to think and feel and love.

This doesn't mean that communicators consider animals to be humans and treat them accordingly. "My dog has his own bed and runs around and sniffs manure, but that's not what I do," Smith says. "You have to show them how they fit in the household. If you don't lay the rules out very clearly, they'll run all over you."

Noting her deepening interest, a friend gave Kunz a special present—a workshop with an animal communicator. That, she says, "opened my eyes and took away my cynicism." Motivated and moved, she took more workshops and started practicing on any animal who would let her: strays at the cat shelter where she volunteered, dogs who belonged to friends, even animals she'd never met before. Increasingly, she felt she was getting through. "I'd ask the animal what her favorite color was, I'd get the answer blue, and her owner would say, 'Yes, her food bowl is blue.'"

Kunz requests a picture of the animal to help her focus and get connected, as well as a list of questions from the owner. Because she's a "very verbal person," she gets mostly words, though sometimes she will get a physical sensation, like feeling nauseated and starting to cough when she talked to an animal who turned out to be ill.

Slowly, as she began to trust herself and her ability, she took on paying clients. They aren't enough for her to leave her day job, but they definitely are a start. And while Kunz has her occasional moments of doubt, they are fewer and fewer. "For a long time I thought—and sometimes still do think—'Oh, I'm making that up,'" she says. "But sometimes I get things that are so random or outside my usual thought process that I know it isn't me."

Ease

There is such a thing as trying too hard to make a connection, says Smith, and strained concentration is not going to get you talking to your animals any faster. An onslaught of sudden, alright-come-and-get-it energy can be more a turnoff than an invitation, particularly if your dog is not accustomed to it.

Instead, try to mete that intention out more gently over your interactions. Strive not to be focused like a laser beam on communicating just once or twice. Instead, try to cultivate a general sense of openness. Try to stay tuned in to your animals in general, not just when *you* feel the urge.

There isn't one big "aha" moment when the lights get turned on and you instantly become a communicator. There is no big cosmic tap on the shoulder. Instead, insights come slowly, a kind of sure, steady knowing. If that sounds vague, perhaps that's because it is.

DO IT YOURSELF

If you are trying to communicate with your animals without an intermediary, one of the most difficult concepts to get down is how, exactly, you go about it. The desire for clear, step-by-step instructions is understandable. "We're a very mechanical society, so people are looking for, 'How do I grab on to it?'" says Smith. "But intuitive ability isn't something you grab on to, it's something you open up to."

A good analogy is learning how to ride a bicycle. To do that successfully, you need a sense of balance and equilibrium—something that can't be explained or learned through words. It's gained through experience. So you add training wheels onto your two-wheeler and start pedaling. As you teeter and wobble, the bike will tilt to one side or another and the training wheels will help right you. But the more you ride with the training wheels, the more you will learn how to balance yourself. At some point, you will be riding the bike yourself without need for the wheels. Chances are you're not conscious of this and have a hard time telling where the training wheels end and your own sense of maintaining balance begins.

Animal communication is sort of like that. At the beginning, most communicators suggest that you try having a conversation with your animal and just trust what comes back. It might be an image or an intuition. Perhaps you are actually communicating, perhaps you are still wobbling. The point is, the more you do it, the more you will acquire that elusive skill.

Many communicators suggest using tools such as meditation and guided imagery to help get in tune with your animal. Visualization is important; practice creating images and sending them. The next step is your version of training wheels: Say something to your animal—Smith suggests "hello" as a logical start—then imagine she says hello back. Ask a question, then wait for the answer. You may not know if the answer you get is the animal or if it is your own internal voice answering, and communicators say it does not matter. Accept and acknowledge what you get without worrying about the source. With the bicycle, it doesn't matter what the actual mechanism is that keeps you from

Animal Communication Resources

Penelope Smith has written *Animal Talk: Interspecies Telepathic Communication* and *When Animals Speak: Advanced Interspecies Communication* (Beyond Words Publishing, $14.95 each). Videotapes and audiotapes are available at her website, www. animaltalk.net. Smith also publishes *Species Link*, a quarterly journal about animal communication, available from Anima Mundi Inc., P.O. Box 1060, Point Reyes, CA 94956, (415) 663-1247.

Other books include:

The Animal Connection: A Guide to Intuitive Communication With Your Pet by Judy Meyer (Plume, $10.95).

The Language of Animals: 7 Steps to Communicating With Animals by Carol Gurney (Dell Books, $13.95).

Straight From the Horse's Mouth: How to Talk to Animals and Get Answers by Amelia Kinkade (Crown, $22).

You Can Talk to Your Animals by Janine Adams (Howell Book House, $14.99).

losing your balance and falling off. The point is that you are doing it—you are gliding through space and your body is feeling what it would feel like to ride a bike and keep your equilibrium.

With communication, the point is not to focus on whether what you are getting is real or imagined, but to just get it. Eventually, with enough practice and repetition, you will realize that you have been doing it on your own for much longer than you thought.

Chapter 10

Cancer: A Journey of Healing

"Cancer" is one of the most terrifying words a dog owner can hear, and for good reason. Among diseases, cancer is the number-one canine killer in this country: Twenty-three percent of dogs will eventually die from it, a statistic that zooms to 45 percent if the dog is over the age of 10. And those numbers do not seem likely to drop any time soon.

Despite the numbers, canine oncology is still a relatively new field. Only recently have most of the nation's veterinary schools focused on it as a specialty, and at the beginning of 2000, there were fewer than 120 veterinary oncologists in the entire country.

There is also the sense, unspoken but very real, that a dog with cancer is incurable. Oftentimes, the only solution offered is euthanasia. To add to the difficulty, many general practitioners are not up-to-date on conventional cancer treatments, let alone holistic ones. Much of that has to do with how aggressive and toxic early cancer treatment was, says Barbara E. Kitchell, an associate professor of oncology at the College of Veterinary Medicine at the University of Illinois in Urbana. "In the early days of

oncology in veterinary medicine, the adverse-effect rate was suf-
ficiently high that a lot of veterinarians in training programs were
turned off to the whole idea of accepting it," she says. As a result,
some vets—and their clients—view cancer treatment for dogs as
possibly worse than the disease itself.

But it's a mistake, say canine oncologists, to draw parallels
between human cancer care and that of dogs. If you have ever gone
through cancer treatment with a human family member, those
painful mental snapshots—debilitating weakness and nausea, the
loss of hair and seemingly any ounce of energy—do not fore-
shadow what awaits your dog. "Our approach to treating animals
is very different from what it is with people," stresses Antony
Moore, head of the Harrington Oncology Program at Tufts
University in North Grafton, Massachusetts. "If you're 35 and have
breast cancer, you can have aggressive therapy because if you live,
you'll have another 50 years. So you'll take doses that are not going
to kill you—but just barely.

"In dogs, most of our patients are older. If you get an eight-
or nine-year-old dog who might have life expectancy of 10
years—to put him through that doesn't make sense. And owners
are uniformly more interested in giving quality of life rather than
length of life. As a result, we treat cancer very much like a chronic disease such as heart disease—something to be managed."

While many veterinarians are on the same page about their
treatment goals—not to cure the cancer, but to control it, with a
focus on the quality, not the quantity of time left—they differ
dramatically in the methods they use. Much of this has to do with
the way they perceive cancer's root cause.

From a holistic point of view, cancer is the ultimate manifes-
tation of imbalance. A healthy immune system is able to regulate
cell growth, destroying abnormal cells before they create problems. In fact, your dog's body creates potentially cancer-causing
cells every day. When the immune system is compromised or
weak, these rogue cells are permitted to grow unchecked, until
finally they take over, replacing normal cells and causing cancer.

While conventional vets generally agree that a physical malfunction permits cancer to germinate and spread, the traditional
cures for cancer—surgery, radiation and chemotherapy—focus

on killing the aberrant cells by external means, such as cutting them out with a scalpel or zapping them with a laser beam. While there might be casualties (in the form of healthy cells that get destroyed in the process), that is the price to pay for winning the war.

The holistic vet, by contrast, reasons that just as the body created the cancer, it has the ability to eliminate it. Instead of focusing primarily on killing the rogue cells, the holistic approach advocates supporting the body with good nutrition, micronutrients and other therapies, so that once the body is back in balance, it has the tools to deal with the cancer.

"We're not going after the cancer per se—we're going after the immune system," says Martin Goldstein, a veterinarian in Salem, New York, and the author of *The Nature of Animal Healing: The Definitive Holistic Medicine Guide to Caring for Your Dog and Cat*. It's all a matter of perspective. Goldstein says he sees his animal charges as cancer patients—not patients with cancer. There's an important difference: The latter suggests that the cancer and the patient are two separate entities; the former acknowledges that they are inextricably linked.

All that said, oncology is an area where many holistic vets straddle the line between an allopathic and a holistic approach. If a cancer is life-threatening or spreading rapidly, a holistic vet may feel there simply isn't enough time to let the body heal itself and may opt for a conventional treatment such as surgery or even— when the success rates are proven and the dog in question might benefit from it—chemotherapy. After all, holistic medicine is not about rejecting allopathic tools, but rather about using them judiciously when the individual case warrants it.

Keep in mind that you may have to seek out second, or even third and fourth opinions before you find the cancer regimen that feels right to you. Many traditional vets are simply not equipped to treat cancer, whether traditionally or holistically, and you may have to travel to a specialized practice or teaching hospital with experience in canine oncology. As for holistically oriented oncologists, they are probably harder to locate than a surefire cure for the disease itself. You may find yourself consulting with both an oncologist and a holistic vet who specializes in cancer care before settling on a final approach, which may be purely holistic or which may use holistic modalities in conjunction with conventional therapy.

Cancer treatment for humans is an inexact science at best, and with dogs the road map is no clearer. The treatments you pursue will depend on the individual dog, the type and stage of cancer, your financial situation and how aggressive you want to be. "You don't know how a given patient will respond until you provide a therapy," Kitchell says. "We tell people every animal we treat is its own clinical trial. Statistics are created off the bell curve of a general population, and I don't know where your dog fits on that curve."

As with human health care, you can never do enough research or ask enough questions. Be a savvy health-care consumer.

CONVENTIONAL THERAPIES

There are three major approaches that traditionally trained veterinary oncologists use to treat cancer, depending on the type of cancer, its location and the degree to which is has metastasized, or spread. They are listed here, more or less in order of the degree of damage they do to the body, from least to greatest.

Surgery

Surgery is the simplest solution for dealing with cancer, but often the most impractical, since many cancers are not well defined, have grown too large or are in an inoperable location. Because a vet often cannot be sure that surgery has removed all the cancer cells, a second treatment with either radiation or chemotherapy is frequently recommended.

Radiation

Radiation is another treatment used when cancers have not spread. Because radiation can and does damage healthy tissue, the treatments are broken up into small doses, or "fractionalized." A dog must be anesthetized for each treatment—a concern for older or very frail dogs. Side effects can include tissue death, organ dysfunction and blindness.

Chemotherapy

Once cancer has spread and is no longer localized, chemotherapy is often the treatment oncologists turn to. While chemotherapy does kill cancer cells, it also kills normal ones, creating the potential for side effects and toxicities. From a holistic point of view, chemotherapy is counterintuitive because it further weakens the immune system at a time when it needs just the opposite—to be strengthened and bolstered.

Still, some holistic vets decide on chemotherapy when they encounter a form of cancer—lymphoma, for example—where the success rates with chemo are high. And many holistic vets will seek to mitigate the aftereffects of chemotherapy with therapies that boost the immune system and help flush out toxins.

Other Conventional Therapies

While surgery, radiation and chemotherapy are the most accessible cancer treatments, they are not the only ones available. The nation's veterinary schools are always conducting trials and studies, exploring cutting-edge treatments that might one day become mainstream. Here's a sample.

Anti-angiogenesis. This is a battle tactic generals over the millennia have used to great effect: Surround the enemy, then starve him out. Anti-angiogenic drugs work to cut off the blood supply to tumors, effectively severing their lifeline. They do this by inhibiting the development of new blood vessels to supply the tumor. While there are literally dozens of anti-angiogenic drugs being tested, the research is still very preliminary.

Bone marrow transplants. Some types of chemotherapy are especially damaging to fast-dividing cells, such as those in the bone marrow. This leaves oncologists with a dilemma: The higher the chemo dose, the more cancer it will kill, but the more bone marrow it will destroy, too. To get around this, healthy bone marrow is removed before the chemotherapy, then replaced after the chemo has destroyed the marrow left behind.

Radioactive beads. Instead of subjecting a dog to repeated radiation treatments, which require anesthesia, small radioactive

Resources for Conventional Cancer Therapies

These organizations are good starting points for finding information about and links to clinical trials and university studies. While these are experimental treatments and might be geographically unfeasible for some, they are well worth exploring.

The Veterinary Cancer Society
P.O. Box 1763
Spring Valley, CA 91979-1763
www.vetcancersociety.org

The Perseus Foundation
9810 Dairyton Court
Gaithersburg, MD 20879
(301) 417-2721
www.perseusfoundation.org

Morris Animal Foundation
45 Inverness Drive East
Englewood, CO 80112-5480
(800) 243-2345 or (303) 790-2345
www.morrisanimalfoundation.org

beads are inserted near the tumor to give out a slow, steady dose of radiation.

Stereotactic radiosurgery. Like bone marrow transplants and radioactive beads, this is another treatment that has been used on human cancer patients with good success, and is now being used on dogs. Using a three-dimensional computer-generated mapping system, radiation is delivered to the precise location of the cancer.

Tumor vaccines. Just like regular vaccines, tumor vaccines prompt the immune system to defend itself against an intruder. But then the vaccines must also work to get the body to realize that the cancer is abnormal and begin fighting it as well. As treatments go, tumor cell vaccines are still "horizon" therapies, and much work has yet to be done.

Gene therapy. Another experimental field of research, gene therapy involves getting the dog's cells to accept new genes that can reprogram them to fight cancer.

HOLISTIC THERAPIES

In life, we like our reality neatly packaged. We crave definitives: yes or no. Maybes make us nervous. But if we're honest with ourselves, we know that nothing is absolute. Cancer is only a death sentence for your dog if you choose it to be. There is nothing wrong with pursuing ways of helping your dog cope with her cancer even if you know they will not cure it. The goal is to make her feel good in the remaining time she has.

After you have all your information in hand, you will have to decide whether you want to follow the conventional courses of treatment outlined earlier, pursue an experimental treatment at one of the veterinary universities, or try a natural approach using complementary medicine. It's not an either-or decision. You can choose to do conventional therapy along with holistic modalities to help support your dog during the process.

As strong as it may be, resist the urge to try and find a miracle cure for cancer. Your dog's disease took quite a while—perhaps a lifetime—to develop, and there is no magic wand to make it go away. Your dog might go into complete remission, and that would be wonderful. But statistically, it's likely the cancer will reoccur.

So remember your goal: To give your dog the best possible quality of life for as long as possible. You will need a vet to help you sort through all the options available. In the end, you may decide you want two veterinarians on board—a traditional vet and a holistic one. What's important is that you maintain the flow of information, letting each vet know what the other is doing, even if it is met with disapproval or disbelief.

Following are some therapies and remedies that holistic vets often use with animals who have cancer. What they all have in common is a focus on rebuilding the body and giving it the tools to do its job—return to health. In this sense, cancer isn't the primary focus; it's just a terrible expression of how out of balance and defenseless the body has become.

Some of the other modalities discussed in this book—including homeopathy and acupuncture—are also used by some practitioners to treat cancer. Consult with a veterinarian who has extensive experience using them with cancer patients.

These therapies and supplements are starting points in your discussions about the universe of options out there. You cannot do them yourself. Instead, seek out vets familiar with these therapies and see what they think about your dog's individual situation. Many times, a vet will recommend a tapestry of approaches, alternating and combining modalities to gain the benefit of their synergy, rather than just relying on one "big gun."

Antioxidant Therapy

Nancy Scanlan, a holistic vet in Sherman Oaks, California, has had success using groups of antioxidants to both prevent and treat cancers. As evidence, she points to cancer studies done mostly in impoverished countries in Eastern Europe, where issues of affordability and accessibility have prompted doctors to explore multiple antioxidants as a way of controlling cancer.

Antioxidants are a big buzz word in natural medicine because of their ability to destroy free radicals—unstable atoms that can create cell mutations and sometimes, cancer. But taking a single antioxidant—for example, massive doses of vitamin E—may actually do more harm than good, because once the vitamin E uses itself up as an antioxidant, it can convert to a pro-oxidant, which promotes oxidation and can worsen the cancer.

The key, says Scanlan, is not to use antioxidants individually, but in groups. Working together, in synergy, they can have a discernible anti-cancer effect. With the guidance of a nutrition-savvy vet, you may choose to use Scanlan's regimen (see page 188) alone to treat a slow-growing cancer. She also recommends it be used in conjunction with radiation and certain kinds of chemotherapy that destroy cancer cells using free radicals.

If you are using chemotherapy, ask the oncologist which type your dog is getting, and only suspend the antioxidants if it's the free-radical-producing kind. In that case, careful timing is key: High levels of antioxidants during the radiation or chemo treatments can lessen their effectiveness, because the antioxidants will engage the free radicals before they have had time to kill the cancer cells. As a result, Scanlan stresses suspending your dog's antioxidant regimen the day before the treatment, the day of the treatment itself and the day after. After that three-day hiatus, resume the antioxidants to speed the healing of any damaged healthy tissue.

Here are the antioxidants Scanlan recommends. Her website includes a list of which chemotherapy agents are free-radical generators (www.drnancysplace.com, Sherman Oaks Veterinary Group, 13624 Moorpark St., Sherman Oaks, CA 91423).

Vitamin C. Administer twice a day, gradually increasing to bowel tolerance (in other words, if your dog's stool gets loose, decrease the amount until you have found the maximum amount that will not cause diarrhea). If your dog has urinary problems or tends to form stones, opt for sodium ascorbate, which is a less acidic form of vitamin C. Make sure it's *sodium* ascorbate and not *calcium* ascorbate, which can lead to more stones.

Vitamin E. Recent studies have suggested that 800 IUs of vitamin E is a maximum safe dose for humans. Using that as a guide, Scanlan recommends administering a proportionate amount to your dog based on body weight. So a 40- to 50-pound dog should get about 400 IUs a day; a five-pound Chihuahua, 50 IUs daily.

Mixed carotenoids. While betacarotene is often hailed as an antioxidant, Scanlan points to several studies that show pure betacarotene might increase the risk for several types of lung cancer. As a result, she recommends mixed carotenoids, which should be readily available at most health-food stores (as should all of the supplements mentioned here). Stay away from formulations that contain vitamin A, as it can be toxic in large doses. Scanlan's recommended dose is 500 IUs per 10 pounds of dog.

IP-6. This is a special form of the B vitamin inositol, with antioxidant properties. Giving two 600 mg capsules twice a day would be appropriate for a large dog.

Coenzyme Q10. In very high doses, this antioxidant can cause nausea or even vomiting. Scanlan recommends a minimum dose of roughly 1 mg per pound of body weight, although you can

IMMUNE SYSTEM CHECKLIST

Since cancer needs a weakened immune system to take hold, enhancing your dog's immune system should be your first priority, no matter what anti-cancer regimen you ultimately decide on. Here are some areas to review.

Diet. The less processed, the better, with a homemade diet being optimal. Try to buy the best quality ingredients possible, especially pesticide- and hormone-free meats.

Water. Switch to bottled spring water to reduce exposure to the kind of impurities that can sneak by in tap water.

Vaccines. I discussed the problems of overvaccination in Chapter 7. If your vet wants to vaccinate your dog in the middle of her cancer battle, it would be a good idea to seek a second opinion.

Flea and tick killers. Steer clear of chemical flea collars that contain such toxic ingredients as the nerve poisons DDVP, propoxur, Diazinon and carbaryl. Do your best to keep fleas and ticks at bay holistically by planting insect-repelling plants such as marigolds and pennyroyal. Consult mail-order garden catalogs for nematodes—microscopic organisms that eat flea larvae in your lawn. Two substances help dehydrate fleas: Diatomaceous earth can be distributed indoors and out, and borate powder can be sprinkled in the carpet and under couch pillows. Be sure to vacuum frequently.

Make your dog an unappealing host by adding garlic to his food (be sure not to feed an excessive amount); apple cider vinegar and brewer's yeast are also said to be useful supplements. Finally, you can spray him with essential-oil combinations formulated especially for keeping creepy-crawlies at bay.

give more than that if you do not see adverse reactions; some dogs cannot tolerate even that minimum dose. If problems with nausea occur, discontinue the CoQ10 and reintroduce it at a lower dose once the dog is feeling better.

Alpha-lipoic acid. This is a versatile antioxidant, effective at eliminating both fat- and water-soluble free radicals. It's also thought to help heighten the effectiveness of other antioxidants, such as vitamins E and C. Scanlan's suggested minimum dose is 1 mg per pound of body weight.

Outdoor contaminants. Are you spraying your garden with insecticides and pesticides? Dogs are forever sniffing and grazing on our lawns, and they can easily absorb chemicals through the pads of their feet. Having a perfectly manicured lawn is a small reward for the amount of environmental havoc you are wreaking. So what if all your neighbors garden with chemicals? Progress has to start somewhere. And by gardening organically, you are ensuring that the plants and grasses your dog comes in contact with are safe. If you must use an insecticide, seek out those made with pyrethrins, which are derived from chrysanthemums.

Secondhand smoke. If you're a smoker, stop. Easier said than done, of course, but you're not just harming yourself: A recent study done at Tufts University showed that cats exposed to secondhand smoke had a significantly higher risk of contracting lymphoma. Your dog not only breathes carcinogens in the air, but he licks them as they settle on objects all over the house.

Indoor contaminants. Harsh household cleaners may leave your floors and furniture sparkling, but keep in mind your dog comes into close contact with them through his paws and pads. Explore more environmentally friendly cleaners.

Also keep in mind that toxic fumes are emitted from all sorts of sources—new latex-backed rugs, dry-cleaned clothing and polyurethaned floors. While this doesn't mean you should never take that suit to the dry cleaners, you do need to stop and think about the cumulative effect of all the toxic cleaners and materials you have in your household.

Herbs

There are many herbs from many different traditions that are said to have cancer-fighting properties, often by enhancing the immune system. Some herbs work best in combination, and they can be rotated to keep your dog's body from getting into a rut with the same unchanging regimen. Because they are such powerful healing agents, any herbs, no matter how beneficial, should be used with caution and under a doctor's supervision.

Astragalus or **Huang Qi** (*Astragalus membranaceus*). Among the most popular and widely used of Chinese herbs, astragalus helps normalize the immune system. For that reason, it is often used to help mitigate the damage done by chemotherapy or radiation.

Cat's Claw (*Uncaria tomentosa*). This South American herb has many anti-cancer properties, helping combat tumors and boost the immune system.

Chaparral (*Larrea tridentate*). Unless you live in the Southwest, the place you're most likely to have seen this scrubby shrub is on shoot-'em-up Westerns. But this low-desert plant was used by indigenous peoples for treating tumors. Because this herb can be toxic to the liver in large quantities, it should be used with extra care.

Garlic (*Allium sativum*). We've already talked about how garlic's uses extend far beyond the Italian restaurant menu. Its abilities to stimulate immune function are arguably unrivaled in the plant world. It's an inexpensive and invaluable supplement for your dog's diet, not just in the case of a cancer diagnosis, but throughout his entire life.

Milk Thistle (*Carduus marianus*). In cases where cancer has metastasized to the liver or where drugs may be compromising liver function, this herb helps repair and protect that organ from toxicities.

Mushrooms. Shiitake mushrooms don't just make delicious appetizers—they, along with other mushrooms, have anti-cancer effects and are important boosters of the immune system. Because it may be difficult to persuade your dog to eat them in any quantity, medical mushrooms are available as a supplement, such as MGN-3.

Pau d'Arco (*Bignoniaceae tabebuia*). Another South American herb, this tree bark has anti-cancer properties. Since it can be taxing on the liver, some vets suggest alternating it after several weeks with cat's claw.

Red Clover (*Trifolium pratense*). There is research to show that red clover inhibits carcinogens, making this lowly highway herb a promising contender in the fight against cancer.

Turmeric (*Curcuma longa*). This mild-tasting root was used in Asia for centuries as a blood cleanser, and it is thought to slow or arrest the growth of tumors.

Essiac Tea

Pronounced *EZ-iac*, this blend of herbs was popularized by Canadian nurse Rene Caisse, whose surname spelled backward gave it its name. Legend says the remedy, which contains burdock root, Turkish rhubarb, slippery elm and sheep sorrel, had its origins with the Ojibway people. While Caisse was working as a nurse, an old woman passed on the recipe for the restorative tea, and later Caisse opened a cancer clinic and began using it with cancer patients. Although she started off with the initial support of some local physicians, government pressure eventually forced her to shut her doors.

> ### Essiac Tea Resource
>
> *The Essiac Report: Canada's Remarkable Unknown Cancer Remedy* (Royal Publications, $19.95).

Since claims that essiac cures cancer have never been proven by clinical trial, it is sold as a nutritional supplement. Currently, essiac-like teas are marketed under the names Tea of Life and Flor-Essence, among others. Formulas for making the tea at home are also widely available on the Internet, with seemingly as many variations as there are herbs. Many formulas use substitutes such as yellow dock for the sheep sorrel, which is an integral part of the formula.

"Although I have not seen great success with essiac given by mouth, I have found that compresses of concentrated tea can help if a cancer has broken through the skin," says Scanlan. "Initially, it can make part of the cancer shrink and the skin will partially or completely grow back over it. This is a temporary effect, but it sometimes lasts for weeks or, occasionally, months."

Because, like many herbal teas, essiac is bitter, it may be difficult to get your dog to ingest a significant amount of it. It is available in tincture and pill form, although some maintain that only the tea form is effective. Ask your holistic vet for guidance in administering it.

Hoxsey Formula

Like essiac, this is another story of a cancer cure that met great resistance from the medical powers that be—and one that comes with a legend of its own. The story goes that in the mid–1800s, a farmer from Illinois named John Hoxsey noticed that his horse had a cancerous growth on his leg. Turned loose in a field, the horse sought out the herbs in a particular corner, and eventually, the tumor shrank and disappeared.

Passed down through the Hoxsey family, the horse-healing formula was popularized by Harry Hoxsey, who opened cancer clinics in the early part of the 20th century. Hounded by the American Medical Association and other mainstream medical groups, Hoxsey closed his clinics. In the 1960s, his head nurse opened the Bio-Medical Centre in Tijuana, Mexico, where the treatment is still available.

Despite its controversial history, Hoxsey formula does contain some herbs that have body-cleansing and immune-boosting properties, including burdock root, red clover, prickly ash bark and licorice root.

D'Arcy Naturals sells an herbal formulation based on Hoxsey's original formula, as well as a Boneset version that is intended to treat or help prevent osteosarcoma.

Hoxey Formula Resource

D'Arcy Naturals
1-800-RXDARCY
(800-793-2729)
www.darcynat.com

Glandulars

Glandulars are extracts from the gland tissue of mammals, most often cows. They are prescribed to boost the health and functioning of the corresponding organ in the dog by providing vital

More Cancer Resources

Why Is Cancer Killing Our Pets? by Deborah Straw (Healing Arts Press, $14.95).

Pets Living With Cancer: A Pet Owner's Resource by Robin Downing, DVM (American Animal Hospital Association, $19.95).

The Nature of Animal Healing: The Definitive Holistic Medicine Guide to Caring for Your Dog and Cat by Martin Goldstein (Knopf, $25).

enzymes and nutrients. So, for example, since immune-system response is related in large part to the thymus, a holistic vet might suggest a thymus glandular as part of your dog's supplementation schedule.

Glandulars are not accepted across the board by holistic vets. Some think the idea that consuming the extract of a gland you are trying to strengthen is too simplistic to be biologically feasible. Also, since glands can be repositories for toxicities, it is crucial to make sure your glandulars come from animals that were naturally raised.

Shark Cartilage

This is just what it sounds like—cartilage from one of the ocean's fiercest predators. The theory is that when taken as a supplement, shark cartilage is anti-angiogenic—that is, it inhibits the development of blood vessels that supply the tumor, essentially starving it. Available in powdered form, shark cartilage has two drawbacks, one immediate, the other long-range: It is expensive, and conservationists worry about the impact its popularity will have on the world's shark populations.

Goldstein says ecological concerns have prompted him to use vascustatin, a dietary supplement sold under the name Angioblock, instead. Made of an extract of the common weed bindweed (*Convolvulus arvensis*), its anti-angiogenic properties are said to be 100 times more potent than shark cartilage.

NUTRITION

While it is fighting cancer, a dog's body needs to be given every opportunity to strengthen itself, and good nutrition is a cornerstone. Researchers now know that cancer tumors are carbohydrate junkies—they thrive on sugary snacks, grains, and starchy fruits and vegetables. A "cancer diet" developed at Colorado State University's veterinary school in Fort Collins, Colorado (and funded by Hills Pet Nutrition and the Morris Animal Foundation) had success with lymphoma remission by severely reducing the amount of simple sugars in the diet. The diet also included small amounts of complex carbohydrates, high quality but modest amounts of protein, and certain types of fat, including those high in omega-3 fatty acids.

Holistic vets do not agree about whether a raw diet is appropriate for canine cancer patients. Some worry that a sick dog will be more susceptible to the ordinary bacteria and parasites that a healthy dog's system can deal with handily. Even so, any dog with cancer can benefit from a home-cooked diet, because the wholesome, fresh food is easier to digest and does not contain the mother lode of preservatives and chemicals present in most commercial dog foods. Also, you can control the quality and precise source of the proteins your dog is eating—something that definitely cannot be said for kibble.

Good cancer-fighting vegetables include carrots and members of the broccoli family. Ideally, pulp the raw veggies before feeding so they are digestible. If you can't process them that finely, steam them lightly instead.

If it is at all possible for you to feed your dog a homemade diet, do so, especially since many holistic vets feel that a lifetime of eating overprocessed food of dubious quality helps give rise to our dogs' cancer to begin with. If you must feed a commercial diet, Science Diet n/d is specifically formulated to follow the Colorado State cancer diet guidelines.

LETTING GO—BUT NOT YET

Sadly, when it comes to cancer care in animals, there's little middle ground. We think of animals as either sick or well; they are either hospitalized or romping happily at home.

Hospice Resources

The Nikki Hospice Foundation for Pets
400 New Bedford Drive
Vallejo, CA 94591
(707) 557-8595
www.csum.edu/pethospice/
A referral service for veterinarians who offer supportive hospice services.

Angel's Gate
18 Josephine Lane
Northport, NY 11768-2708
www.angelsgate.org
One of the only residential hospices for animals in the nation, with a decidedly holistic bent.

It's important to understand that those extremes are not the only options. There is a way for sick animals to stay home and live out their final months, weeks and days. It's called hospice.

Hospice care for humans has been slow to gain acceptance in this country, and the concept for animals has been even less explored. But that's a matter of culture, not capability. Veterinarians have a wide assortment of palliative techniques and drugs at their disposal to help ease an animal through her final time free of pain and suffering. The challenge is to get vets thinking in terms of palliative care, not the black-and-white extremes of curing or euthanizing.

Recently, recognizing the need to give our animals a way to finish out their lives naturally, surrounded by the people and places they love, the American Veterinary Medical Association developed recommended guidelines for hospice care. Still, if your vet is new to the concept, you might have to push him to provide you with the tools you need to help your animal through to a "good death."

"A lot of people say, 'I don't want my animal to suffer,'" says Eric Clough, a veterinarian in Merrimack, New Hampshire, who is an active advocate of hospice, teaching his techniques to vets across the country. "But the definition of suffering is the loss of

Pet Loss Resources

Pet Loss Support Page
www.pet-loss.net
Includes a state-by-state directory of animal-loss resources.

Cornell University Pet Support Hotline
(607) 253-3932
www.vet.cornell.edu/public/petloss/
Staffed 6 p.m. to 9 p.m. EST, Tuesday through Thursday

The National Pet Loss Hotline
(800) 946-4646 (punch in pin number 140-7211 and then your own phone number)
Free nationwide bereavement consultations around the clock.

Pet Loss: A Spiritual Guide by Julia Harris (Lantern Press, $14.95).

psychological resources for coping—and I'm not sure I can really describe that for animals. What we really mean when we say 'I don't want my animal to suffer' is 'I don't want him to be in pain.' And pain we can always take care of." Indeed, says Clough, even though they are often reluctant to prescribe a controlled substance such as morphine for fear it might be abused by human caretakers, vets can prescribe narcotics.

By explaining in detail the kind of physical symptoms you might encounter, a vet can tell you what to do to cope with chronic nose bleeds, how to give injections or how to deal with sudden lameness or vomiting. Clough also recommends that dog owners seek out human hospice agencies to see if they offer any volunteer training, which is often given free of charge and provides information that applies to dogs as well.

Here, in the final chapters of your dog's life, you will likely have to be her strong advocate, pushing for the tools you need, seeking out compassionate vets who understand the hospice concept and want to be a partner in it.

Hospice care is a complicated three-way process between you, your vet and your dog. Having helped your dog live a healthy life, it's only fitting that both you and your vet help your dog bring her life to a close—on whatever timetable she chooses.

MOURNING

"It's just a dog."

No, it's not.

Losing an animal is a deep, deep loss—one that can't be papered over with a few days devoted to "getting over it." A person's grief, like a fingerprint, is an intensely personal thing. No two of us grieve alike, no two of us experience loss in the same way.

Increasingly, as the emotional and even spiritual roles of animals in our lives become recognized, the resources for mourning them have grown. Bereavement groups and support counselors specializing in the loss of animal companions are available nationwide.

It's difficult enough to mourn the passing of a beloved animal. It's even worse to do so feeling you're alone or freakish because of the depth of your pain. Talking with others who understand and empathize is a first, and important, step.

Chapter 11

Allergies: More Than Skin Deep

....

Is your veterinarian a gardener or a mechanic?

Traditional Chinese Medicine, which was discussed in Chapter 4, uses that analogy to describe how Western and Eastern doctors approach illness. The Western doctor is the mechanic: Like a technician trying to narrow the problem down to the smallest of its parts, his goal is finding the broken belt or the spent spark plug. Locating and fixing that dysfunctional piece, he concludes, will get the whole machine up and running.

The Eastern doctor is the gardener. When his plants start to wilt or their leaves begin to drop, he does not narrow his focus, but expands it. He realizes many factors go into determining the health of a plant—the amount of fertilizer and water it gets, how crowded its roots are, the hours of sunlight it is exposed to. While a certain fungus or insect might be the culprit in terms of the specific disease at hand, the gardener also understands that a healthy, hardy plant will be more likely to withstand such external attacks.

Of the two approaches, the holistic one, as you have probably already surmised, is the gardener. It's an important distinction to keep in mind as we discuss one of the most common and frustrating medical problems affecting dogs—allergies.

When we humans get allergies, they are usually expressed with nasal or respiratory problems, such as a running nose, sneezing and wheezing. Dogs, by contrast, often manifest their allergies dermatologically—with skin rashes and irritations that might prompt chronic chewing, licking or scratching, or copious shedding or hair loss. Other signs of allergies include chronic ear infections, runny eyes and digestive problems such as vomiting and diarrhea.

The first step in treating allergies is to determine whether they are, indeed, the problem. Skin disorders such as mange and metabolic diseases such as hypothyroidism often produce similar signs in dogs, and should first be ruled out by your veterinarian.

One common approach to allergies is to try to eliminate the allergen—that is, the substance that makes the dog react. Switching to a hypoallergenic diet, keeping your dog indoors with air filters running when the pollen count is high, bathing frequently—all those tactics are aimed at keeping allergens from igniting a response in your dog.

While such preventive measures are often helpful in dealing with allergies, many holistic vets believe they are just Band-Aids on a larger, deeper problem. Allergies, after all, are a sensitivity to everyday substances—things your dog would normally come into contact with and would normally have no reaction to. An allergen isn't an allergen until your dog's body decides it is, and begins to mount a defense against what, under normal circumstances, it would regard as benign.

In that sense, then, allergies are a matter of perspective, and it is your dog's immune system that makes the judgment call—deciding, for example, whether the wheat flour in a dog biscuit is a yummy ingredient or the trigger for a flank covered with hives.

What makes an immune system overreact in this way? That's a difficult question, since every dog is unique and his genetic background and individual circumstances affect how he reacts. But one helpful analogy is to think of the immune system as a kid during recess in the school yard. Imagine you are a fellow classmate, and are approaching him from behind. You tap him on the shoulder and he turns around—and socks you in the jaw. Is that a normal reaction? In most school yards, hopefully, not. But if our imaginary

Allergy Resources

The Allergy Solution for Dogs by Shawn Messonnier (Prima Publishing, $14.95).
A holistic approach to dealing with allergies in dogs.

kid has had a tough time at recess—bullies stealing his lunch, teasing him, tripping him when he's not looking—he is going to be supersensitive to any unknown interaction.

Immune systems are sort of like that kid in the school yard. They can get beat up so often and so regularly that inevitably, they overreact from the stress and the pressure. And that overreaction has much more to do with what challenges and assaults came before the tap on the shoulder. The tap itself is just the trigger.

Holistic veterinarians are not unanimous in how they treat allergies. Some—especially those located in areas where allergens are plentiful and who see severe and chronic cases—also use conventional modalities such as drugs and allergy shots. Others do not. As always, seek out the veterinarian and approach that works best for you and your dog.

And while it seems that cancer and allergies are unrelated subjects, you will find a significant amount of overlap in the holistic approach to managing these conditions. That's because allergies and cancer are theoretically just gradations of the same problem—the immune system's inability to cope with the pressures it faces.

NAME THAT ALLERGY

Obviously, the first step in dealing with an allergy is to figure out what the dog is allergic to. Allergies can fall into several categories.

Inhalant allergies. Also called atopy, this is an allergy to everyday airborne particles. One of the most common causes of

IDENTIFYING ALLERGIES

When it comes to food allergies, finding the problematic ingredient is technically a process of addition rather than elimination. Starting off with a diagnostic diet that contains two ingredients that the dog has never been exposed to, the owner slowly adds new food components to the menu and notes the reaction to each addition.

But with atopic, or inhalant, allergies, it's impossible to stop all the exposure your dog has to everyday allergens such as grass or pollen or mold, and then add them back into his life one by one.

As a result, atopy is often diagnosed with two different types of testing. Both should be conducted at times of the year when seasonal allergies are at their peak. Neither type should be performed on dogs who have recently been on corticosteroids or antihistamines.

Blood tests. In this testing, blood is screened for antibodies for a wide range of common allergens. The two standard blood tests used for allergy testing in dogs are the ELISA test (enyzme-linked immunoabsorbent assay) and the RAST (radioallergosorbent test).

Generally speaking, the ELISA test is considered more accurate by many veterinarians. Both tests, however, can produce false positives.

Intradermal skin testing. This type of testing is considered far more accurate than blood testing—but it is also more invasive. After the dog is sedated, antigens—that is, potential allergy-inducing substances—are injected into a shaved area of the skin. The injection sites are later examined for reactions.

allergies in dogs, atopy can be often seasonal, as with pollen, or year-round, as with mold or dust. Airborne particles can come into contact with the dog through the respiratory system or the skin.

Food allergies. Although dog owners are quick to suspect them, food allergies are actually not all that common, and account for only about 10 percent to 15 percent of all allergies. Unlike inhalant allergies, they are not seasonal, and pruritus, or itchiness, is often focused on one area, such as the ears or feet.

Food allergies can appear seemingly out of nowhere, because they generally develop over time and exposure. Certain breeds are prone to food allergies, including Soft Coated Wheaten Terriers, Cocker Spaniels, English Springer Spaniels, Labrador Retrievers, Boxers, Collies, Dalmatians and German Shepherd Dogs.

One way to identify a food allergen is with a hypoallergenic diet, more appropriately called an elimination diet. The dog is taken off his regular food and fed a very simplified diet, usually comprising one protein and one starch that he has never been exposed to, such as duck and potatoes. If the dog does well on the restricted diet, new foods are added one by one and the reactions noted.

Flea allergies. It's not the flea, but the protein in the flea's saliva, that triggers an allergic reaction. Keeping fleas at bay is one obvious preventive measure. Keep in mind that chemical repellents and collars may eliminate the pests in the short term, but may be yet another irritant, further weakening your dog's immune system in the long run.

ALLERGY OR INTOLERANCE?

Food allergies are often confused with food intolerances. The difference is immunologic: A food allergy is a reaction by the immune system to a specific food, usually a protein such as beef, while a food intolerance is a chemical sensitivity to something in the diet, whether a specific ingredient, an additive or a preservative.

ALLERGY APPROACHES

When it comes to allergies, there usually is no single culprit in this immunological whodunit. Instead, the best approach often is a multi-layered one, starting first and foremost with strengthening the immune system.

Many of the approaches outlined here focus on boosting overall health in the expectation that allergies will resolve themselves when the imbalance is addressed. Other approaches target the symptoms of allergic reactions by using drugs to reduce

THE WRITE STUFF

With allergies and other chronic problems, a detailed history of your dog's exposures and reactions can be extremely helpful in pinpointing problems and the causes of flair-ups.

"Keep a diary," advises veterinarian Shawn Messonnier. While writing down the daily minutiae of what your dog ate or where he cavorted may seem futile to you, it can help illuminate patterns when looked at over a whole year.

inflammation and itching. In and of themselves, they are not holistic. But they are included here because they, like any tool, have their place. If, for example, an allergy is serious enough and a dog is in significant discomfort, a holistic veterinarian might very well turn to a drug to bring relief. Every dog is an individual, and every case brings with it a unique set of parameters.

Nutrition

"The very first thing we look at is diet," says veterinarian Susan Wynn, who sees lots of dogs with allergies in her Georgia practice. "No doubt about it, dogs on poor diets have worse symptoms. An improved diet will make most dogs comfortable."

Wynn's definition of "improved" depends on the client: Dogs who are on grocery-store brands or low-quality kibble are moved up to a homemade diet, or at the very least a super-premium brand of kibble.

"If there is evidence to suspect that there is a food allergy," she says, "then we recommend a hypoallergenic elimination diet"—in other words, a very simplified diet that only includes a handful of new ingredients, so the allergy-inducing food can be identified.

Herbalist Gregory Tilford echoes the importance of a good diet, pointing out that allergies are "second to poor nutrition and poor waste elimination. And you're really chasing your tail—no pun intended—if you're not addressing them." Most commercial dog foods, he says, "use low-grade proteins, which the body doesn't recognize as food and has a hard time eliminating."

AVOIDANCE

If you know what triggers an allergy, stay away from it. This is simple common sense. With food allergies, this means embarking on an elimination diet to figure out what specific food is creating the reaction. With flea allergy dermatitis, it means keeping your home and yard scrupulously flea-free. While keeping pollen and dust at bay are more complicated propositions, the more you can limit your dog's exposure to those allergens, the better.

"If there's one thing to impress on people, it's that bathing is the most important thing for dogs with skin disease," says Messonnier. That's not just because hypoallergenic shampoos containing oatmeal and aloe vera are soothing to inflamed skin, but because they clean the coat, washing off potentially irritating allergens. "The more you can bathe," he says, "the better dogs respond." Baths two or three times a week—or even every day if the skin is very itchy or red—can offer temporary relief.

While Tilford is a strong believer in a raw diet, he adds that because every dog is different, raw food may not be the answer across the board. But in his opinion, a homemade diet—whether raw or cooked—is ideal.

Vaccinations

Many holistic veterinarians are careful about the number and kind of vaccinations they give the animals in their care. With an allergic animal, whose immune system is already crying "uncle," vaccines mean adding more stress to an already overburdened system. The label on the vaccine says it all: "Use only on healthy dogs."

"Minimize vaccines," stresses veterinarian Shawn Messonnier. "Don't give a dog more foreign protein in his system if his skin is itchy and red."

In addition to vaccines, reevaluate all the other stressors on your dog's immune system. These can include flea and tick sprays and chemical-laden disinfectants, fertilizers and insecticides used around the house and garden.

Fatty Acid Supplements

Fatty acids are a buzzword these days. We all know they're supposed to be good for our dogs, and when used properly, they can be. But, as with most things, you need to understand how they work.

There are two types of essential fatty acids that you hear about constantly: omega-3 and omega-6. Omega-6 fatty acids are often found in dog food, and they are a mixed bag in terms of how they work in the body: Certain omega-6 fatty acids, such as gamma-linolenic acid (GLA), are anti-inflammatory, but others can actually cause inflammation. Safflower oil, canola oil and corn oil all contain omega-6 fatty acids that are inflammatory, so they should be avoided in allergy-prone dogs.

Omega-3 fatty acids are not found in commercial diets because they cannot survive the manufacturing process, so they must be added to a diet as a supplement. Omega-3s such as eicosapentaenoic acid (EPA) and docosahexaenoic acid (DHA) have been shown to have an anti-inflammatory effect, and so can be good guys in your dog's battle against allergies when added to his diet.

Two often-cited sources for omega-3 fatty acids are flax seed oil and fish body oil, which is derived from cold-water fish such as salmon. (Although it sounds similar to fish body oil, cod liver oil does not fall into this category.) While flax seed and fish body oils are often considered interchangeable, there is a significant difference: Flax seed oil contains alphalinolenic acid (ALA), which, when converted biochemically, turns into the inflammation-fighting EPA and DHA fatty acids. But whether a dog's body can actually prompt that conversion and benefit from it is still up for debate.

"The research that has been done is mostly on fish oil and its components," says Wynn, referring to studies of the anti-inflammatory effects of EPA and DHA. "The only research I'm aware of suggests flax seed oil doesn't raise DHA levels in the blood." While that doesn't mean flax seed oil has no benefit, so far there is no evidence that flax seed oil will have therapeutic value in trying to control inflammation caused by allergies. Meanwhile, the benefits of omega-3s from fish body oil are not in doubt.

If you are buying a mix of fatty-acid supplements, choose wisely and read the label to make sure you are getting the omega-3 fatty acids and the *correct* kind of omega-6s. Evening-primrose oil and borage oil are excellent sources of GLA, the "good" omega-6.

Acupuncture and Homeopathy

Because they are a sign that something is awry in the immune system, allergies can be helped by any modality that focuses on rebuilding health and restoring balance. Acupuncture and homeopathy are approaches that stress the importance of this internal equilibrium. Both might be helpful in trying to alleviate your dog's allergies.

Herbs

In their role as body regulators and boosters, herbs can help an allergy-stricken animal reach equilibrium. Wynn finds she is most successful with Chinese herbs, while herbalist Tilford offers this list of commonly available Western herbs, many of which support liver and gall bladder function.

Alfalfa. A popular and effective nutritive herb, alfalfa is often used in older animals for conditions such as arthritis. Its anti-inflammatory effect makes it valuable in allergy-prone dogs.

Burdock. This cleansing herb helps flush toxins from the system and reduce inflammation.

Dandelion root. Like burdock, this herb is a diuretic, helping remove toxins and waste products. It also stimulates and supports liver function.

Licorice root. This herb has been touted as the herbal answer to the steroid prednisone. There are several contraindications with licorice root, including heart disease and hypertension, and long-term effects may include decreased potassium levels and high blood pressure. For this reason, some practitioners use deglycyrrhizinated licorice (DGL), which does not contain blood-pressure-raising glycyrrhizin.

Nettle. Consider this herb for dogs with seasonal allergies. It has a mild antihistamine effect. Some dogs might be sensitive to the herb itself, so be sure to have your dog monitored by an herb-savvy veterinarian.

Red clover. Red clover contains bioflavonoids, which are thought to help boost immunity. It can be used internally and externally for skin problems.

Spirulina. This nutritious blue-green algae supports the immune system and is a source of the anti-inflammatory essential fatty acid GLA.

Orthomolecular Medicine

We all need a balanced diet—that much we agree on. But what is your definition of "balanced"?

Orthomolecular medicine takes good nutrition a step further: It not only considers nutrition to be a primary factor in maintaining good health, but it recognizes biochemical individuality. In other words, different dogs require different levels of vitamins, minerals and other nutrients.

Messonnier says he uses "any combination of a hundred products," from glandular extracts to antioxidants, in dogs with allergies. These nutraceuticals—including vitamins, minerals, enzymes, herbals and glandulars—can help strike the right nutritional balance, restoring health in the process.

NAET

Nambudripad's Allergy Elimination Techniques (NAET) is an allergy-elimination system created by Devi S. Nambudripad, a medical doctor from Buena Park, California, who is also an acupuncturist, chiropractor and kinesiologist. Plagued by allergies ever since her childhood in South India, Nambudripad began to explore how Traditional Chinese Medicine—specifically,

---

NAET Resources

Say Goodbye to Illness by Dr. Devi S. Nambudripad (Delta Publishing Company, $24).

NAET Department
6714 Beach Boulevard
Buena Park, CA 90621
www.naet.com
This is Dr. Nambudripad's clinic

Veterinary NAET
1637 16th Street
Santa Monica, CA 90404
(310) 450-2287
www.vetnaet.com

acupuncture and acupressure—could reprogram the body to stop reacting to a specific allergen.

The NAET method uses kinesiology, or muscle response testing (described in Chapter 6), to identify which substances the dog is sensitive to. Then acutherapy is done in the presence of the antigen responsible for the allergic reaction, so the body can be rebalanced and taught to ignore the allergens it has been reacting to.

In veterinary NAET, a human surrogate (usually the owner) receives the acupressure treatment, while his or her hands are in contact with the allergic dog. Through this closed circuit, the benefits of the treatment are transferred to the canine patient.

Immunotherapy

This is a fancy way of saying "allergy shots." Once an allergen has been identified, hyposensitizing injections are given over a period of weeks or months. With constant, steady exposure to this source of his allergies over the course of weeks or even months, the dog eventually develops immunity. Even after the initial series of shots, boosters may be required, so owners must make a significant time commitment.

Holistic vets disagree about allergy shots, and even conventional vets are not all convinced they are effective for dogs. Wynn says there are some cases in which she does not recommend them—usually in the case of older animals with long histories of taking steroids. Still, "sometimes the best chance we have of really managing disease is with allergy shots," she says, especially with animals who do not respond to neutraceuticals and herbs. "You're using the body's own mechanisms, and if it works, you get a better chance of a longer, deeper cure."

Corticosteroids

These drugs—which can be either injected or given orally—are very effective at addressing severe allergy symptoms such as inflammation and itching. But they only address the symptoms, not the allergic reaction itself. Short-term side effects of steroid use include increased water consumption and urination, hyperactivity and diarrhea. Depending on the dose given, long-term

EAR, HERE

Allergies often express themselves as chronic ear infections or itchiness, which will cause a dog to shake her head or scratch her ears repeatedly. Especially if a dog has long or drop ears, she can develop traumas on the ear flap, or pinna. These damaged blood vessels develop into fluid-filled swellings called hemotomas, and severe ones sometimes need to be surgically removed. Regular swabbing with a soothing herbal wash (you'll find a popular one at www.halopets.com) can help keep head shaking to a minimum as you get the allergies under control.

use of steroids can cause serious health problems, including kidney disease and impaired liver function.

The popular corticosteroid prednisone has become a dirty word of sorts among holistic devotees, symbolic of an approach that wants to sweep symptoms under the rug instead of dealing with them. But it would be unfair and counterproductive to suggest that prednisone and other drugs like it do not have any place in a holistic veterinarian's repertoire. In severe cases where the animal is acutely uncomfortable, a vet may very well turn to prednisone to provide some much-needed relief and get the physical situation under control. "Too many people think 'holistic' means no drugs, and 'holistic' really means what works for the patient," says Messonnier. "Any drug can be used safely if you follow the manufacturer's warnings and guidelines."

It is the sustained, reflexive use of the drug in any and all allergy cases that should be a cause for concern. Steroids are powerful drugs, and we are only beginning to understand the effects of their prolonged use. Wynn points to the suspected connection between corticosteroid use and leaky gut syndrome, in which the mucosal lining of the bowel wall is eroded away due to inflammation from allergies, allowing undigested food proteins to seep into the bloodstream and triggering an immune response. Anti-inflammatories such as prednisone, the theory goes, prompt the gut to absorb even more things that it shouldn't, which, in turn, is thought to worsen the whole inflammatory situation and possibly spark further allergies.

The best judge of whether a drug like prednisone is needed ought to be your dog, says Messonnier. "Let's do what your dog's body needs—it will tell you if and when she needs that dose of prednisone. And if she doesn't need it, what are you doing it for?"

Antihistamines

To keep allergic reactions in check, some veterinarians recommend some of the same over-the-counter antihistamines that you might use for a bout of hay fever, including Benadryl, Chlor-Trimeton and Tavist. As with steroids, antihistamines only address the symptoms of the allergy, not the cause itself. And they are not as powerful as corticosteroids, which is both good and bad. While they do not do as much harm to the body in the long run, they also are not as effective in alleviating symptoms.

Chapter 12

Veterinarians: Finding the Perfect One

What exactly is a holistic veterinarian?

At first glance, it seems like a simple enough question. And here's a simple enough answer: A holistic vet is any veterinarian who is a member of the American Holistic Veterinary Medical Association.

But if you visit that group's website and scroll through the directory of members, you'll notice a wide range of modalities offered. Some vets only do acupuncture and chiropractic, others concentrate solely on homeopathy. Some use flower essences and reiki; even more would look at you askance if you asked about them.

Also, some self-described "holistic" vets practice in a way that seems inconsistent. For example, while they may offer complementary therapies such as chiropractic, they may also sell commercial dog food in their waiting rooms. Or, while they offer acupuncture and Chinese herbs, they will also administer a full roster of annual vaccinations, year in and year out.

The truth is, there are varying levels of "holistic," and the key is for you to find the vet whose style of practicing and prescribing meshes with yours.

That can be difficult at a time when many conventionally trained vets do not see the value of complementary medicine—which they are not exposed to in veterinary school, or at least not to any great degree. Indeed, those who choose a holistic path do so on their own initiative, seeking out seminars and certifications on their own time.

"It's hard" to be a holistic vet, says veterinarian Allen Schoen, acknowledging that many allopathic colleagues can be dismissive of modalities they don't understand and aren't willing to try. Conversely, "there are vets who say they're completely holistic, and they do more harm because they don't acknowledge when an allopathic approach is needed." That is a key point to remember: A truly holistic vet doesn't disregard tools such as drugs or surgery if they are of benefit to the animal.

We each have our own interests and talents, and veterinarians are no different. Inevitably, each holistic veterinarian develops a particular focus and expertise, which means he or she won't be able to offer every modality in the holistic universe. "You've got to have a philosophy about what you're going to treat with, what you going to recommend, from hundreds of available therapies," says veterinarian Susan Wynn. "The skeptics have a great point when they say one is as good as another if you don't have proof. How do you choose from seemingly random choices?"

For her part, Wynn looks for one of two things—science and consensus. Acupuncture, for example, has both. Its medical benefits have been documented, and virtually everyone accepts it. The benefits of a homemade diet have not been studied, but there is such consensus among holistic vets about its benefits that Wynn feels comfortable recommending it.

It's also important to remember that no matter how well-received or excruciatingly documented, a holistic therapy is only of benefit if the practitioner is using it properly. Consider Veterinarian X. He's a traditional vet who's never tried or explored any of the modalities described in this book, but he has a deep connection with his patients. He notices their individual quirks and behaviors, he greets them with affection and a general concern for their health. While he has an arsenal of drugs at his disposal, he is careful how he uses them. He can order a battery of tests to diagnose a problem, but he also relies on what each individual dog is telling him. He uses common sense. He takes his time talking to owners, listening to their concerns, understanding what they are saying instead of just hearing.

Is he using holistic modalities? No. But he is using a holistic approach. And given a choice between him and another veterinarian who has the word "holistic" on his business card but whose intention in offering chiropractic or acupuncture is to make a buck, what decision would you make?

Labels only tell us so much. Every veterinarian is unique, and every relationship that vet has is special. Much of the success of such a relationship depends on the level of mutual respect and trust you can reach with the person who is your dog's primary care provider. And, like most things in life, that is a two-way street.

"Part of the whole approach to healing is having that beginner's open mind. The minute we begin feeling we have all the answers is the minute we've failed as a holistic person," says veterinarian Donna Kelleher. "I feel like I'm constantly learning. And anyone who's really honest about it feels that way, too.

"It's totally about steps"—for the dog's owner as much as the veterinarian. Conventional medicine, whether intentionally or not, trains practitioners to "take the power away from the person," says Kelleher, while a holistic approach empowers the caretaker, giving her a role in her animal's health care and helping that caretaker grow and thrive in that capacity. "That's what doctor means," Kelleher says. "It means teacher."

Think about your own health care for a moment. While you probably have a general practitioner who takes care of your everyday health issues and wellness care, chances are you have other professionals whom you rely on—acupuncturists, nutritionists, chiropractors . . . the list goes on and on. We seek them out at different times because we need their expertise in a particular area, especially where keeping ourselves centered and balanced is concerned.

Why should it be any different for our dogs?

VETTING THE VET

Do you have the right veterinarian? If you have to ask the question in the first place, you probably already know the answer. Still, here are some questions to ask yourself.

Am I comfortable with my vet's base of knowledge? To paraphrase Ann Landers, half of all veterinarians graduated at the bottom of their class. Not every vet has the newest diagnostic gizmo in his office or can offer the latest cutting-edge treatment. But she should, at minimum, be current on the trends and topics in veterinary medicine, keeping up-to-date with publications such as the *Journal of the American Veterinary Medical Association* and other peer-reviewed publications.

Knowing what one doesn't know is also important. Your vet should be ready and willing to refer you to a top-notch specialist when she realizes she has reached the end of her expertise. Sending you to a specialist is not a sign of weakness or incompetence. In fact, it's just the opposite.

Am I comfortable with my vet's personality? Brains aren't everything in medicine. A true healer has an emotional connection with his patients and clients. It's important that you "click" with your vet, that you feel comfortable sharing information and arriving at decisions together. If your encounters make you uneasy or anxious, then your personalities may not be suited for one another. That doesn't make anyone right or wrong. That's just the way it is.

No vet is an expert in everything. You'd be very fortunate to find a holistic vet who practiced even half of the modalities mentioned in this book. Some may specialize in just one or two areas. So while one vet may do acupuncture and Chinese herbs, he may be totally unversed—and uninterested—in flower essences and essential oils. Still another might be a classical homeopath, not combining his homeopathic remedies with any other treatment. One might consult an animal communicator if he felt a dog's illness had a deep emotional root; his colleague across town might think that totally off-base.

The point is that vets, like people, take different paths. Some believe in only one way to heal, others are more eclectic. There

Am I comfortable with the vet staff? A vet sets a tone in the way her office is run and the way her staffers, from receptionists to technicians, treat clients. Your vet's office should be a welcoming environment. You don't need her to be Oprah, but you do need her to temper some of the sterility and standoffishness that are common at medical offices.

Am I comfortable with the vet's accessibility? You don't want to be paging your vet about every sniffle or snort that you hear from your dog. But you do want to know that she will return your calls within a reasonable time. And if you call needing an emergency appointment, she should trust your judgment enough to take you seriously and try to see your animal as soon as possible.

Do I trust this vet? This is really the question at the heart of this chapter. It's simple and complicated at the same time. Your relationship with your vet is like any other connection between two people: It grows over time and experience and it allows for mistakes and misunderstandings, as long as there is common ground—the well-being of your animal.

People can have a lot of unspoken motives about why they do what they do. They're in it for the money, for the control, for the ego boost, for a whole host of reasons that might be less than stellar. Trust your instinct when it comes to this: If your relationship with your vet just feels right, then it probably is.

is nothing wrong with using different vets for different purposes, as long as you are honest and up-front about it, and designate one person to be your "gatekeeper." And if geography makes it impossible to find a holistic vet in reasonable proximity, put technology to use. Many holistic veterinarians are available for phone or e-mail consultations.

WHY IT'S NOT EASY

In a perfect world, all veterinarians would focus only on healing their patients, with no other concerns or distractions. But we live in the real world and, like it or not, there are mitigating factors.

Money

James Herriott and other country-vets-with-hearts-of-gold notwithstanding, the reality is that veterinary practices are businesses, not nonprofit organizations. Vets need to keep cash flowing, and some of the reflexive practices that are objectionable from a holistic standpoint, such as annual vaccinations, have a strong economic component. If you didn't think you needed to get your dog vaccinated year in and year out, you might decide to skip your annual office visit—not good news for the vet's bottom line.

While financial concerns will always loom large for vets, the good news is that holistic medicine will not send them to the poorhouse. Holistic care provides just as lucrative a revenue stream, whether it's for titering or chiropractic adjustments or acupuncture treatments. With its emphasis on preventive care and overall health, a holistic practice isn't synonymous with a bankrupt one. In fact, quite the opposite.

As soon as so-called conventional vets figure that out, you'll begin to notice more and more practices that label themselves holistic.

Veterinary practices, like supermarkets or tuxedo-rental stores or any other commercial endeavor, respond to market demand. If enough customers ask those stores for mango-flavored yogurt or chartreuse cummerbunds, they will eventually begin to stock them for fear their business will go elsewhere. And if enough patients request complementary veterinary care for their animals, veterinarians will offer it.

Generally speaking, this is a good thing, because, freed from the disapproval of their peers, some veterinarians will explore these modalities with open hearts, open minds and a true desire to heal. Others, however, will just be in it for the money. Since intention is a crucial part of healing, that's something to reflect on. Whether a vet is actually holistic, or is just calling herself that because it's the latest marketing buzzword, is for you to figure out.

A final thought on money: Vets, unlike lawyers, do not charge by the hour—although perhaps they should. Often, taking a holistic approach means talking over possible scenarios and options, and this can quickly run longer than the allotted time for an office visit. The end result is that you feel bum-rushed and the vet feels stressed, because his workload is backing up and the natives are getting restless in the waiting room. Time is money, and you should be willing to pay for it. Most vets will happily agree to setting up a dedicated time for a consultation, and you should just as cheerfully be willing to pay for it.

Fear

Veterinarians operate within a rigid medical system that exalts exactness and uniformity. For a vet to go beyond the conventional protocols and procedures to explore new, "untested" ones can be stressful, especially in the beginning. Also, many vets cling to old habits based on the emotional impact of one experience: For example, a vet who has lost a puppy to distemper will probably feel very strongly about vaccinating well into adulthood. Similarly, I know holistic vets who support their clients feeding a raw food diet, but, after seeing just one overeager eater asphyxiate on a chicken neck, insist that bones be fed ground instead of whole.

"The vets see the screwups— they dig out bones at three in the morning that punctured a dog's intestine because it was fed cooked," says Kelleher. "They see these things and they can't forget them. They smell the parvovirus and can't get that out of their mind when it comes time to vaccinate."

Experience aside, a large component of fear is financial, and for good reason. We live in a reflexively litigious society, with many people believing they are entitled to a perfect outcome to every situation—and if that doesn't materialize, then someone must pay. Vets don't want to be the ones who are sued, and they are less vulnerable in a lawsuit if they followed "conventional veterinary practices." As a result, their decisions and policies tend to be conservative. Considering that their livelihood is on the line, can you blame them?

Ego

Some people, including some veterinarians, are convinced of the infallibility of the methods they have already learned. They see new ideas and new modalities as a challenge to their body of hard-won knowledge.

In this sense, veterinarians are sort of like gardeners. Some are convinced it's better to work only with the tried-and-true perennials, never venturing to try an exotic annual. But others are more adventurous, constantly exploring new cultivars and willing to gamble on an unknown, if they think the risk is outweighed by the possible benefits.

It's this latter kind of vet you want to seek out—someone who is not convinced of his own infallibility and who still believes that there is a universe of things to be learned in the world.

VET CHECK

Here's a to-do list for finding (or, if you like a challenge, molding) the perfect veterinarian.

Set Up an Interview

If you were responsible for hiring employees at your workplace, you wouldn't dream of bringing someone on board without at least one interview. Your veterinarian is a very important person in your dog's life, with an equally important job.

When you're looking for a vet, her technical knowledge should count for a lot. Just because a vet is holistic shouldn't mean she doesn't keep up-to-date with the latest studies and findings in her field. In fact, you should expect quite the opposite. A holistic approach is a complementary one, not an alternative one. It is not a matter of either-or. There is a valid and important place for conventional allopathic medicine in your dog's care, and you want a vet who is well-versed and up-to-date on all the current technology and ideas.

At the same time, don't discount the importance of the dynamic between you and your vet. Good relationships depend on good communication, and if you feel uncomfortable or intimidated or unheeded, reconsider. All the technical expertise in the world will not matter if, in the crunch, you cannot trust and feel comfortable with the person who holds your dog's health in her hands.

Do Your Homework

The world is filled with instant experts—a dubious blessing for which we have the Internet to thank. But in order to talk intelligently about your dog with your vet, you need to have real knowledge and a deep understanding of the subject at hand.

On the most basic level, most vets simply don't have the time to sit down and give you a dissertation on, say, vaccinations. It's a subject that is nuanced and controversial and, minimally, it will take a couple of hours of reading before you can discuss it intelligently with anyone, let alone a medical professional. Also, most people need time and concentration to absorb such a large amount of information, and it's better off done in more than one sitting.

All this isn't to say that you shouldn't expect your vet to give you in-depth explanations about decisions involving your dog. But if there is a subject that you know in advance will come up—such as the right time to spay or neuter, or the kind of vaccine schedule you want to use, or how you want to treat a chronic condition such as a persistent ear infection—it makes sense to have as many facts as possible beforehand so your conversation can go beyond just grasping the basics.

On a deeper level, coming in prepared and conversant on a subject tells a vet two things: First, you are not someone who goes off half-cocked without fully researching a subject, and so neither will you be someone who is willing to accept an answer that does not make sense to you; and second, this is not a hierarchical relationship, but rather a collaboration between equals. While you will never have the medical knowledge or expertise of a veterinarian unless you go to vet school, you are still your animal's caretaker, and so have a responsibility to be as informed as possible.

If you do your homework, you will probably be pleasantly surprised at how open your vet is to your ideas. Veterinarians are confronted every day with people who latch on to things without bothering to take the time to research them, and they are naturally skeptical about the latest health fad. If something you are proposing has risks or drawbacks, be sure to mention them, so your vet knows you are being realistic and can be sure you've done enough research to see both sides of the equation.

Take Responsibility

Just as you need to trust your vet's judgment, she needs to trust yours. It's important for your vet to know that you make decisions based on your dog's best interests—as best you can determine them from the facts before you. And you need to be very clear that you are willing to take responsibility for your decisions if something goes wrong.

A perfect example of this is emergency vet fees. The family dog gets hit by a car and he is rushed into the vet, who is told, "Do whatever you can to save him, please, he's like a member of the family." The vet pulls out all the stops, the dog's life is saved, and the family is presented with a huge bill. Despite the fact that the vet can document every line-item charge, the family refuses to pay.

It's a scenario that has played itself out so often in virtually every practice that most vets now require clients whose animals might need extensive care to sign a form indicating they are aware of what the final tab might be. Some practices even require a deposit up-front. Clients get angry that the vet staff is focusing on money at such an emotional time, but the fact is that vets do not bank on their clients' sense of responsibility because experience has shown them otherwise.

Similarly, you can't expect to start blaming your vet if you make a decision about your dog's care and then something goes wrong. If you are willing to do your research and take credit for the wonderful, healthful effects a particular decision of yours has on your dog, then you should be willing to take responsibility for mistakes, if they happen.

Find a Community

It's difficult to make a major decision about your dog's health care in a vacuum. Many traditional vets, for example, strongly discourage a raw food diet, often because they don't have much experience with it, have heard one horror story or don't have the confidence that their clients can do it properly. Or your dog might develop a breed-specific condition that your vet has had little experience with.

In such cases, it helps to find other dog people who have gone through the same thing and who can give you sound advice about how they proceeded. Spending time on a raw-food list on the Internet, for example, will enable you to do some research and explore your options before you buy

Resources

American Holistic Veterinary Medical Association
2218 Old Emmorton Road
Bel Air, MD 21015
(410) 569-0795
www.ahvma.org

your first chicken wing. You'll find starting points, especially references to books and websites, where you can consider a variety of opinions and approaches.

Similarly, if you have a purebred dog, talk to long-time breeders about the health problems and peculiarities of that breed. While vets see many kinds of dogs over the course of their careers, they often do not have deep, extensive knowledge about every breed. A good vet, in fact, will ask you questions about your breed, if you are knowledgeable enough to answer them.

As with anything, apply common sense and look for corroborating sources whenever you obtain information from the 'Net, and remember that anything you learn there is in no way a substitute for veterinary advice.

Appendix A

A Job to Do

The wonderful thing about your relationship with your dog is that it's not just a two-way exchange. Dogs are pack animals, and so are we humans. And given the chance, we gravitate toward communities that reflect our interests and obsessions.

In other words, dog people find other dog people. And dog people organize plenty of sports and activities where your dog can sharpen and show off his skills. Whether it's agility or tracking, herding or obedience, these events are not just for a handful of super-motivated insiders who want to collect ribbons or titles. They are for everyone who loves their dog and whose dog loves having a job to do, whether it's fetching a dumbbell or herding a duck.

Dogs are dogs, no matter what their pedigree, but one reality you will find as you explore performance events is that many of them are restricted to purebreds only. In most cases, that is because a purebred registry sanctions those events, and so only allows those dogs registered with it. Other organizations, however, such as the United Kennel Club and the Australian Shepherd Club of America, take all comers.

Rather than getting caught up in what your dog can't do, focus instead on what she can do. Seek out those organizations that support your kind of dog. If you want to do obedience or agility, two of the most popular canine sports, there are organizations that will let most any four-legger compete, with or without "papers."

One caveat: The point of these events is to go out and have fun with your dog. Winning isn't everything; most of the time, it isn't even anything. But if you make that the barometer by which you gauge your success, you're setting yourself up for frustration and failure. You won't have a good time. And neither will your dog.

OBEDIENCE

Someday, perhaps, someone will rename this area of canine endeavor to something that better reflects the reciprocity of the animal–human bond. "Obedience" not only sounds negative and compulsory, but it also belies the true spirit of the exercises. Dog and human are supposed to be upbeat, happy and relaxed, comfortable and joyful in their performance together. Sometimes you will see handlers in the ring who are stressed and unhappy, never so much as smiling at their dog. Often, the dog lags behind and looks miserable. Surprising? Not if you put yourself in the dog's place.

In competitive obedience, you are scored on how well you and your dog execute a number of basic obedience commands: Heel on leash and off, come when called, stand for examination from the judge, and long sits and downs in a group of other dogs are just a few of the exercises novice dogs will encounter. In more advanced obedience, the work gets progressively harder, with the dog off leash and facing exercises such as jumps and retrieves, and, at the most advanced levels, scent discrimination.

Unfortunately, the sport often prompts a lot of drilling and obsession with perfection. Also, the competitive obedience culture has lots of unspoken do's (do gently lead your dog by the collar in between exercises) and don'ts (don't push his butt down to get him to sit—that's points off). These are best learned in an obedience class, not the ring itself.

Most important, if you are going to do obedience with your dog, remember why you are doing it. Obedience showcases your relationship—or lack thereof.

The most basic obedience accomplishment a dog can achieve is the Canine Good Citizen certificate. This test is administered by the AKC (you'll find contact information in the Registries box on page 236), and is the only AKC sport that is open to all dogs, purebred and mixed, with papers and without. The test requires a dog to pass 10 basic requirements:

- Accept the approach and touch of a friendly stranger
- Sit politely while being petted
- Permit grooming from a stranger
- Walk on a loose leash
- Move calmly through a crowd of people
- Sit and lie down on command, and stay
- Come when called
- React calmly to the presence of another dog
- React appropriately to a startling distraction
- Stay calmly with another person while the handler goes out of sight

The next levels of AKC obedience are restricted to purebred dogs, but if you have a mixed breed or a breed the AKC does not register, there are other options. Both the United Kennel Club (UKC) and the Australian Shepherd Club of America (ASCA) welcome mixed breeds in their obedience events. The American Mixed Breed Obedience Registration (AMBOR) is a registry devoted to helping "All-American" dogs achieve titles; the group also sanctions its own obedience trials. Visit their websites (listed in the Registries box on page 236) to learn more about each group's obedience trials, which may involve everything from heeling in a figure-eight pattern to retrieving a dumbbell.

RALLY-O

A brand-new sport, this is sort of obedience meets Simon Says. Created by Charles L. (Bud) Kramer of Manhattan, Kansas, Rally Style Obedience is a good fit for those who are put off by traditional obedience's emphasis on flawless performance, and who

Rally-O Resource

Bud Kramer's home page, www.personal.ksu.edu/~kramerc/ home.htm, explains this fledgling sport in depth. You can also contact him at:

401 Bluemont Circle
Manhattan, KS 66502
kramerc@ksu.edu

welcome the opportunity to give repeat commands (a no-no in traditional obedience, where you get only one chance to give your dog a command) and effusive praise in the ring.

Inspired by Rally Car Racing, Rally-O requires dog and handler to follow a sequence of directional signs, performing the exercise posted on each. The AKC plans to offer Rally Style Obedience as a regular class in 2003.

AGILITY

A kind of canine obstacle course, agility requires more than the physical suppleness its name implies. Speed, coordination, precise footwork and closely honed teamwork are required of both dog and handler, who have to navigate an obstacle course, from tunnels to seesaws to jumps, taking the obstacles in a specific order. The faster you can complete the course with the least number of errors, the higher your score.

Agility's growing popularity is reflected in the number of organizations that offer it. All of the registries listed at the end of this chapter—AKC, UKC, ASCA and AMBOR—sanction agility trials. Only the AKC requires participating dogs to be purebreds.

HERDING

The AKC restricts its herding trials to breeds whose original function was to drive, tend or herd livestock. Other herding organizations and clubs also limit participation. The American Herding Breed Association, for example, has a list of approved herding breeds. (Included in the list are multipurpose breeds with herding backgrounds, and it also accepts herding breed mixes.)

Agility Resources

Clean Run magazine is a monthly must-read. Visit the site for supplies such as course designs and training gear.
35 North Chicopee Street, Unit 4
Chicopee, MA 01020
(800) 311-6503
Outside the U.S.: (413) 532-1389
www.cleanrun.com

These three organizations run agility trials that are open to all dogs, regardless of pedigree.

North American Dog Agility Council (NADAC)
11522 South Highway 3
Cataldo, ID 83810
(208) 689-3803
www.nadac.com

North American Dog Racing Association (NADRA)
P.O. Box 84
Fenton, MI 48430
(810) 210-5315
www.nadra.itgo.com

United States Dog Agility Association (USDAA)
P.O. Box 850955
Richardson, TX 75085-0955
(972) 487-2200
www.usdaa.com

But any dog can take a Herding Instinct Test, which gauges whether or not he has the drive to work livestock. Generally, most tests involve exposing a dog to sheep—sometimes the sheep are behind a fence, sometimes the dog is let loose among them—and observing if the dog shows at least five minutes of "sustained interest" in the woolly creatures. There is no national organization that administers these tests; they are usually offered periodically by local herding clubs. To find one near you, try visiting an Internet search engine, and type the words "Herding Instinct Test," along with your state name. You can also contact any of the registries mentioned in this chapter for a list of affiliated herding clubs.

Herding Resources

American Herding Breed Association
277 Central Avenue
Seekonk, MA 02771
www.ahba-herding.org

American Tending Breeds Association
31 Mt. Lebanon Road
Port Murray, NJ 07865
www.atba-herding.org

United States Border Collie Handlers' Association
2915 Anderson Lane
Crawford, TX 76638
www.usbcha.com

If your dog shows herding instinct, you don't have to stop there. Inquire if the herding club has beginners' seminars or arrange for private lessons.

FLYBALL

Invented in California in the 1970s, this doggie sport is basically a four-dog relay race using a tennis ball, with two teams competing side by side on a 51-foot course. Each individual dog must cross the start line and clear four hurdles spaced 10 feet apart to reach a spring-loaded box, which, when stepped on properly, shoots out a tennis ball. The dog catches the ball, goes back over the hurdles and recrosses the start line, upon which another dog starts the process. The first team to have all four dogs complete an error-free course wins the heat.

Flyball Resource

North American Flyball Association (NAFA)
1400 W. Devon Avenue, #512
Chicago, IL 60660
www.flyball.org

Disc Dog Resources

International Disc Dog Handlers' Association
1690 Julius Bridge Road
Ball Ground, GA 30107
(770) 735-6200
www.iddha.com

SkyHoundz
1015C Collier Road
Atlanta, GA 30319
(404) 350-9343
www.skyhoundz.com

DISC DOGS

Tossing a Frisbee to your pup isn't just a game to idle away an hour in the park. It has become an official sport. There are many local and regional disc dog clubs all over the country where your dog can hone his catching and retrieving skills. Perhaps most popular are choreographed freestyle competitions, where dogs do twists and back-flips, and ricochet off their handlers.

FREESTYLE

Think of this as "dancing with dogs." Handlers and dogs perform choreographed routines to the music of their choice, incorporating such obedience and trick moves as weaving through legs, backward scoots and tail chasing. Music selection and choreography play a part in a judge's scoring, and so does costuming. So if you and your dog are going to be Fred and Ginger, you'll need to look the part, too.

Freestyle Resource

World Canine Freestyle Organization
P.O. Box 350122
Brooklyn, NY 11235-2525
(718) 332-8336
www.worldcaninefreestyle.org

WEIGHT PULL

Dogs have been used for draft work since ancient times. Wearing a special padded harness that is attached to either a sled (in snow) or wheeled cart, a dog pulls a load (the size of the load depends on the weight of the dog) a distance of 16 feet within 60 seconds. As the competition progresses, weights are added in increments.

Huskies, Rottweilers and Pit Bulls are commonly entered at weight pulls, but events held by the UKC and the International Weight Pull Association are open to all breeds. Competitors have included everything from Cocker Spaniels to Chinese Cresteds. The winning dog does not necessarily pull the most weight, since size and body weight are factored into the final decision, so all these breeds have a chance to shine. In addition, the American Dog Breeder's Association (members.aol.com/bstofshw, P.O. Box 1771, Salt Lake City, Utah 84110) holds competitions for American Pit Bull Terriers, and many sledding clubs sponsor similar events for the northern breeds.

Weight Pull Resources

International Weight Pull Association
www.iwpa.net
Toni Yoakam, (313) 848-8636,
Mushnmom1@aol.com
Debbie Lee, (252) 357-0942,
debiwpa@albemarlenet.com

TRACKING

Dogs have superior noses. They smell scents the way we see color—in great and exquisite detail. Although your dog may be a super sniffer when he's out on walks or in the park, it takes consistency and training to teach him to follow a trail and find a dropped article—usually a glove—left by a track-layer. Tracking tests take place in urban, suburban

TRACKING RESOURCES

All of the registries listed in the box on page 236 offer tracking tests; the AKC's are only for purebred dogs.

and rural areas, and each provides its own challenges to the dog—and handler.

Tracking may be unique among the dog sports in that it is the only one where the handler has no idea what the dog should do. Humans never follow an invisible scent track the way a dog can, so we must simply trust our dog to get it right.

BREED-SPECIFIC TRIALS

Some breeds of dogs were bred to do specific jobs that are no longer in demand today. Most Dachshunds, for example, no longer go to ground to flush badgers, and most retrievers have swapped a mouthful of grouse for a tennis ball.

But there are several organizations dedicated to awakening those instincts in dogs and keeping their tradition alive in performance events. Participation is often restricted to specific breeds. For example, Golden Retrievers cannot compete in lure coursing trials, which are only for sighthounds. But interested dog owners can find a local lure coursing club, attend a trial just for fun, and perhaps have their dog participate in a fun run at the end of the day.

Earthdog

Terriers and Dachshunds were bred to "go to ground"—to flush out and kill vermin in their underground burrows. In earthdog trials, dogs enter an artificial den and work the quarry at the end of the trench. (Usually, the "quarry" is a rat safely ensconced in a cage. If you are concerned about the rodent's psychological trauma, factor that in before attending or participating.) The AKC holds these trials, as does the American Working Terrier Association (www.dirt-dog.com/awta, N14330 County Hwy G, Minong, Wisconsin 54859).

Lure Coursing

For sighthounds only, these events are basically rabbit hunts without the rabbit. In the bunny's place is a white plastic kitchen garbage bag, which zooms on a string around a pulley-rigged course up to 1,000 yards long.

Registries

American Kennel Club (AKC)
Operations Center
5580 Centerview Drive
Raleigh, NC 27606
(919) 233-9767
www.akc.org
Headquarters:
260 Madison Avenue
New York, NY 10016
(212) 696-8200

For purebreds only, the AKC offers conformation (the physical judging of a dog, which is what most people think of when they think "dog show"), obedience, agility, tracking and the Canine Good Citizen test for all breeds. Eligible breeds are able to compete in herding, lure coursing, hunting and retriever events, earthdog trials and coonhound events. If you have a purebred dog who does not have AKC papers, you can apply for an Indefinite Listing Privilege (ILP) number, which will permit your dog to compete in performance events but not conformation. Mixed breeds and unregistered purebreds can only participate in the Canine Good Citizen test.

American Mixed Breed Obedience Registration (AMBOR)
179 Niblick Road #113
Paso Robles, CA 93446
(805) 226-9275
www.amborusa.org

The AKC holds lure-coursing trials, as does the American Sighthound Field Association (www.asfa.org, 7045 SE 61st Street, Tecumseh, Kansas 66542). Most sighthounds except Whippets can participate in speed-related straight-racing competitions with the Large Gazehound Racing Association (www.lgra.org, 1839 Mecklenburg Road, Ithaca, New York 14850). Whippets, in turn, can compete with the Whippet Racing Association (www.whippetracing.org, 4300 Denison Avenue, Cleveland, Ohio 44109-2654) and the North American Whippet Racing Association (www.nawra.com, 1340 Shepherds

This registry enables mixed breed dogs to compete for titles in a variety of sports.

Australian Shepherd Club of America (ASCA)
P.O. Box 3790
Bryan, TX 77805-3790
(800) 892-ASCA
www.asca.org

Although this registry is breed-specific, it permits other purebreds as well as mixed breeds to compete in its performance events, including obedience, herding, agility and tracking.

United Kennel Club (UKC)
100 East Kilgore Road
Kalamazoo, MI 49002-5584
(269) 343-9020
www.ukcdogs.com

Like the AKC, the UKC holds conformation shows and perform-ance events such as obedience and agility, hunting tests for retrieving breeds and coonhound events. It also offers weight pull. The UKC will give a Limited Privilege Listing to purebred dogs who do not have registration papers, allowing them to compete in obedience and agility trials, but not conformation events. Mixed breeds can compete in UKC obedience and agility.

Creek Drive, Lucas, Texas 75002), among others. Sighthounds can also compete in oval track racing with the National Oval Track Racing Association (www.notra.org).

Field Trials and Hunting Tests

These AKC and UKC events test a dog's sporting ability to work effectively in the field. Field trials are competitive; hunt trials are not.

Water Work

Breeds developed for water rescue, such as Newfoundlands (Newfoundland Club of America, www.newfdogclub.org, 107 New Street, Rehoboth, Massachusetts 02769) and Portuguese Water Dogs (Portuguese Water Dog Club of America, www.pwdca.org) compete in water exercises that include retrieving. Some exercises are open to dogs of other breeds.

Holistic Remedies by Condition

Here is a quick reference chart to some of the remedies and modalities mentioned in this book and the conditions they are often associated with. Keep in mind that this list is not comprehensive, and should not be used for diagnostic or treatment purposes. As with any health concern involving your animal, consult a veterinarian or other qualified animal-care practitioner.

CONDITION	HOLISTIC REMEDY
Abscess	Homeopathy: Hepar sulphur (p. 53), Ledum (p. 53)
Absent mindedness	Flower essences: Clematis (p. 110)
Adjustment problems	Flower essences: Honeysuckle (p. 111)
Aggressive behavior (sudden)	Homeopathy: Belladonna (p. 51)
Allergic reactions	Homeopathy: Apis mel (p. 51), Sulphur (p. 56)

CONDITION	HOLISTIC REMEDY
Allergies	Nutrition: Diet/Raw feeding (p. 2)
	Herbs: Alfalfa (p. 209), Burdock (p. 209), Dandelion root (p. 209), Licorice root (p. 209), Nettle (p. 209), Red clover (p. 210), Spirulina (p. 210)
	Orthomolecular medicine (p. 210)
	Nambudripad's Allergy Elimination Technique (p. 210)
Allergies (food)	Nutrition: Diet (p. 206)
Allergies (skin)	Essential oils: Lavender (p. 40), Niaouli (p. 42)
Anal gland infection/ problems	Nutrition: Diet/Raw feeding (p. 6) Homeopathy: Hepar sulphur (p. 53), Merc sol (p. 53)
Antibacterial/germicide	Herbs: Aloe vera (p. 29), Garlic (p. 31)
	Essential oils: Oregano (p. 41)
	Homeopathy: Thuja (p. 56)
Anxiety (extreme)	Flower essences: Rescue Remedy (p. 106)
Anxiety (general)	Herbs: Valerian (p. 33)
	Essential oils: Lavender (p. 40)
	Homeopathy: Nux vomica (p. 53)
Anxiety (high pressure)	Flower essences: Elm (p. 110)
Anxiety (performance)	Flower essences: Gelsemium (p. 53)
Anxiety (separation)	Homeopathy: Pulsatilla (p. 54)
Anxiety (transition)	Flower essences: Walnut (p. 116)
Apathy	Flower essences: Wild Rose (p. 117)
Arthritis	Herbs: Burdock (p. 30), Licorice (p. 32)
Attention-seeking behavior	Flower essences: Heather (p. 111)
Bad breath	Herbs: Parsley (p. 32)
	Nutrition: Diet/Raw feeding (p. 6)
Bee stings	Homepathy: Ledum (p. 53)

CONDITION	HOLISTIC REMEDY
Bites (without bleeding)	Homeopathy: Ledum (p. 53)
Bloat /Gastric torsion	Seek immediate veterinary assistance
	Homeopathy: Colocynthis (p. 52), Carbo Veg (p. 52)
	Flower essences: Sweet Chestnut (p. 115)
Blood clotting	Herbs: Yarrow (p. 34)
Blood pressure (general)	Herbs: Hawthorn (p. 31)
Bonding (difficulty)	Flower essences: Water Violet (p. 116)
Bones (broken)	Homeopathy: Silicea (p. 56)
Bronchitis	Essential oils: Eucalyptus (p. 39)
Burns (minor)	Herbs: Aloe (p. 29), Calendula (p. 30)
	Essential oils: Lavender (p. 40)
	Homeopathy: Urtica Urens (p. 56)
Cancer (general)	Antioxidant therapy (p. 188), herbal treatments (only under veterinary supervision), Essiac Tea (p. 193), Hoxey Formula (p. 194), glandulars (p. 194), shark cartilage (p. 195), dietary treatments (p. 196)
Cardiovascular problems	Herbs: Hawthorn (p. 34)
Central nervous system (problems)	Essential oil: Helichrysum (p. 40)
Circulation (promotion of)	Homeopathy: Arnica (p. 51)
Coat (improved)	Nutrition: Kelp (p. 21)
Colitis	Herbs: Licorice (p. 32), Slippery Elm (p. 33)
Concentration problems	Flower essences: Impatiens (p. 112)
Congestion	Homeopathy: Silicea (p. 56)
Conjunctivitis	Homeopathy: Euphrasia (p. 52)
Constipation	Nutrition: Pumpkin (p. 21)
	Homeopathy: Nux Vomica (p. 53)
Coughing (general)	Herbs: Coltsfoot (p. 30)
	Homeopathy: Sulphur (p. 56)

CONDITION	HOLISTIC REMEDY
Cough (Kennel)	Homeopathy: Bryonia (p. 51), Drosera (p. 52)
Cuts (minor)	Herbs: Aloe (p. 29), Calendula (p. 30)
	Essential oils: Lavender (p. 40)
Dependency	Flower essences: Cerato (p. 108), Chicory (p. 109)
Destructive behavior	Flower essences: Willow (p. 120)
Detoxifier (general)	Herbs: Dandelion (p. 31), Garlic (p. 31), Licorice (p. 32)
Development problems	Flower essences: Chestnut Bud (p. 109)
Diarrhea	Nutrition: Pumpkin (p. 21)
	Herbs: Hawthorn (p. 31), Slippery Elm (p. 33)
	Homeopathy: Sulphur (p. 56), Merc sol (p. 53)
Digestive Problems	Nutrition (p. 22)
	Essential oils: Peppermint (p. 42)
Diverticular disease	Herbs: Licorice (p. 32)
Dominant behavior	Flower essences: Vine (p. 116)
Doubt	Flower essences: Larch (p. 112)
Dry skin	Nutrition: Kelp (p. 21)
Ear Infections	Nutrition (p. 6)
	Essential oils: Niaouli (p. 42)
	Homeopathy: Belladonna (p. 51), Sulphur (p. 56)
Eczema	Herbs: Burdock (p. 30)
Emotional Trauma	Homeopathy: Aconite (p. 50)
Erratic behavior	Flower essences: Scleranthus (p. 115)
Exhaustion	Homeopathy: Cocculus (p. 52)
	Flower essences: Olive (p. 113)
Eye irritation	Homeopathy: Euphrasia (p. 52)
Fatigue	Homeopathy: Carbo Veg (p. 52)

CONDITION	HOLISTIC REMEDY
Fear	Homeopathy: Aconite (p. 50)
	Flower essences: Aspen (p. 108), Mimulus (p. 112), Rescue Remedy (p. 106), Rock Rose (p. 114)
Fertility Problems	Nutrition: Apple cider vinegar (p. 21)
Fever	Herbs: Yarrow (p. 34)
	Homeopathy: Aconite (p. 52), Belladonna (p. 51)
Flatulence/gas	Homeopathy: Nux Vomica (p. 53), Sulphur (p. 56)
Fleas/flea prevention	Herbs: Garlic (p. 31)
	Essential oils: Lemon (p. 41), Peppermint (p. 42)
Fluid retention	Homeopathy: Apis Mel (p. 51)
Focus (loss of)	Flower essences: Clematis (p. 110)
Gastric upset	Homeopathy: Nux Vomica (p. 53)
Gastritis	Herbs: Licorice (p. 32)
Gingivitis	Homeopathy: Merc Sol (p. 53)
Grumpiness	Flower essences: Wild Rose (p. 117), Willow (p. 120)
Guilt	Flower essences: Pine (p. 113)
Heart problems (general)	Herbs: Hawthorn (p. 31)
Heatstroke	Homeopathy: Belladonna (p. 51)
High blood pressure	Herbs: Garlic, Hawthorn (p. 31)
Hives	Homeopathy: Apis Mel (p. 51), Rhus Tox (p. 55), Urtica Urens (p. 56)
Homesickness	Flower essences: Honeysuckle (p. 111)
Hot spots	Herbs: Aloe (p. 29)
Hygiene (poor)	Flower essences: Crab Apple (p. 110)
Hygroma	Homeopathy: Apis Mel (p. 51)
Hyperactivity	Flower essences: Vervain (p. 116)
Indigestion (with gas)	Homeopathy: Carbo Veg (p. 52)

CONDITION	HOLISTIC REMEDY
Immune System (boosting)	Nutrition: Vitamin C (p. 21)
	Herbs: Garlic (p. 31)
	Essential oils: Frankincense (p. 39), Lemon (p. 41)
Impatience	Flower essences: Impatiens (p. 112)
Indigestion	Herbs: Ginger (p. 31)
	Homeopathy: Nux Vomica (p. 53)
Infection (general)	Herbs: Yarrow (p. 34)
	Essential oils: Oregano (p. 41)
	Homeopathy: Hepar Sulphur (p. 53)
Inflamed joints	Homeopathy: Ledum (p. 53)
Insect bites	Herbs: Aloe (p. 29), Calendula (p. 30)
Insect stings (not bee)	Homeopathy: Apis Mel (p. 51)
Insecurity	Flower essences: Chicory (p. 109)
Insomnia	Flower essences: White Chestnut (p. 117)
Intestinal tract (inflammation)	Herbs: Slippery elm (p. 33)
Irritability	Flower essences: Beech (p. 108)
Jealousy	Flower essences: Holly (p. 111)
Kidney, tonifying	Herbs: Burdock (p. 30), Dandelion (p. 31)
Laziness	Flower essences: Hornbeam (p. 112)
Lesions	Herbs: Calendula (p. 30)
Lethargy	Flower essences: Hornbeam (p. 112)
Lick granulomas	Herbs: Aloe (p. 29)
Listlessness	Flower essences: Gentian (p. 110)
Liver, tonifying	Herbs: Burdock (p. 30), Garlic (p. 31), Milk thistle (p. 32)
Mange	Homeopathy: Sulphur (p. 56)
Mastitis	Homeopathy: Belladonna (p. 51)
Milk production/lactation	Herbs: Raspberry (p. 32)

CONDITION	HOLISTIC REMEDY
Mistrust	Flower essences: Aspen (p. 108)
Mood swings	Flower essences: Scleranthus (p. 115)
Motion sickness/nausea	Herbs: Ginger (p. 31)
	Essential oils: Peppermint (p. 42)
	Homeopathy: Cocculus (p. 52)
	Flower essences: Scleranthus (p. 115)
Nerve damage	Essential oils: Helichrysum (p. 40)
	Homeopathy: Hypericum (p. 53)
Obsessive behavior	Flower essences: Crab Apple (p. 110)
Odor ("doggy smell")	Nutrition: Diet/Raw feeding (p. 6)
Overprotectiveness	Flower essences: Chicory (p. 109)
Overvaccination	Homeopathy: Thuja (p. 56)
Pain (mouth)	Homeopathy: Chamomilla (p. 52)
Pain (movement related)	Homeopathy: Bryonia (p. 51)
Pain (tail & paw)	Homeopathy: Hypericum (p. 53)
Panic	Herbs: Valerian (p. 33)
	Essential oils: Lavender (p. 40),
	Homeopathy: Aconite (p. 50)
	Flower essences: Aspen (p. 108), Rescue Remedy (p. 106), Rock Rose (p. 114)
Paralysis (fear related)	Homeopathy: Gelsemium (p. 53)
Pneumonia	Herbs: Coltsfoot (p. 30)
Poison ivy	Herbs: Calendula (p. 30)
	Homeopathy: Rhus Tox (p. 55)
Pregnancy	Herbs: Raspberry (p. 32)
Pregnancy (false)	Homeopathy: Pulsatilla (p. 54)
Puncture (without bleeding)	Homeopathy: Ledum (p. 53)
Rashes	Homeopathy: Rhus Tox (p. 55)
Regeneration dead tissue	Homeopathy: Silicea (p. 56)
Resentment	Flower essences: Willow (p. 120)

CONDITION	HOLISTIC REMEDY
Respiratory problems (general)	Essential oils: Eucalyptus (p. 39)
Respiratory infection	Herbs: Coltsfoot (p. 30)
Restlessness	Flower essences: White Chestnut (p. 117)
Rigidity (emotional/mental)	Flower essences: Rock Water (p. 114)
Scar tissue	Essential oils: Helichrysum (p. 40) Homeopathy: Silicea (p. 56)
Sedative/tranquilizer	Herbs: Valerian (p. 33)
Self control (loss of)	Flower essences: Cherry Plum (p. 109)
Self-esteem (low)	Flower essences: Larch (p. 112)
Separation anxiety	Flower essences: Red Chestnut (p. 114)
Shock	Homeopathy: Aconite (p. 50) Flower essences: Rescue Remedy (p. 106), Star of Bethlehem (p. 115)
Shyness	Flower essences: Aspen (p. 108), Larch (p. 112), Mimulus (p. 112)
Sinusitis	Essential oils: Eucalyptus (p. 39)
Skin eruptions	Homeopathy: Hepar sulphur (p. 53)
Skin irritations	Herbs: Aloe (p. 29), Calendula (p. 30) Homeopathy: Sulphur (p. 56)
Sleepiness	Homeopathy: Cocculus (p. 52)
Soreness	Homeopathy: Arnica (p. 51)
Sprains/strains	Homeopathy: Arnica (p. 51)
Staph infection	Essential oils: Oregano (p. 41)
Stomach problems (general)	Herbs: Dandelion (p. 31), Ginger (p. 31), Slippery elm (p. 33)
Stress	Herbs: Valerian (p. 33) Essential oils: Lavender (p. 40)
Stress (extreme)	Flower essences: Rescue Remedy (p. 106)

CONDITION	HOLISTIC REMEDY
Stress (situational)	Flower essences: Elm (p. 110)
Sunstroke	Homeopathy: Belladonna (p. 51)
Suspicion	Flower essences: Holly (p. 111)
Tartar/Cleaner Teeth/ Bad Breath	Nutrition: Diet/Raw feeding (p. 6)
Teething	Homeopathy: Chamomilla (p. 52)
Territorialism	Flower essences: Rock Water (p. 114), Vine (p. 116)
Thyroid problems/ hypothyroid	Nutrition: Kelp (p. 21)
Timidity	Flower essences: Centaury (p. 108), Cerato (p. 108)
Toxins (environmental)	Herbs: Burdock (p. 30)
Training problems	Flower essences: Chestnut Bud (p. 109), White Chestnut (p. 117)
Tumors (external)	Essential oils: Frankincense (p. 39)
Unconsciousness	Homeopathy: Carbo Veg (p. 52)
Urinary problems (diuretic)	Herbs: Yarrow (p. 34)
Urination (problems with)	Herbs: Dandelion (p. 31)
Uterus (strengthening)	Herbs: Raspberry (p. 32)
Virus (prevention)	Herbs: Garlic (p. 31), Licorice (p. 32)
Vomiting (nervous)	Homeopathy: Nux Vomica (p. 53)
Vomiting (overeating)	Homeopathy: Nux Vomica (p. 53)
Vomiting (general)	Herbs: Ginger (p. 31) Essential oils: Peppermint (p. 42)
Warts	Essential oils: Frankincense (p. 39)
Weight problems	Homeopathy: Carbo Veg (p. 52)
Worry	Flower essences: Mimulus (p. 112), Red Chestnut (p. 114)

Index

N

W

Y

Z